Homeland Security Technologies for the 21st Century

Homeland Security Technologies for the 21st Century

Ryan K. Baggett, Chad S. Foster,
and Brian K. Simpkins, Editors

Praeger Security International Textbook

 PRAEGER™

An Imprint of ABC-CLIO, LLC
Santa Barbara, California • Denver, Colorado

Library of Congress Cataloging-in-Publication Data

Names: Baggett, Ryan K., editor. | Foster, Chad S., editor. | Simpkins, Brian K., editor.
Title: Homeland security technologies for the 21st century / Ryan K. Baggett, Chad S. Foster, and Brian K. Simpkins, editors.
Description: Santa Barbara, California : Praeger, [2017] | Series: Praeger security international textbook | Includes bibliographical references and index.
Identifiers: LCCN 2016044271 (print) | LCCN 2016059964 (ebook) | ISBN 9781440831423 (hardback : alk. paper) | ISBN 9781440833533 (pbk. : alk. paper) | ISBN 9781440831430 (ebook)
Subjects: LCSH: United States. Department of Homeland Security. | National security—United States. | Terrorism—United States—Prevention.
Classification: LCC HV6432.4 .H664 2017 (print) | LCC HV6432.4 (ebook) | DDC 363.32028/4—dc23
LC record available at https://lccn.loc.gov/2016044271

ISBN: 978-1-4408-3142-3
EISBN: 978-1-4408-3143-0
Paperback ISBN: 978-1-4408-3353-3

21 20 19 18 17   1 2 3 4 5

This book is also available as an eBook.

Praeger
An Imprint of ABC-CLIO, LLC

ABC-CLIO, LLC
130 Cremona Drive, P.O. Box 1911
Santa Barbara, California 93116-1911
www.abc-clio.com

This book is printed on acid-free paper ∞
Manufactured in the United States of America

For Ben and Sam, you are destined for greatness; For Missy, because of you, these endeavors are possible.—Ryan Baggett

To my wife (Leah) and children (Gavin, Gabrielle, and Graham) as a family is life's greatest gift.—Brian Simpkins

Contents

Acknowledgments

WE WANT TO THANK ALL of those involved in the writing of this book, especially the contributing authors Kris Bowerman, Bob Coullahan, David Lamensdorf, Jay English, and Scott Rockwell. We sincerely appreciate the time and effort you put into this first edition, your patience as we labored through the development and editing process, and, most importantly, your friendship. Second, we thank our colleagues from the U.S. Department of Homeland Security (DHS), other federal departments and agencies, and responders from the field who we have had the great fortune of getting to know and collaborating with for many years on technology grant programs. A special "shout out" is in order for Al Fluman, David Larimer, Denis Gusty, Bill Kalin, John Panella, and Eddie Broyles. Finally, students enrolled in the Homeland Security Program at Eastern Kentucky University (EKU) provided the initial spark and motivation to produce this edition. Your success in life, including college and the profession of homeland security, is central to our higher education calling.

CHAPTER ONE

Introduction

Technology Securing the Homeland

Brian K. Simpkins and Chad S. Foster

Learning Objectives

After reading this chapter, readers should be able to:

- Summarize the fundamental concept of homeland security technology.
- Summarize why technologies are important in securing the nation.
- Analyze how the implementation of homeland security technologies presents both advantages and risks.
- Analyze why effective leadership and management is needed to implement technology within homeland security partners.
- Apply knowledge obtained through chapter to discussion questions.

Key Terms

Homeland Security Partner
Strategic Planning
Technology
Transformational Leadership

Introduction

When we look at the future of public safety, there is a lot that can be done to make things safer and more effective, and the technology exists to make it happen.[1]

September 11, 2001: Law enforcement and fire service agencies responding to the World Trade Center attacks are unable to talk with each other due to a lack of interagency/interoperable communications. Incident management and response is further hampered by two-way radio signal issues within the high-rise buildings. Evacuation orders for the North Tower from law enforcement agencies subsequent to the collapse of the South Tower are not heard by or relayed to fire service agencies due to the interoperability issues, the shear amount of radio traffic on specific radio channels, and the number of radio channels being used. Primary and redundant communications systems as well as backup power generators are lost due to their placement in the basement areas of office buildings thereby making them inaccessible.[2]

June 10–11, 2010: The Ouachita National Forest in Arkansas receives heavy rainfall the evening of June 10, especially in the Little Missouri River watershed that includes the Albert Pike Recreation Area. The National Weather Service issues multiple flash flood warnings throughout the night for impending storms, but visitors are unaware of the danger due to the lack of radio reception and cell phone service in the isolated wilderness area. The U.S. Forest Service is also unable to alert visitors to the danger due to a lack of an alert and warning system within the Albert Pike Recreation Area. During the early morning hours of June 11, the area experiences historic localized rainfall causing the Little Missouri River to rise from three feet to approximately 23 feet in about four hours. U.S. Geological Survey stream gauges record the onslaught of quickly rising floodwaters, but the data is not reported in real time and is not connected to an early warning system. As a result, 20 fatalities occur within the Albert Pike Recreation Area as individuals sleeping in cabins, campers, and tents are caught off guard and are inundated by rapidly rising floodwaters.[3]

Despite the differences in the events above—a terrorist attack versus a natural disaster—both scenarios showcase how the lack of available and necessary technology, and the incapacitation of technology, can have profound impacts on incident response and situational awareness. Although communications and alert and warning systems are only two examples of the multiple technology types being utilized in homeland security today, they continue to be salient ones. As technology becomes a more integral part of human life in the 21st century, homeland security partners[4] are now finding it necessary to implement technologies for the benefit of the communities they serve. However, understanding technology can be a difficult task, which is a problem this book aims to address. For starters, what is technology?

What Is Technology?

Defining "technology" would seem a logical way to begin the book. Further, one would think that defining "technology" would be easy in today's digital world. However, if one researches for a standard definition of "technology," he or she would soon be discouraged as there are numerous definitions being utilized, but nothing standardized, across different industries and communities of practice. The following technology definitions serve as an example:

- The application of scientific advancements to benefit humanity[5]
- The use of science in industry, engineering, etc., to invent useful things or to solve problems[6]
- Application of knowledge to develop tools, materials, techniques, and systems to help people meet and fulfill needs[7]
- A body of knowledge devoted to creating tools, processing actions, and extracting of materials[8]
- The advancement in theoretical knowledge, tools, and equipment that drive industry[9]
- The practical application of science to commerce or industry[10]

For the purpose of this book only, "homeland security technologies" are defined as applications of knowledge and innovations, mostly hardware and software systems, that enable homeland security partners to accomplish their missions. This book does not attempt to solve the technology definition conundrum; rather it provides a greater and practical understanding of homeland security technologies in a larger context. This understanding is warranted because technologies within the homeland security field may not be what people think.

Why Is Homeland Security Technology Important?

[Homeland security] is all a continuum. Local security impacts the city, which influences the state, which drives the nation. Homeland security is . . . community security.[11]

Advancements in homeland security technologies since the early 2000s have been remarkable partly due to the digital revolution and the Internet of Things (IoT) movement that has transformed many aspects of society. In fact, the impact of this revolution on homeland security partners has been quite possibly more significant than in other public sectors. It presents new opportunities to achieve greater efficiencies (e.g., cost and time savings) and higher quality services that are achieved through quicker response times and access to information.[12] Some common characteristics of newer technologies from an opportunity perspective include the following:

- **Enhanced Awareness and Intelligence:** Technologies now provide homeland security partners with enhanced situational awareness, as well as smart, intelligent systems made possible through advanced algorithms, pattern recognition software, and access to data.
- **Greater Mobility:** Small, networked devices make it possible to monitor areas, vehicles, cargo, etc., for threats. Examples include cameras and sensors equipped to unmanned aerial surveillance (UAS) systems along the border.
- **Stronger Predictions:** Many newer homeland security applications aim to prevent and mitigate threats and hazards by predicting their occurrence. Examples include systems that relate airline passenger information to watch lists and no-fly lists to alert authorities, and modeling and simulation tools for predicting hurricanes and other natural hazards.

The U.S. Department of Homeland Security (DHS) Science and Technology Directorate (S&T) continues to make a concerted effort to invest in the research and development (R&D) of technologies to strengthen homeland security capabilities both now and in the future.[13] Recent incidents illustrate the effectiveness of new technologies and illustrate their tremendous benefit, such as the role of social media in two different incident types: 2013 Boston (MA) Marathon Bombing and 2014 Oso (WA) Mudslide.[14] These events illustrate the benefit of technology investments and utilization to the Whole Community, thereby increasing the protection and resiliency of the nation.[15] In sum, all homeland security technologies, including those discussed in this book, as a whole contribute to helping ensure the nation's homeland security partners and their communities can effectively and efficiently plan and prepare for, protect against, respond to, mitigate the effects of, and recover from incidents and disasters.

Despite the advantages, technologies have also presented risks to those charged with defending the homeland. It was also well-known during the writing of the first *National Strategy for Homeland Security* in 2002 that such technologies as information networks enabled adversaries by providing them a platform to plan attacks, raise funds, and spread propaganda, which continues today in the fight against adversaries like Islamic State in Iraq and Syria (ISIS). Another threat is the intrusion into and manipulation of industrial control systems (e.g., supervisory control and data acquisition [SCADA] networks) that control critical infrastructure systems.[16] The paradox and challenge for those on the front lines of homeland security today is effectively using innovation and technologies to achieve benefits, while at the same time denying and responding to those same advantages in the hands of ever-evolving and sophisticated adversaries.

The new risks and vulnerabilities created by technological advances harkens to the "gift of fire" concept.[17] Although fire can heat a home and cook food to help humans survive, it can also burn a house down and kill humans directly by flame or indirectly by smoke. Similarly, technological advancements within the homeland security field can create efficiencies of scale and force multipliers, and many of the technologies described in this book are intended to capitalize on these opportunities. However, their limitations and ability to be improperly used either directly or indirectly must be realized. Of course, homeland security technologies may be defeated by terrorists or those with malicious intentions, or fail on accident (e.g., New Orleans levee and flood wall system). Interwoven within the chapters are explanations of these limitations, which include cost–benefit analysis and moral and ethical considerations associated with the implementation of select technologies.

Leading and Managing Innovations and Change

Benefiting and managing risks associated with technologies requires more than basic knowledge of the technologies themselves. At a fundamental level, many agencies simply lack the willingness or institutional capacity to innovate. A vendor representative recently pointed out to an author that "public agencies are one generation behind the rest of the field." How to maintain version after version of software, for example, is a shared challenge.

At the same time, simply adopting technologies without proper due diligence is risky, potentially costly, and downright unacceptable for many categories of technologies, especially those that impact citizen and responder safety and security. It is argued that a "technological determinism" exists in society fueled by the propaganda of high-tech companies, excitement of technologists, and need to remain competitive.[18] Even the term "technological solutionism" has been used to critique the digitization ideology.[19] Further yet, individuals have voiced concerns that new technologies are automatically adopted without critical thought and study of the possible spatial and social impacts as well as impacts at the agency/organizational and individual levels.[20] Similarly, others have noted that planning for technologies is often conducted by technicians and engineers who maintain a "world view" confined to their domain with little external monitoring and measurement of impacts.[21] Finding the proper balance between the extremes—from failing to innovate to mindlessly innovating—is a difficulty. As emphasized by Baggett in chapter 3, proper strategic planning can pay dividends to homeland security agencies and organizations for striking this balance.

How do homeland security organizations manage the fast pace of technological change to reap benefits and mitigate costs, and to essentially remain significant today? For example, English discusses in chapter 10 how public safety answering points (PSAPs) and other institutions charged with communicating with the public are feeling many pressures to innovate. While maintaining traditional landline capabilities, for example, they are now being asked to accurately locate mobile callers both outdoors and indoors, receive and respond to text messages to 9-1-1, and manage new social media platforms for communicating with those in distress.

Kumle-Hammes offers transformational leadership and having a change-ready organizational culture as two key ingredients for managing change within the workplace.[22] It also requires a flexible strategic planning framework as Baggett indicates in chapter 2. There is a significant body of research on transformational leadership as well as other leadership theories. Rowe and Guerrero define transformational leadership as "an involved, complex process that binds leaders and followers together in the transformation or changing of followers, organizations."[23] A transformational leader is one who:

- develops an organizational culture open to change by empowering subordinates to change;
- encourages transparency in conversations related to change; and
- supports members of the organization in trying to innovate and different ways of achieving organizational goals.[24]

The competency framework offered by Quinn, Faerman, Thompson, and McGrath includes eight roles for a *managerial leader* deemed critical for ensuring the success of an organization. Aspects of transformational leadership overlap with, among others, the *innovator* and *director* roles. An effective *innovator* promotes change and encourages adaptation by championing and selling ideas, fueling and fostering innovation, and implementing and sustaining change.[25] Of course innovating is not conducted in a proverbial vacuum. The effective managerial leader must also develop and communicate a vision, set goals and objectives, and motivate self and others.[26]

Strategic planning is one of many innovation tools offered by Cohen, Eimicke, and Heikkila.[27] Strategic planning is much broader than simply adopting new technologies to accomplish the organization's goals. If not the centerpiece for a supporting strategy, however, technologies are often viewed as enablers of the desired change given their widespread use in society today. In addition to supporting strategic planning, technologies may be used to reengineer processes and improve quality.

McCrimmon notes that it's not only the person at the top who can or should provide leadership within an organization. He notes that the world is "too complex and fast changing for one person to provide all of the answers"[28] and organizations that solely rely on top-down models may be viewed as a liability today. Instead, effective leaders facilitate and enable team members to generate ideas for new directions. It is more about the content of the idea, and less about who generates or delivers it.[29] Baggett's approach to conducting needs assessments is consistent with this portrayal of leadership. It is often those on the front lines (e.g., the field, operations centers) who have the technical skills required to operate and benefit from new technologies, so it seems reasonable they would be the source for many ideas in the homeland security mission space.

Though any employee may influence change, Kumle-Hammes suggests that only top-level managers may alter an entire organization's culture. Regardless, synergies appear to exist between the concepts of leadership and culture. Among others, she recommends that organizations establish a participatory hierarchy that encourages teamwork for solving problems, and open communications to build trust and provide every worker a voice.[30]

Through proper leadership, organizational culture, and strategic planning, homeland security partners may have the wherewithal or conditions required to effectively manage change and technological innovations. Figure 1.1 below provides a concept diagram that compares two innovation paradigms. The top image displays an organization incapable of managing innovation and change despite the internal and external pressures that both resist and demand change. The bottom image displays an organization that is capable of managing innovation and change through proper leadership, organizational culture, and strategic planning.

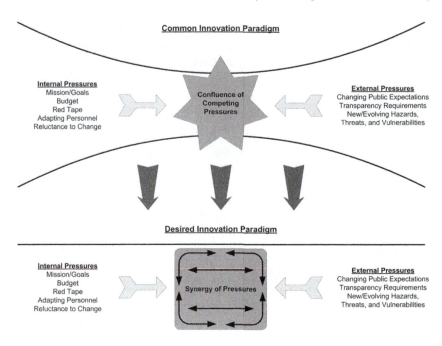

Figure 1.1   Technology Innovation Paradigm.

Overall Intent and Perspective

The overall intent of this book is to provide an overview of select home-land security technologies for those entering or currently working in the homeland security field in the public or private sectors—the target audience. Therefore, this book has two main objectives. The first objective is to provide the aforementioned familiarization and basic, practical under-standing of homeland security technology. The second objective is to provide information and viewpoints that allow readers to think critically about assessing, implementing, and operating homeland security technologies. Aside from the homeland security student, the book is intended for individuals in technical fields of study (e.g., geographic information systems [GIS], computer science, engineering) seeking information on standards and theories underlying homeland security technologies. Further, it is important that those who grew up in the digital area who are now entering the homeland security field have a foundational understanding of technology. This is because there will be expectations placed on them to understand, assess, implement, and/or operate technologies within their organizations.

To achieve the overall intent, this book utilizes an applied perspective—putting technologies into practice. It also covers topics that are presented in a problem-to-solution fashion for the benefit of purchasers and users of technologies, and others looking to implement innovations. Note that the authors embrace the concept of the homeland security enterprise, so technologies presented in this book may be of interest to homeland security partners at the local, state, federal, and tribal levels as well as the private sector. This is important as information contained within this book can be utilized by any organization that performs a homeland security function.

Structure of the Book

To accomplish the overall intent of the book from the defined perspective, the authors invited a diverse and experienced group of individuals representing all aspects of the homeland security field to provide contributions. This group investigated various theories behind use of technologies and assessed the importance of technologies for meeting goals and objectives (e.g., smarter and more capable systems, achieving economies of scale and force multipliers) while at the same time citing example applications at all levels of practice using an all-hazards approach. The book provides key features and commentary for the benefit of homeland security professionals and students alike through discussions of:

- Homeland security technologies from the viewpoint of contemporary homeland security mission areas and user applications as opposed to purely technical interpretations of the technologies as commonly found in contemporary references
- Various theories behind use of technologies and the importance of technologies for achieving goals and objectives
- Sample applications of technologies using an all-hazards framework and use cases at all levels of practice, including those commonly found in the public and private sectors
- Opportunities and risks associated with homeland security technologies for identifying technology needs and characteristics
- Standards and technologies that promote interoperability, compatibility, and system safety
- Technology trends and impacts on contemporary and future homeland security practices

The discussions above are interwoven within and among chapters that address "old" technologies—those that have persisted for many years but continue to be improved—and "new" technologies that are now being used in—or are in the process of being transitioned for wider use in—the homeland security field.

The authors explore fundamental questions underlying several technology areas identified in collaboration between the editors and contributors who have expertise in one or more areas of homeland security technologies. Though the book presents a small sample of technology areas, it is the authors' intent that readers become stronger critical thinkers and better prepared to analyze other technology areas as a result of the readings in this book. The learning objectives and discussion questions presented in each chapter will help the reader become a critical thinker. In collaboration with multiple authors, the book covers the following chapters:

- **Chapter 2—Ethical and Privacy Implications of Technology:** This chapter identifies important ethical and privacy implications homeland security partners must consider when implementing technology. This discussion helps partners understand and be aware of consequences (intended and unintended) as well as impacts of using technology.
- **Chapter 3—Homeland Security Technology Assessment and Implementation:** This chapter details an eight-step technology implementation process to include needs assessment, project planning, and operational evaluation. Technology training and maintenance are also discussed to illustrate that the overall technology implementation process is more than simply buying and using a technology.
- **Chapter 4—Perspectives in Homeland Security Training: Enhancing Training Access and Delivery through Technology:** This chapter identifies how training barriers can be overcome through utilizing technology-based solutions to achieve training goals and objectives. The discussion includes guidance on how to implement technology-based training solutions through the Planning, Analysis, Design, Development, Implementation, and Evaluation (PADDIE) framework.
- **Chapter 5—Social Media's Role in Supporting the Homeland Security Mission:** This chapter provides an introduction into the use of social media by homeland security partners through identifying the categories of social media applications and their associated benefits. Challenges related to the use of social media are also discussed along with important implementation considerations.
- **Chapter 6—Physical Security Technologies: Protecting Assets and Critical Infrastructure through Technology:** This chapter identifies technologies utilized by public and private homeland security partners to protect assets and critical infrastructure. The discussion illustrates that although standard physical security techniques continue to be enhanced through technological advancements, new physical security technologies are now enabling partners to be more efficient and effective at securing some of the nation's most important assets.

- **Chapter 7—Cybersecurity Threats and Technology Applications in Homeland Security:** Cybersecurity threats are a key concern for homeland security partners that must be identified and mitigated. This chapter identifies many of those threats to information and hardware and software while summarizing various technologies and risk management strategies used to thwart these challenges. This chapter provides a nontechnical overview in an effort to provide situational awareness to partners.
- **Chapter 8—Unmanned Aircraft Systems in Homeland Security:** This chapter examines the evolution and operational uses of UAS. Additionally, challenges related to training, implementation, and legal issues are identified. Overall, the chapter provides an important overview on impacts, benefits, and consequences of UAS use by homeland security partners.
- **Chapter 9—Chemical, Biological, Radiological, Nuclear, and Explosive (CBRNE) Detection Systems and Data Interoperability:** CBRNE threats and events pose unique and complex problems to homeland security partners. This chapter discusses the detection systems that are designed to address, overcome, or mitigate CBRNE threats and events. Included within the chapter is a discussion on the importance of sensor data interoperability and standards.
- **Chapter 10—Public Safety Communications: The Technology behind the Call:** Despite the type of emergency, an individual's first reaction is to call 9-1-1. However, most individuals fail to realize the complexities of modern 9-1-1 technology. This chapter provides a basic understanding of 9-1-1 technology utilized in conventional 9-1-1 and enhanced 9-1-1 (E9-1-1) systems at PSAPs. The chapter also addresses the challenges associated within implementing Internet Protocol (IP)-based communications systems and provides a view into the Next Generation 9-1-1 (NG9-1-1) technology.
- **Chapter 11—Mobile Communications and Decision Support Applications:** The convergence of voice and data communications—not long ago considered separate sectors—offers users in the field working in many different capacities with significant capabilities. This chapter traces the evolution of communications technologies to the present day, and provides a summary of hardware used to support mobile applications and software systems that aim to enhance situational awareness and decision making.
- **Chapter 12—Fire Protection Systems for Infrastructure Protection:** This chapter explains the various types of fire protection systems being utilized within critical infrastructure throughout the nation. Within the overview, relative standards are discussed in addition to technologies related to alarm system communications, computer fire modeling, personal protective equipment (PPE), hazardous materials response, and urban search and rescue response.
- **Chapter 13—Conclusion: The Future of Homeland Security Technology:** This chapter explores select "megatrends" in the form of both risks and opportunities that appear to be steering the course of innovations in the homeland security field.

In addition to written discussions on the topical area, each chapter incorporates common elements to assist with critical thinking, learning, and application. For example, each chapter includes learning objectives, which articulate the knowledge the author wants the reader to obtain via the chapter. This is assisted through the identification of key terms in each chapter. The key terms should not be viewed as a simple glossary but rather as key terms and concepts that should become part of the reader's professional vocabulary. Lastly, each chapter includes discussion questions and case study analyses that enable the reader to think critically about the information provided in the chapter and apply obtained knowledge through stated questions.

Conclusion

Readers will quickly realize that technology is now a major element of homeland security at all levels. The state of technology has eclipsed the simple use of laptops and tablets and is now on a trajectory to turn what was once considered purely science fiction into reality. For example, wearable technology (e.g., cameras, sensors, communication devices, etc.); System of Systems; IoT; big data; and wireless, small, and mobile technology are just some of the major trends within the rapidly changing field of homeland security technology.[31] Further, technology transfer was once the exclusive realm of military technology transitioning to the public safety and security community, especially law enforcement. Today's homeland security agencies and organizations are also transitioning to and utilizing technologies that were developed primarily for the general public, such as social media and networking platforms. However, homeland security partners must not fall into complete dependence on technology because technology can fail. Although this book will discuss the importance and benefits of technologies, partners must not forget about the people, policies, and procedures underlying the use of the technologies. However, an understanding of technology is warranted because technology development and implementation is a constant force that has profound effects on homeland security partners. Or, as David Ihrie, chief technology officer at the Center for Innovative Technology, states:

> The future is coming really fast. If you look at the convergence of the Internet of Things, robotics, and artificial intelligence, 10 years from now the world is going to look very different than it does now. Emergency response folks are going to be living in a very different world.[32]

Discussion Questions

1. Explain the "gift of fire" concept by discussing a current technology and explain how it presents both advantages and risks to homeland security.
2. Select and research a U.S. incident or disaster that occurred prior to 9/11. Explain how current technology would have greatly aided in the protection against, response to, and recovery from the incident or disaster.
3. Assess your organization and determine if it is capable of managing innovation and change through proper leadership, organizational culture, and strategic planning.

Notes

1. McKay, "Welcome to the Future," 10.

2. National Commission on Terrorist Attacks upon the United States, *9/11 Commission Report.*

3. Holmes and Wagner, *Flood of June 11, 2010, in the Upper Little Missouri River Watershed, Arkansas*; Woodyard, Young, Amos, and Bandy, *Review Team Report*; U.S. Forest Service, *Recreation Visitor Safety Report.*

4. For the perspective of this book, "homeland security partners" includes all public and private agencies and organizations that have a responsibility in responding to an incident and/or disaster.

5. Greisler and Stupak, *Handbook of Technology Management in Public Administration*, 3.

6. Merriam-Webster, "Technology."

7. Greisler and Stupak, *Handbook of Technology Management in Public Administration*, 3.

8. Ramey, "What Is Technology—Meaning of Technology and Its Use," para. 1.

9. Greisler and Stupak, *Handbook of Technology Management in Public Administration*, 3.

10. Ibid., 4.

11. Stone, "A New World," 16.

12. Eastern Kentucky University Justice and Safety Center, *SAVER Program Report: Ruggedized Computers Selection and Procurement Guide,* 1.

13. U.S. Department of Homeland Security, *Science and Technology: A Foundation for Homeland Security,* 4.

14. Massachusetts Emergency Management Agency, *After Action Report for the Response to the 2013 Boston Marathon Bombings*; Gilgoff and Lee, "Social Media Shapes Boston Bombings Response"; Pittman, "The Story Behind #530slide: Social Media During Emergency Response."

15. U.S. Department of Homeland Security, *Science and Technology: A Foundation for Homeland Security,* 4.

16. U.S. Department of Homeland Security, *The 2014 Quadrennial Homeland Security Review.*

17. Baase, *A Gift of Fire.*

18. Dabinett, "Reflections on Regional Development Police in the Information Society," 232.

19. Morozov, *To Save Everything, Click Here.*

20. Ibid.; Dabinett, "Reflections on Regional Development Police in the Information Society."

21. Andrew and Petkov, "The Need for a Systems Thinking Approach to the Planning of Rural Telecommunications Infrastructure," 89.

22. Kumle-Hammes, "Transformational Leadership in the PSAP: The Importance of Being Change Ready."

23. Rowe and Guerrero, "Transformational Leadership," 167.

24. Ibid., 172.

25. Quinn, Bright, Faerman, Thompson, and McGrath, *Becoming a Master Manager,* 20.

26. Ibid., 20.

27. Cohen, Eimicke, and Heikkila, *The Effective Public Manager,* 115–128.

28. McCrimmon, "The Ideal Leader," 116.

29. Ibid.

30. Kumle-Hammes, "Transformational Leadership in the PSAP."

31. Stone, "A New World."

32. Ibid., 21.

Bibliography

Andrew, T., and D. Petkov. "The Need for a Systems Thinking Approach to the Planning of Rural Telecommunications Infrastructure." *Telecommunications Policy* 25 (2003): 75–93.

Baase, S. *A Gift of Fire: Social, Legal, and Ethical Issues for Computing Technology* (4th ed.). Upper Saddle River, NJ: Pearson. 2012.

Boyette, C. "Robots, Drones, and Heart-Detectors: How Disaster Technology Is Saving Lives." *CNN.* Last modified October 5, 2015. http://www.cnn.com/2015/08/24/us/robot-disaster-technology/.

Chapman, S. "How Digital Technology Is Revolutionising Disaster Response." *World Economic Forum.* Last modified April 21, 2015. http://www.weforum.org/agenda/2015/04/how-digital-technology-is-revolutionising-disaster-response.

Cohen, S., W. Eimicke, and T. Heikkila. *The Effective Public Manager: Achieving Success in Government Organizations* (5th ed.). San Francisco, CA: Jossey-Bass. 2013.

Dabinett, G. "Reflections on Regional Development Policies in the Information Society." *Planning Theory and Practice* 3, no. 2 (2002): 232–237.

Eastern Kentucky University Justice and Safety Center. *SAVER Program Report: Ruggedized Computers Selection and Procurement Guide (Cooperative Agreement # EMW-2005-CA-0378 awarded by DHS)*. Richmond, KY: Eastern Kentucky University. 2012.

Federal Emergency Management Agency. *A Whole Community Approach to Emergency Management: Principles, Themes, and Pathways for Action (FDOC 104-008-1)*. Washington, DC: Federal Emergency Management Agency. 2011.

Gilgoff, D., and J. Lee. "Social Media Shapes Boston Bombings Response." *National Geographic*. Last modified April 17, 2013. http://news.nationalgeographic.com /news/2013/13/130415-boston-marathon-bombings-terrorism-social-media -twitter-facebook/.

Goodier, R. "The Next Generation of Technology for Disaster Preparedness and Relief." *Engineering for Change*. Last modified October 10, 2014. http://www .engineeringforchange.org/the-next-generation-of-technology-for-disaster -preparedness-and-relief/.

Greisler, D., and R. Stupak (eds.). *Handbook of Technology Management in Public Administration*. Boca Rotan, FL: Taylor and Francis. 2007.

Holderman, E. "Technology Plays an Increasing Role in Emergency Management." *Emergency Management*. Last modified June 26, 2014. http://www.emergen cymgmt.com/training/Technology-Increasing-Role-Emergency-Management .html.

Holmes, R., and D. Wagner. *Flood of June 11, 2010, in the Upper Little Missouri River Watershed, Arkansas: Scientific Investigations Report 2011–5194*. Reston, VA: U.S. Department of the Interior, U.S. Geological Survey. 2011.

International Telecommunication Union and the Organization for Economic Co-operation and Development. *M-Government: Mobile Technologies for Responsive Governments and Connected Societies*. Geneva, Switzerland: ITU. 2011.

Jackson, B. "Technology Strategies for Homeland Security: Adaptation and Coevolution of Office and Defense." *Homeland Security Affairs* 5, no. 1 (2009): 1–16.

Kumle-Hammes, M. "Transformational Leadership in the PSAP: The Importance of Being Change Ready." *Public Safety Communications* 81, no. 6 (June 2015): 18–21.

Massachusetts Emergency Management Agency. *After Action Report for the Response to the 2013 Boston Marathon Bombings*. Boston, MA: Massachusetts Emergency Management Agency. 2014.

McCrimmon, M. "The Ideal Leader." In *Cases in Leadership* (4th ed.), ed. W. Rowe and L. Guerrero, 115–119. Thousand Oaks, CA: Sage Publications. 2016.

McKay, J. "Welcome to the Future." *Emergency Management* 1, no. 11 (Winter 2016): 10.

Merriam-Webster. "Technology." *Merriam-Webster*. Accessed February 2016. http:// www.merriam-webster.com/dictionary/technology.

Miller, R. "Hurricane Katrina: Communications and Infrastructure Impacts." In *Threats at Our Homeland: Homeland Defense and Homeland Security in the New Century—A Compilation of the Proceedings of the First Annual Homeland Defense* and *Homeland Security Conference*, ed. B. Tussing, 191–204. Carlisle Barracks, PA: U.S. Army War College. 2006.

Morozov, E. *To Save Everything, Click Here.* New York, NY: Public Affairs. 2013.

Moynihan, T. "The New Tech of Disaster Response, From Apps to Aqua-Drones." *Wired.* Last modified August 29, 2015. http://www.wired.com/2015/08/fema -disaster-tech/.

National Commission on Terrorist Attacks upon the United States. *The 9/11 Commission Report.* Washington, DC: National Commission on Terrorist Attacks upon the United States. 2004.

Pittman, E. "The Story Behind #530slide: Social Media During Emergency Response." *Emergency Management.* Last modified April 16, 2014. http://www .emergencymgmt.com/training/530slide-Social-Media-Emergency-Response .html.

Quinn, R., D. Bright, S. Faerman, M. Thompson, and M. McGrath. *Becoming a Master Manager: A Competing Values Approach* (6th ed.). New York, NY: John Wiley & Sons. 2015.

Ramey, K. "What Is Technology—Meaning of Technology and Its Use." *Use of Technology.* Last modified December 12, 2013. http://www.useoftechnology .com/what-is-technology/.

Rowe, W., and L. Guerrero. "Transformational Leadership." In *Cases in Leadership* (4th ed.), ed. W. Rowe and L. Guerrero. Thousand Oaks, CA: Sage Publications. 2016.

Select Bipartisan Committee to Investigate the Preparation for and Response to Hurricane Katrina. *A Failure of Initiative, 109th Congress*, R. REP. NO. 109–377 (2006).

Stone, A. "A New World." *Emergency Management* 1, no. 11 (Winter 2016): 16–21.

U.S. Department of Homeland Security. *National Preparedness Goal* (2nd ed.). Washington, DC: U.S. Department of Homeland Security. 2015.

U.S. Department of Homeland Security. *Science and Technology: A Foundation for Homeland Security.* Washington, DC: U.S. Department of Homeland Security, Office of Science and Technology Policy. 2005.

U.S. Department of Homeland Security. *The 2014 Quadrennial Homeland Security Review.* Washington, DC: U.S. Department of Homeland Security. 2014.

U.S. Forest Service. *Recreation Visitor Safety Report: October 18, 2010.* Washington, DC: U.S. Forest Service. 2010.

Woodyard, D., H. Young, M. Amos, and J. Bandy. *Review Team Report: Inquiry Regarding June 11, 2010 Flash Flood Incident Albert Pike Recreation Area Ouachita National Forest.* Washington, DC: U.S. Department of Agriculture. 2010.

CHAPTER TWO

Ethical and Privacy Implications of Technology

Ryan K. Baggett

Learning Objectives

After reading this chapter, readers should be able to:

- Explain the concepts of ethics and privacy and summarize the importance of their application to technology development and implementation.
- Apply the considerations in investigating ethics when developing or implementing technology.
- Compare and contrast the various types of technology assessments and identify the key components of each assessment.
- Compare and contrast the concepts of privacy and security and describe the merits of each in a homeland security setting.
- Explain the ethical issues identified in the example technologies within the chapter and describe potential alternatives for mitigating ethical conflicts.

Key Terms

Big Data
Civil Rights/Civil Liberties Impact Assessment
Ethics
Information Fusion Centers

Internet of Things
Privacy
Privacy Impact Assessment
Surveillance
Technological Impact Assessment
Technology Transfer

Introduction

> Laws and institutions must go hand in hand with the progress of the human mind. As that becomes more developed, more enlightened, as new discoveries are made, new truths disclosed, and manners and opinions change with the change of circumstances, institutions must advance also, and keep pace with the times.[1]

In the ever-changing global society, it is difficult to identify areas of everyday life that have not been fundamentally changed by technology. These changes are seemingly implemented to improve one's life (through areas such as medical advancements, convenience, or financial gain) but also have the potential to cause ethical challenges that must be addressed for successful implementation. However, it must be noted that laws and ethical practices have evolved over centuries as a result of technological innovation. For example, the steam engine and the building of the railroads in the 18th and 19th centuries led to the development of property rights and contract law. Many of the cases at that time were centered around property (on which tracks would be built) and eminent domain (the power of the state to forcibly acquire land for public utility).[2]

As such, the goal of this chapter is to provide a foundation on which readers can objectively assess both the ethical and privacy implications of technology. In building the foundation, the chapter will identify fundamental concepts, provide applicable frameworks, and present various topical areas for evaluation. Although provided examples will include both mainstream and homeland security technologies, it is intended that readers will carefully examine the information and determine what precautions and/or actions they might take if they were responsible for technology implementation. Further, it is also envisioned that readers will consider the information presented when making technology decisions in the future.

Ethics

The definition of "ethical behavior" is often debated based on variations in religion, politics, and cultural/societal norms. Although multiple definitions of ethics exist, a few commonalities include:

- A system of moral principles
- An area of study dealing with ideas regarding good and bad behavior
- A branch of philosophy dealing with what is morally right or wrong
- Governing a person's or group's behavior, such as how one should act in a range of situations
- Studying the conduct and moral judgment of a particular person, religion, group, profession, etc.

When discussing ethics as a field of study, technology ethics looks at the ethics involved in the development of a new technology (whether it is right or wrong to invent and implement a technological innovation) and the ethical questions raised because of the ways in which technology extends or restrains the power of individuals.[3] In 1990, Guy (1990) identified the basic characteristics of complex ethical decisions. First, the decision affects two or more values, and when compared, a greater return to one value can only be acquired through a loss to the other. Next, uncertainty is certain and consequences cannot be predicted. Last, decision-making power is distributed over a plethora of individuals and organizations.[4]

In investigating ethics in technology, decision makers should take into account several key considerations (as adapted from work developed by Brown University):[5]

Recognize the Ethical Issue and Gather Relevant Information: First, decision makers must determine if there are any specific ethical implications of the technology under consideration. It is important to completely understand the facts about the operation of the product before attempting to determine ethical implications. This step would include reviewing available, trusted information on the technology (from various sources) and potentially talking with current users.

Consider the Parties Involved: After information about the technology is obtained and potential ethical implications are identified, decision makers must ensure that consideration is given to those who might be affected by the technology. This effect might be positive or negative, depending on the circumstances. This step may include a focus group of those potentially affected to discuss the reason(s) for the technology's implementation and potential implications that may arise as a result.

Formulate Actions and Consider Alternatives: Next, potential actions must be identified and can be evaluated by asking various questions:

- What action will produce the most good and do the least harm? (Utilitarian Approach)
- What action treats people equally? (Justice Approach)
- What action serves the community as a whole, not just some members? (Common Good Approach)

Make a Decision and Act: After examining all the potential actions, decision makers must determine which one best addresses the situation at hand and then make a decision. It is noted that it may be uncomfortable to make certain decisions based on the ethical issues at hand. However, there are times when action must be taken, and utilizing a multistepped approach will afford the decision maker the due diligence necessary for an informed decision.

Reflect on the Outcome: The final step is to continuously evaluate the results of the decision and take note of any consequences (intended or unintended). The decision maker can determine if any changes need to be made following technology implementation (continuous improvement cycle) based on the results of the consequences.

It is important that ethical decision-making guidelines be used in technology implementation, and decision makers can clearly assess moral principles and probable consequences in ethical dilemmas. Challenges in these areas, if left unattended, can cause significant damage to an organization's/agency's morale and its relationships with constituents and community. Another area in technology implementation that should be considered carefully, along with ethics, is privacy.

Privacy

Privacy (in relationship to technology) is one's right to be left alone from personal intrusions and the ability to determine how much of one's personal information should be communicated to third parties. Privacy is another important factor that should be taken into consideration when new technologies are implemented. From a historical perspective, early work on privacy in the United States can be traced back to Warren and Brandeis's *The Right to Privacy*. As described by Kevin Macnish, the book is regarded as one of the first attempts to "define the concept of privacy, where the authors claim that the right to privacy is an instance of the 'right to be let alone' and establish limits to that right, arguing that it is not absolute."[6]

Developments in technology then gave rise to defining legal cases, such as *Katz v. United States* (1967), which related privacy and surveillance to the Fourth Amendment of the U.S. Constitution (forbidding unreasonable search and seizure by the state). *Eisenstadt v. Baird* (1972) then established that the right to privacy involves the right to make important choices without government intervention, drawing a connection between privacy and autonomy. When these areas are taken into consideration, a likely discussion may center on the balance of privacy versus security.

The Balance of Privacy and National Security

In December 2015, 14 people were killed and 22 were seriously injured during an attack in San Bernardino, California. In February 2016, Apple rejected a court order asking it to assist the Federal Bureau of Investigation (FBI) in obtaining encrypted data on the iPhone used by one of the shooters in the attack. Prosecutors noted that they needed Apple's help accessing the phone's data to find out who the shooters were communicating with and who may have helped plan and carry out the attack. In its response, Apple noted:

> Through the court order, the FBI has asked us to create a backdoor to the iPhone which would circumvent several important security features. While we believe the FBI's intentions are good, it would be wrong for the government to force us to build a backdoor into our products. And ultimately, we fear that this demand would undermine the very freedoms and liberty our government is meant to protect.[7]

Apple's decision to reject the court order undoubtedly considered the security of the nation (potentially preventing further attacks) and the privacy of Apple customers (ensuring that freedoms and liberties are protected). However, the discussion on privacy and security did not start with the Apple court order. In fact, the U.S. statesman Benjamin Franklin stated in 1775 that "those who give up essential liberty to purchase a little temporary safety deserve neither liberty nor safety."[8] In fact, this debate can be seen in historical events such as the Alien and Sedition Acts of 1798, the suspension of the writ of habeas corpus by President Abraham Lincoln, the Red Scare in the 1920s, and even the Uniting and Strengthening America by Providing Appropriate Tools Required to Intercept and Obstruct Terrorism Act of 2001 (USA PATRIOT Act).

The September 11, 2001, attacks led to the rapid congressional approval of the USA PATRIOT Act. Critics claim that the act "gives the Attorney General and federal law enforcement unnecessary and permanent new powers to violate civil liberties that go far beyond the goal of fighting international terrorism."[9] Advocates for the act note that "America needs the

USA PATRIOT Act because it helps prevent terrorism and lets counter-terrorism agents use tools that have been in place for decades with the inclusion of elaborate safeguards against abuse."[10]

Also in the field of homeland security/intelligence was the 2013 classified documents leak by National Security Agency contractor Edward Snowden. The information revealed global surveillance programs that were being conducted by the NSA, the Five Eyes (an intelligence alliance between the United States, United Kingdom, Australia, Canada, and New Zealand), and global telecommunication companies. The document dissemination focused the nation's attention on security policies and again questioned the effect of the measures on their basic constitutional liberties. Whatever the individual's perspective may be regarding the balance between privacy and security, it is imperative that factual information is collected and analyzed through an objective assessment process.

Technology Assessments

In order to explore how multifaceted impacts might be understood, controlled, and mitigated, there are several areas that must be investigated. We need to look into social/technology assessment, the transfer of the technology as it is placed into practice, and the techniques/processes that are available for control within the legal, political, institutional, and attitudinal environment within which the technology is placed as a way of protecting our rights to life, liberty, and pursuit of happiness.[11]

Technological Impact Assessment

Most cultures would likely agree that the development and application of powerful emerging technologies should have a foundation on a comprehensive evaluation of the advantages and disadvantages that the technology might generate. A technological impact assessment (TIA) can be defined as the "systematic study of the effects on society that may occur when a technology is introduced, extended, or modified with emphasis on the impacts that are unintended, indirect or delayed."[12] It should be noted that a TIA is not an anti-technological approach, but rather an interdisciplinary approach to prevent potential damages caused by the implementation of new technologies. The results of a TIA, a form of a cost-benefit analysis, should be utilized by decision makers. However, an objective TIA is often difficult to conduct due to a wide range of ethical perspectives, research variables that delineate between positive and negative consequences for a specific technology, and overall design that may overgeneralize the results of the assessment.[13]

Privacy Impact Assessment

One key consideration of technology privacy is data or information privacy and the collection of Personally Identifiable Information (PII) or Sensitive Personal Information (SPI). With the prevalence of identity theft and other cybercrimes (including financial), individuals should be concerned about the release/sharing of information that can be used to identify, contact, or locate them. One decision tool to identify and mitigate privacy risks is the Privacy Impact Assessment (PIA) utilized by the federal government. The PIA is used when developing or procuring any new technologies or systems that handle PII; when creating a new program, system, or technology that may have privacy implications; or when updating existing systems that may result in privacy risks. The PIA will ensure compliance with legal and privacy requirements, determine risks and effects, and evaluate protections and alternatives to mitigate privacy risks.

Civil Rights/Civil Liberties Impact Assessment

The U.S. Department of Homeland Security houses an Office for Civil Rights and Civil Liberties (CRCL) to support the department's mission to secure the nation while preserving individual liberty, fairness, and equality under the law. One of the tools the office uses is a Civil Rights/Civil Liberties Impact Assessment that may be required by statute, requested by department leadership or staff, or initiated by the Office for CRCL. According to the DHS, "The policy analysts who write CRCL Impact Assessments review various department programs, policies, or activities to determine whether these department initiatives have an impact on the civil rights or civil liberties of those affected by the initiative. CRCL policy analysts consider various types of questions when drafting an impact assessment to include the impact on particular groups or individuals, the influence of government, notice and redress, alternatives, and safeguards." In the course of conducting the impact assessment, and in the final written document, CRCL may make recommendations for change.[14]

21st-Century Emerging Ethical Dilemmas and Policy Issues in Science and Technology

The 21st century has seen a wide variety of astonishing advances in technology innovation, many of which have associated ethical dilemmas. These advances have occurred in many different areas that include, but are not limited to, biotechnology, computing, robotics, medicine, telecommunications, finance, artificial intelligence, and genetics. For example, the debate on stem cells and embryo research and genetically modified organisms has involved scientists, policy makers (which includes politicians), and religious groups. Additionally, artificial intelligence and robotics continue to expand capabilities in various areas of society as well as raise the question of privacy.

In an effort to advance science and technology, the John J. Reilly Center for Science, Technology, and Values at the University of Notre Dame develops an annual list of emerging ethical dilemmas and policy issues in science and technology. The center explores conceptual, ethical, and policy issues where science and technology intersect with society from different disciplinary perspectives. The ten items from the 2016 list are highlighted below in no particular order:[15]

1. **Lethal Cyber Weapons:** In 2015, the U.S. Cyber Command contracted a project to produce "lethal cyber weapons"—logic bombs with the ability to cause critical infrastructure to self-destruct. Additionally, the U.S. Department of Defense (DoD) has released information on cyber weapons and potentially lethal applications, including a nuclear plant meltdown, opening a dam upstream from a populated area, and disabling air traffic control services.[16] While ethical issues in weaponry are not new for the United States (atomic bombs in WWII), the mechanisms and strategies are.

2. **Exoskeletons for the Elderly:** An exoskeleton is a lightweight scaffolding that fits over the user's arms, legs, and torso to improve strength and speed. The technology started with a goal to relieve back pain for those who work manual labor jobs. The ethical question is whether extending labor years and automating the elderly are in the best interest of society.

3. **Artificial Wombs:** This technology allows for the process of ectogenesis, or the ability to grow a fetus outside of a woman's body. Advocates of the technology note that artificial wombs give the capacity to remove women from the medical risks of childbirth. Opponents to the technology argue the technology on religious and moral grounds.

4. **Artificial Intelligence Toys:** Mattel has released plans for a new Barbie doll called "Hello Barbie." This toy is constantly connected to Wi-Fi and interacts with children on a variety of topics (based on previous conversations that are stored). Parents can be sent a transcript of the conversation based on the information that is exchanged by the child with the doll. Not only does this toy have privacy implications for the children, but child development specialists are concerned that an interactive doll may fulfill friendship roles in some children and also lead to unhealthy interactions that are incapable of conflict.

5. **Digital Labor:** Many online marketplaces give individuals the opportunity to work with a significant amount of autonomy. Although some may find the ability to work from home appealing, the lack of protections provided by

digital labor have sparked ethical discussions. One of the most challenging aspects is the blur between work time and home time. Without labor rights for the digital labor community, the ability to take advantage of this work-force could be heightened.

6. **Bone Conduction for Marketing:** Bone conduction is not a new technology and has been essential in the development of hearing aids, modern head-phones, and Google Glass. These technologies work by passing sounds through a transducer that sits on the user's skull. However, marketing com-panies now have begun to use bone conduction to transmit advertising. In fact, AT&T has filed patents for technology that can be used to target ads to users of mobile devices by learning their body language.

7. **Genetic Engineering:** Clustered regularly interspaced short palindromic re-peats (CRISPR) allow scientists to make precise, targeted changes to the ge-nome of living cells that will be inherited by future generations. Advocates state that genetic engineering in humans is meant to eradicate a variety of devastating, heritable diseases. However, critics (including bioethicists) have argued against the prospect because of concerns about use of the technology for purely cosmetic enhancements, unforeseen side effects of changing the DNA, and equality of access to this technology.

8. **Disappearing Drones:** Inbound, Controlled, Air-Releasable, Unrecoverable Systems (ICARUS) are drones that self-destruct after performing their task. Although the utilization of unmanned aerial systems is presented in chapter 8, one concern with self-destructing drones is the inability to identify the individual and/or country behind their use. This lack of evidence should be considered not only in international uses, but also in domestic scenarios with the increasing citizen use of drone technology.

9. **Head Transplants:** By 2017, an Italian doctor has promised to perform the world's first head transplant. While skeptics believe the technology is decades away from successful execution, the doctor expresses his confidence in vari-ous surgical advances in the last decade. In considering ethical issues, the human brain may not be able to adequately comprehend the implications of such a transplant. Memory and identification immediately arise from the lim-itless ethical dilemmas that will likely commence.

10. **Rapid Whole-Genome Sequencing:** In an effort to identify and hopefully treat potential problems in newborns, the process of rapid whole-genome sequencing has been conducted. Medical researchers collect DNA from both the newborn and his or her parent, whose genomes give them a starting point for identifying mutations. Once the DNA is sequenced, doctors can assess the newborn's symptoms in order to narrow down their search. A diagnosis based on genome sequencing is then given to the doctors and parents; the sequence data is stored anonymously for future research. It has been noted that knowl-edge of these genes confers no benefits on the newborn at this point in time, and instead may give parents uncertainties of raising children with poten-tially fatal diseases. Further ethical concerns include genome ownership,

privacy, equality of access, and accessing genomic information not related to the diseases in the current case.

Internet of Things

One additional technological advancement that should be included in any discussion of technology ethics is the Internet of Things (IoT). The IoT is a network of physical objects that are embedded with electronics, software, sensors, and network connectivity to enable those objects to collect and exchange data.[17] These objects (devices, buildings, vehicles, etc.) can be controlled remotely across existing network infrastructure. Developers cite advantages such as real-time marketing, enhanced situational awareness, process optimization, and resource consumption optimization. However, despite the convenience and utility of IoT devices, several ethical, privacy, and security implications should be considered.

Clubb, Kirch, and Patwa (2015) note that networks allow a continuous data feed from IoT devices that can be collected and analyzed, producing various possibilities to include:[18]

- From a smartphone-connected wearable device: detection of sensitive behavioral patterns, moods, habits, stress levels, and potentially, diseases
- From a connected home: vacancy times, data on who is at home (elderly, children, etc.)
- From a connected car: driving habits, routine locations visited by individuals

Through the data produced by the IoT, the disruptive analysis of human patterns could lead to unintended consequences. For example, behavioral patterns could be used against a person, without detection, for life insurance, employment, lending, or other decisions. An individual's poor driving habits could be used to deny automobile insurance or rental car access. Further, home vacancy information (gleaned from IoT data) could be used by intruders for "windows of opportunity."

The international research firm Gartner estimated that by the end of 2015, there would be 3.8 billion connected devices on the IoT, ranging from smart cars, smoke detectors, door locks, industrial robots, streetlights, heart monitors, trains, wind turbines, even tennis racquets and toasters.[19] Networking company Cisco estimates that the number of connected devices on the IoT will rise to 50 billion by 2020, with other companies estimating over three times that amount.[20] Questions on generated data ownership, availability, usage, and admissibility must be addressed, but this area of technology will undoubtedly continue to advance in many aspects of an individual's life.

21st-Century Emerging Ethical Dilemmas in Homeland Security Related Technologies

Technology transfer can be defined as the process of transferring skill, knowledge, and technologies to other institutions to ensure that developments are accessible to a wider range of users who can further develop the technology for other uses. Although technology transfer can describe several transactions throughout a society, the homeland security enterprise has been a key recipient of transferred technology from both the commercial electronics market and the DoD. In some instances, the transferred technologies may have been developed for a specific use, and then altered or customized for homeland security applications. As noted in the previous discussions on ethics and privacy, technologies should be carefully evaluated for consequences (intended and unintended) that may occur as a result of implementation. In the following pages, the areas of video surveillance, big data, information fusion centers, and three-dimensional (3-D) printing will be explored, with a close focus on ethical and privacy implications in homeland security applications.

Video Surveillance

Surveillance involves the act of paying close and sustained attention to another person or object. Ethical considerations in surveillance are not new, with many historical examples in both fiction and nonfiction. From the fictional perspective, George Orwell's *1984* introduced readers to the telescreen, a two-way television that allowed the state visual and auditory access to citizens' lives. They were constantly reminded that "Big Brother was watching them."[21]

Although the function of video surveillance is expanded upon in chapter 6, in its simplest form it is used to observe a certain area. It generally consists of a camera(s) connected to a recording device with variations in hardware and software features. Many major cities are now implementing citywide video surveillance systems to combat terrorism. For example, New York's Lower Manhattan Security Initiative monitors 4,000 security cameras and license plate readers through a combination of public and private cameras. In comparison, London's "Ring of Steel" surveillance system combines nearly a half million cameras to monitor the city. In addition to traditional video surveillance systems, many cities are implementing facial recognition technologies to automatically analyze footage for information. One finding from the investigation into the Boston Marathon Bombing was that even if a city has access to numerous cameras, the overwhelming amount of evidence can be difficult to analyze in an effective manner.[22]

Opponents of video surveillance in public areas claim that video surveillance has not been proven effective, citing reports from the United Kingdom. Further, they argue that public video surveillance is susceptible to abuse in five forms: criminal, institutional, personal, discriminatory, and voyeuristic. Next, because the technology has evolved so quickly, there is a lack of limits or controls on camera use. Finally, critics claim that video surveillance will have a chilling effect on public life and that surveillance will bring profound changes to the character of public spaces.[23]

With regard to the effectiveness of public surveillance, advocates note that many studies cited by critics on the problems with video surveillance are decades old. They note a 2009 Scotland Yard study demonstrating that video surveillance helps solve 70 percent of UK murders. Not only that, but Scotland Yard concluded that video surveillance is as vital for forensic evidence as DNA or fingerprints. As such, security managers note that surveillance is most effective in investigations and not in general crime reduction. Further security professionals warn against designing or justifying surveillance systems as general crime-reducing tools as this practice sets unrealistic expectations that video surveillance is a panacea.[24]

In the end, some surveillance applications are effective and reasonable, while others are questionable and present certain challenges to civil liberties. With that said, there is a clear need for limits, controls, and guidelines. The difficulty lies in the ability to objectively distinguish appropriate from inappropriate uses. As noted by a former Canadian official, "To permit unrestricted video surveillance by agents of the state would seriously diminish the degree of privacy we can reasonably expect to enjoy in a free society."[25] Additionally, Microsoft entrepreneur Bill Gates asked, "Should surveillance be used for petty crimes like jaywalking or minor drug possession? Or is there a higher threshold for certain information? Those aren't easy questions."[26]

Big Data

There is little doubt that many aspects of homeland security have benefited from innovations in technologies, including improved models resulting from access to data. Take, for example, how the increased precision of weather forecasting now affords communities extra days to prepare for severe storms or wintry weather. However, communities have good legal, ethical, and practical reasons to be cautious about overreliance on data-driven solutions to problems.

Data is much more plentiful than in the past, and it presents homeland security partners opportunities to become more efficient in their operation.

It is estimated that the proportion of all information in the world stored in a digital format has increased from 25 percent in 2000 to 98 percent in 2013. This means that less than 2 percent of all information is recorded in nondigital formats such as paper, books, prints, film, etc.[27] Smart policing, intelligence-led policing, predictive policing, and data-driven policing strategies all embrace the use of data to support strategic and tactical operations.[28] Although the precise overlap among these theories or strategies remains unclear, they all aim to respond to new threats involving technologies (e.g., computer crimes, cybercrimes, use of social media and mobile devices among criminals) and leverage technologies for achieving heightened awareness of trends. For example, Mayer-Schonberger and Cukier note that select agencies are now using "big-data analysis to select what streets, groups, and individuals to subject to extra scrutiny."[29]

Due to budget reductions and other reasons, the use of technologies to support the allocation of scarce resources is reasonable. Mayer-Schonberger and Cukier suggest that having access to "big data" may actually reduce risks associated with the profiling of people, places, and things by making decisions less discriminatory and more individualized.[30]

However, inferring one's culpability or intent solely based on locational data used to support "hot spot" policing strategies and others is problematic. Note that correlations among data does not translate into causal relationships. Interpreting relationships and finding meaning within big data requires critical thinking, reasoning, and moral choices. Conducting critical thinking and making moral choices requires more than access to data; it requires sound policies and procedures, professional training, and creative problem solving skills, among many other factors. As Einstein is famous for saying, "Not everything that can be counted counts, and not everything that counts can be counted."[31]

In addition to fears regarding predictive analysis and profiling, big data presents potential privacy risks, such as financial fraud and identity theft, as more and more personal data is digitized and transmitted via the Web.

Information Fusion Centers

An information fusion center is "a collaborative effort of two or more agencies that provide resources, expertise and information to the center with the goal of maximizing their ability to detect, prevent, investigate, and respond to criminal and terrorist activity."[32] As of 2015, there are 53 primary fusion centers and 25 additional recognized fusion centers that have been designated by the state governors.[33] While the events of September 11, 2001, served as a catalyst for many advancements in fusion centers, it should be noted that before the 2001 tragedy, many states and large cities operated units that gathered and shared information focusing on specific areas such as gang activity.

According to DHS, "Fusion centers contribute to the Information Sharing Environment (ISE) through their role in receiving threat information, analyzing that information in the context of their local environment, and disseminating that information to local agencies; and through gathering tips, leads, and suspicious activity reporting (SAR) from local agencies and the public. Fusion centers receive information from a variety of sources, including SAR from stakeholders within their jurisdictions, as well as federal information and intelligence. They analyze the information and develop relevant products to disseminate to their customers. These products assist homeland security partners at all levels of government to identify and address immediate and emerging threats."[34]

With regard to privacy and civil liberties challenges associated with fusion centers, critics have identified various problems. For example, a September 2007 report excerpt reprinted Stanley and Steinhardt's "Even Bigger, Even Weaker" American Civil Liberties Union (ACLU) report,[35] which noted the following issues:

- **Ambiguous Lines of Authority:** The participation of agencies from multiple jurisdictions in fusion centers allows the authorities to manipulate differences in federal, state, and local laws to maximize information collection while evading accountability and oversight through the practice of "policy shopping."
- **Private Sector Participation:** Fusion centers are incorporating private-sector corporations into the intelligence process, breaking down the arm's-length relationship that protects the privacy of innocent Americans who are employees or customers of these companies, and increasing the risk of a data breach.
- **Military Participation:** Fusion centers are involving military personnel in law enforcement activities in troubling ways.
- **Data Fusion = Data Mining:** Federal fusion center guidelines encourage wholesale data collection and manipulation processes that threaten privacy.
- **Excessive Secrecy:** Fusion centers are hobbled by excessive secrecy, which limits public oversight, impairs their ability to acquire essential information, and impedes their ability to fulfill their stated mission, bringing their ultimate value into doubt.

On the other hand, DHS conducted a Civil Rights/Civil Liberties Impact Assessment into fusion centers in 2013; an excerpt from that report has been reprinted from *Civil Rights/Civil Liberties Impact Assessment: DHS Support to the National Network of Fusion Centers:*[36]

- DHS has received only two formal complaints about fusion center activities since the inception of DHS's support to the National Network. Although DHS is unaware of any current civil rights or civil liberties violations, institutional safeguards are required to protect civil rights and civil liberties in the National Network.
- DHS has several important safeguards in place to protect civil rights and civil liberties. Most significantly, it provides useful guidance, advice, training, and technical assistance to fusion centers on the importance of safeguarding privacy, civil rights, and civil liberties; establishes a process for ensuring that fusion centers have in place privacy, civil rights, and civil liberties policies that are at least as comprehensive as the ISE Privacy Guidelines; and collects data on fusion center capabilities through the annual Fusion Center Assessment Program.
- DHS has the potential to implement additional enhancements to protect civil rights and civil liberties throughout the National Network.

In an attempt to ensure the protection of citizens' civil rights with regard to intelligence collection, analysis, and dissemination, Carter and Martinelli (2007) identified seven steps that an agency can practice to ensure the protection of citizens' civil rights and to make a reasonable effort to comply with legal findings and smart practices:[37]

- **Step 1—Policy:** In an effort to align with national standards, agencies are encouraged to develop/adopt and implement policies to include privacy, security, and accepted records management.
- **Step 2—Training:** The National Criminal Intelligence Sharing Plan (developed by the U.S. Department of Justice) includes an outline for an intelligence awareness training program. Not only should the training be conducted in agencies, but personnel should also receive training on all fusion center policies. Carter and Martinelli also note that personnel must understand constitutional rights violations and a "zero-tolerance policy" should be enacted on any infractions.
- **Step 3—Supervision:** It is the role of a supervisor to not only lead by example regarding his or her commitment to the constitutional rights but also hold those under his or her supervision to a high standard in intelligence gathering.
- **Step 4—Public Education:** The delivery of community education will help develop the situational awareness of the public regarding intelligence initiatives. Through these initiatives, it is hoped that the development and spreading of rumors will be mitigated, the public may feel like contributors to their community's security, and relationships can be developed.
- **Step 5—Transparent Processes:** While certain information will be protected in the intelligence process, the process itself should be transparent and clearly understood. This transparency may also lead to stronger relationships and community involvement.

- **Step 6—Accountability Audits:** Carter and Martinelli recommend a two-step process to ensure accountability within an agency. These audits include a supervisor's review/report to be followed by the review of the report by an external auditor.
- **Step 7—Assistance of Legal Counsel:** It goes without saying that legal counsel is a requirement for all intelligence-related/public serving agencies. In an effort to limit potential allegations of rights violations, agencies must follow policies/guidelines, provide effective training opportunities, and use discretion without malice.

Three-Dimensional (3-D) Printing

The process of additive manufacturing, also known as 3-D printing, refers to the formulation of successive layers under computer control to create an object.[38] In his 2013 State of the Union address, President Barack Obama noted that 3-D printing could "revolutionize the way we make almost everything," to include printing prosthetics, violins, and even aircraft parts.[39] In fact, futurologists believe that 3-D printing will bring about the third industrial revolution, succeeding the production line assembly from the 19th century. However, with many technologies comes associated technological risks, given the fact that the same technology that can produce positive life-changing tools can also produce firearms that are incapable of detection.

DHS Intelligence Bulletins have warned that it could be impossible to stop 3-D–printed guns from being made, not to mention getting past security checkpoints. Intelligence on the topic notes that blueprints are readily available that outline the development of guns from melted plastic. The information threatens to reduce the effectiveness of 3-D gun control efforts. "Significant advances in three-dimensional (3D) printing capabilities, availability of free digital 3D printer files for firearms components, and difficulty regulating file sharing may present public safety risks from unqualified gun seekers who obtain or manufacture 3D printed guns," warns the bulletin compiled by the Joint Regional Intelligence Center.[40] 3D Systems, the largest company in consumer and industrial 3-D printing and manufacturing noted:

> We recognize unintended uses of this game-changing technology and take seriously our responsibility as industry leaders to work with legislators to educate and influence them in the good, the bad, and the unintended. We are not a law enforcement agency and cannot prevent someone from shooting a 3D printed gun any more than an automaker can prevent a drunk driver from taking the wheel, but are committed to doing everything that is creative, innovative, and responsible, even if it means some restrictions.[41]

Although the debate may continue with this specific technology, ethical questions regarding the effects of technology on society will undoubtedly continue to surface as long as sophisticated technologies continue to be developed and implemented.

Conclusion

> We now stand in the vestibule of a vast new technological age—one that, despite its capacity for human destruction, has an equal capacity to make poverty and human misery obsolete. If our efforts are wisely directed—and if our unremitting efforts for dependable peace begin to attain some success— we can surely become participants in creating an age characterized by justice and rising levels of human well-being.[42]

"Don't be evil" and "do the right thing" have both been the corporate mottos of Google. Whether Google lives up to this slogan is up to the evaluator, but most technology companies unfortunately do not share this perspective. As explained in chapter 1, technology can act as a double-edged sword, with the same technology yielding both risks and benefits, depending on its use. As such, analysis of function and consequence should be of primary concern for any organization considering the implementation of a technology. Properly selected and implemented technology can make an organization more effective and efficient, but the opposite is true about improperly implemented technology causing hours of shutdowns and resulting in deteriorating community relationships.

This chapter reviewed the concepts of ethics and privacy and identified their importance in technology development and implementation. Additionally, several examples in both the consumer electronics market and the homeland security community were identified, with a focus on ethical and privacy issues. Hopefully the considerations and suggestions noted in this chapter will be applied in both personal and organizational settings in the years to come.

Discussion Questions

1. As the newly elected sheriff of a rural Midwestern county, you have been asked by the county commission to consider the adoption of body-worn cameras for county deputies. The deputies are outraged, stating that administrators will use the cameras to track their every move and try to catch them not doing their jobs. If possible, how could you remedy the

deputy's concerns and help them understand the personal benefits of the cameras?

2. As an analyst for the U.S. Department of Homeland Security's Customs and Border Protection, you have been asked to provide a briefing to DHS administrators on the ethical and privacy concerns of unmanned aerial systems with a focus on ICARUS. What key considerations would you provide using the steps in the investigating ethics in technology process that was presented earlier in the chapter? What alternatives could you deliver?

3. As one of the state's information intelligence analysts, you have been assigned to a regional information sharing initiative in the northeast portion of the state. The Rotary Club has asked for an analyst to come to its monthly meeting to discuss ways in which the club members' privacy would be protected under the new program. What safeguards could you propose to the audience?

Notes

1. Jefferson and Ford, *The Writings of Thomas Jefferson.*

2. Wadhwa, "Laws and Ethics Can't Keep Pace with Technology."

3. Jonas, *Towards a Philosophy of Technology.*

4. Guy, *Ethical Decision Making in Everyday Work Situations.*

5. Brown University, "A Framework for Making Ethical Decisions."

6. Macnish, "Surveillance Ethics."

7. Cook, "A Message to Our Customers."

8. Franklin, *Memoirs of the Life and Writings of Benjamin Franklin.*

9. American Civil Liberties Union, "Does the USA PATRIOT Act Diminish Civil Liberties?"

10. Sales, "The USA PATRIOT Act Is a Vital Weapon in Fighting Terrorism."

11. Bailey, "Technology and Ethics."

12. Baase, *A Gift of Fire.*

13. Huesemann and Huesemann, *Technofix.*

14. U.S. Department of Homeland Security, "Civil Rights and Civil Liberties."

15. John J. Reilly Center, "Emerging Ethical Dilemmas and Policy Issues in Science and Technology 2015."

16. Folk, "U.S. Cyber Command Moves Towards 'Lethal Cyber Weapons.'"

17. ITU, "Internet of Things Global Standards Initiative."

18. Clubb, Kirch, and Patwa, "The Ethics, Privacy, and Legal Issues around the Internet of Things."

19. Scott, "8 Ways the Internet of Things Will Change the Way We Live and Work."

20. Abramovich, "15 Mind-Blowing Stats about the Internet of Things."

21. Orwell, *Nineteen Eighty-Four.*

22. Kelly, "After Boston."

23. American Civil Liberties Union, "What's Wrong with Public Video Surveillance?"

24. Honovich, "Is Public Video Surveillance Effective?"

25. Baase, *A Gift of Fire.*

26. Godell, "Bill Gates: The Rolling Stone Interview."

27. Mayer-Schonberger and Cukier, *Big Data.*

28. Pearsall, "Predictive Policing: The Future of Law Enforcement?"; Wilson, Smith, Markovic, and LeBeau, *Geospatial Technology Working Group Meeting Report on Predictive Policing.*

29. Mayer-Schonberger and Cukier, *Big Data.*

30. Ibid., 161.

31. Isaacson, *Einstein.*

32. U.S. Department of Homeland Security, *Baseline Capabilities for State and Major Urban Area Fusion Centers.*

33. U.S. Department of Homeland Security, "Fusion Center Locations and Contact Information."

34. U.S. Department of Homeland Security, "National Network of Fusion Centers Fact Sheet."

35. Stanley and Steinhardt, *Even Bigger, Even Weaker.*

36. U.S. Department of Homeland Security, *Civil Rights/Civil Liberties Impact Assessment.*

37. Carter and Martinelli, "Civil Rights and Law Enforcement Intelligence."

38. Cummins, "The Rise of Additive Manufacturing."

39. Rosenwald, "Weapons Made with 3-D Printers Could Test Gun-Control Efforts."

40. Winter, "Homeland Security Bulletin Warns 3D-Printed Guns May Be 'Impossible' to Stop."

41. Terdiman, "Why Fear of 3D-Printed Guns Is Overblown."

42. Eisenhower, "Annual Message to the Congress on the State of the Union (January 7, 1960)."

Bibliography

Abramovich, G. "15 Mind-Blowing Stats about the Internet of Things." *CMO by Adobe.* Last modified April 17, 2015. http://www.cmo.com/articles/2015/4/13/mind-blowing-stats-internet-of-things-iot.html.

American Civil Liberties Union. "Does the USA PATRIOT Act Diminish Civil Liberties?" American Civil Liberties Union. Last modified July 2008. http://aclu.procon.org/view.answers.php?questionID=000716.

American Civil Liberties Union. "What's Wrong with Public Video Surveillance?" American Civil Liberties Union. Accessed March 2016. https://www.aclu.org/whats-wrong-public-video-surveillance.

Baase, S. *A Gift of Fire: Social, Legal, and Ethical Issues for Computing Technology* (4th ed.). Upper Saddle River, NJ: Pearson. 2012.

Bailey, R. "Technology and Ethics." Coursera. Accessed March 2016. https://www .class-central.com/mooc/1529/coursera-technology-and-ethics.

Brown University. "A Framework for Making Ethical Decisions." Brown University. Last modified May 2013. https://www.brown.edu/academics/science-and-tech nology-studies/framework-making-ethical-decisions.

Carter, D., and T. Martinelli. "Civil Rights and Law Enforcement Intelligence." *Police Chief Magazine*. Last modified June 2007. http://www.policechiefmagazine .org/magazine/index.cfm?fuseaction=display_arch&article_id=1206&issue _id=62007.

Clubb, K., L. Kirch, and N. Patwa. "The Ethics, Privacy, and Legal Issues around the Internet of Things." University of California-Berkley. Last modified Spring 2015. http://www.ischool.berkeley.edu/files/projects/w231-internetofthingsfinal paper.pdf.

Cook, T. "A Message to Our Customers." Apple, Inc. Last modified February 16, 2016. http://www.apple.com/customer-letter/.

Cummins, K. "The Rise of Additive Manufacturing." *The Engineer.* Last modified May 24, 2010. http://www.theengineer.co.uk/the-rise-of-additive-manufacturing/.

Eisenhower, D. "Annual Message to the Congress on the State of the Union (January 7, 1960)." The American Presidency Project. Accessed March 2016. http:// www.presidency.ucsb.edu/ws/?pid=12061.

Folk, C. "U.S. Cyber Command Moves Towards 'Lethal Cyber Weapons.'" Syracuse University, Institute for National Security and Counterterrorism. Last modified November 10, 2015. http://insct.syr.edu/us-cyber-command-moves-towards -lethal-cyber-weapons/.

Franklin, B. *Memoirs of the Life and Writings of Benjamin Franklin.* Philadelphia, PA: William Duane. 1818.

Godell, Jeff. "Bill Gates: The Rolling Stone Interview." *Rolling Stone*, March 13, 2014.

Guy, M. *Ethical Decision Making in Everyday Work Situations.* New York, NY: Quorum Books. 1990.

Honovich, J. "Is Public Video Surveillance Effective?" *Government Security News*. Last modified January 9, 2009. http://gsnmagazine.com/article/17888/public _video_surveillance_effective.

Huesemann, M., and J. Huesemann. *Technofix: Why Technology Won't Save Us or the Environment.* Gabriola Island, BC: New Society Publishers. 2011.

Isaacson, W. *Einstein: His Life and Universe.* New York, NY: Simon and Schuster. 2007.

ITU. "Internet of Things Global Standards Initiative." ITU. Accessed March 2016. http://www.itu.int/en/ITU-T/gsi/iot/Pages/default.aspx.

Jefferson, T., and P. Ford. *The Writings of Thomas Jefferson: 1788–1792.* New York, NY: G. P. Putnam's Sons. 1892.

John J. Reilly Center. "Emerging Ethical Dilemmas and Policy Issues in Science and Technology 2015." University of Notre Dame. Accessed March 2016. http://reilly .nd.edu/outreach/emerging-ethical-dilemmas-and-policy-issues-in-science-and -technology-2015/.

Jonas, H. *Towards a Philosophy of Technology.* Oxford: Blackwell Publishing. 2013.

Kelly, H. "After Boston: The Pros and Cons of Surveillance Cameras." *CNN.* Last modified April 26, 2013. http://www.cnn.com/2013/04/26/tech/innovation /security-cameras-boston-bombings/.

Macnish, Kevin. "Surveillance Ethics." *Internet Encyclopedia of Philosophy.* Accessed November 2016. http://www.iep.utm.edu/surv-eth/.

Mayer-Schonberger, V., and K. Cukier. *Big Data: A Revolution That Will Transform How We Live, Work, and Think.* New York, NY: Houghton Mifflin Harcourt. 2013.

Orwell, G. *Nineteen Eighty-Four.* London, UK: Penguin Books. 2004.

Pearsall, B. "Predictive Policing: The Future of Law Enforcement?" *National Institute of Justice.* Last modified June 23, 2010. http://www.nij.gov/journals/266 /Pages/predictive.aspx.

Rosenwald, M. "Weapons Made with 3-D Printers Could Test Gun-Control Efforts." *The Washington Post.* Last modified February 18, 2013. https://www .washingtonpost.com/local/weapons-made-with-3-d-printers-could-test-gun -control-efforts/2013/02/18/9ad8b45e-779b-11e2-95e4-6148e45d7adb _story.html.

Sales, N. "The USA PATRIOT Act Is a Vital Weapon in Fighting Terrorism." *The New York Times.* Last modified May 23, 2014. http://www.nytimes.com/room fordebate/2011/09/07/do-we-still-need-the-patriot-act/the-patriot-act-is -a-vital-weapon-in-fighting-terrorism.

Scott, A. "8 Ways the Internet of Things Will Change the Way We Live and Work." *The Globe and Mail: Report on Business Magazine.* Accessed March 2016. http:// www.theglobeandmail.com/report-on-business/rob-magazine/the-future-is -smart/article24586994/.

Stanley, J., and B. Steinhardt. (Reprinted from *Even Bigger, Even Weaker: The Emerging Surveillance Society.* New York, NY: American Civil Liberties Union. 2007.)

Terdiman, D. "Why Fear of 3D-Printed Guns Is Overblown." *C/NET.* Last modified May 9, 2013. http://www.cnet.com/news/why-fear-of-3d-printed-guns-is -overblown/.

U.S. Department of Homeland Security. *Baseline Capabilities for State and Major Urban Area Fusion Centers: A Supplement to the Fusion Center Guidelines.* Washington, DC: U.S. Department of Homeland Security. 2008.

U.S. Department of Homeland Security. "Civil Rights and Civil Liberties." U.S. Department of Homeland Security. Last modified October 5, 2015. https:// www.dhs.gov/topic/civil-rights-and-civil-liberties.

U.S. Department of Homeland Security. (Reprinted from *Civil Rights/Civil Liberties Impact Assessment: DHS Support to the National Network of Fusion Centers.* Washington, DC: U.S. Department of Homeland Security. 2013.)

U.S. Department of Homeland Security. "Fusion Center Locations and Contact Information." U.S. Department of Homeland Security. Accessed March 2016. http://www.dhs.gov/fusion-center-locations-and-contact-information.

U.S. Department of Homeland Security. "National Network of Fusion Centers Fact Sheet." U.S. Department of Homeland Security. Last modified August 21, 2015. https://www.dhs.gov/national-network-fusion-centers-fact-sheet.

Wadhwa, V. "Laws and Ethics Can't Keep Pace with Technology." *MIT Technology Review.* Last modified April 15, 2014. https://www.technologyreview.com/s /526401/laws-and-ethics-cant-keep-pace-with-technology/.

Wilson, R., S. Smith, J. Markovic, and J. LeBeau. *Geospatial Technology Working Group Meeting Report on Predictive Policing (NCJ 237409).* Washington, DC: U.S. Department of Justice, National Institute of Justice. 2009.

Winter, J. "Homeland Security Bulletin Warns 3D-Printed Guns May Be 'Impossible' to Stop." *Fox News.* Last modified May 23, 2015. http://www.foxnews .com/us/2013/05/23/govt-memo-warns-3d-printed-guns-may-be-impossible -to-stop.html.

CHAPTER THREE

Homeland Security Technology Assessment and Implementation

Ryan K. Baggett

Learning Objectives

After reading this chapter, readers should be able to:

- Identify and explain the eight steps of the technology implementation process.
- Summarize and apply the three primary steps that must be taken for a comprehensive needs assessment.
- Explain the various components of a project plan and identify their importance in the technology implementation process.
- Elaborate on the five attributes that must be considered when evaluating technology.
- Articulate the importance in training staff on technology utilization and operation as well as maintaining technology once it is installed.

Key Terms

Affordability
Capability
Deployability
Grants
Implementation

Maintainability
Performance Indicators
Procurement
Project Manager
Standards
Technology Assessment/Evaluation
Usability

Introduction

HOMELAND SECURITY AGENCIES UNDERSTAND THAT in an era of scarce resources, the decision and ability to procure technology takes on an even greater importance. When the lack of resources is coupled with standards requirements, procurement regulations, and a myriad of product choices, the overall process can be overwhelming. Dr. David Brower is credited with stating, "All technology should be assumed guilty until proven innocent."[1] This assertion can be used as a fundamental principle when navigating the assessment and implementation of technology. In fact, it is important to remember that technology in homeland security is a component of the agency's mission, and not a mission in and of itself.

The purpose of this chapter is to provide a comprehensive process for agencies to assess and implement technology into their operations. Simply purchasing the most advanced technology on the market will not ensure efficiency or effectiveness toward fulfilling the agency's mission. A methodical process should be undertaken to increase the opportunities for successful technology implementation. In 2002, the U.S. Department of Justice office of Community Oriented Policing Services (COPS) published a technology guide for law enforcement executives, managers, and technologies. In the forward to the guide, the following overview was provided:

> Technology has long been a two-edged sword for law enforcement. While the benefits of implementing technology are obvious, the obstacles to getting the most from that technology often are not. In a time when growing responsibilities greatly increase the duties of local law enforcement agencies, a natural response is to turn to technology as a force multiplier. Technology can help law enforcement agencies better serve their communities by automating time-consuming tasks, dispatching personnel more efficiently, and improving an agency's ability to collect and analyze data as well

as disseminate it to both internal and external audiences. Implementing technology can be a long and difficult process.[2]

While the guidance was designed for law enforcement over a decade ago, the message is still very applicable to homeland security agencies today. Also located within the guide is an eight-step process for implementing technology projects. While many of the steps are still applicable, several of the steps have been updated and expanded upon by the author in order to provide the foundation for this chapter (see Figure 3.1).

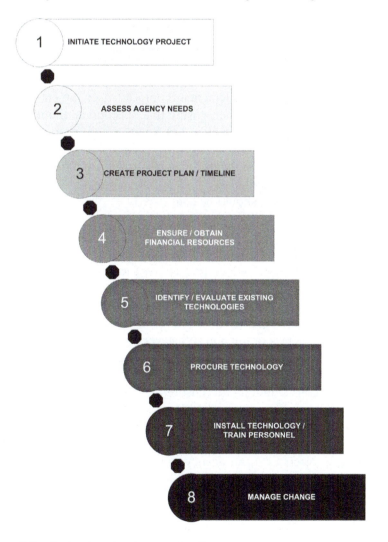

Figure 3.1 Technology Implementation Process.

A comprehensive technology assessment and implementation process is recommended to ensure that an agency finds the new technology useful in that it facilitates tasks and enhances the agency's current mission. The remainder of this chapter will provide additional insights into the process that is presented in Figure 3.1 in order to help the reader understand the various steps necessary for assessment and implementation. On a macro level, the agency must first initiate the process, followed soon thereafter with a determination of the need for the technology in question. If the needs assessment points to a need for the technology, the agency must begin the process of identifying potential technologies and subsequently obtaining evaluation results. Following the identification of a suitable technology, agency administrators must then determine the source of the financial resources for procurement of the technology. If these steps are successfully completed, the actual procurement process can commence. However, the technology implementation process does not end with procurement; the agency must then ensure that appropriate training is conducted for its members who will be utilizing the technology. Finally, the agency should review their policies and procedures to determine if they need to be altered based on the technology's implementation. Further, the technology's lifetime maintenance and operation costs, as well as any future enhancement costs, should be considered.

Initiate Technology Project

The initiation of a technology project lays the foundation for the project's potential success. A project idea may begin as an informal water-cooler conversation after a colleague's return from a conference, a smart practices article from a trade magazine, or a need identified by an employee returning from a specific task or mission. Whatever the impetus behind the idea, a technology project must be handled in a systematic manner to ensure maximum effectiveness for the agency and its employees.

A primary consideration is to ensure that the decision-making structure within the agency is identified in order to successfully govern the project from planning to implementation. There can be many layers of the decision-making structure depending on the size and scope of the technology project. First, an agency must have the full support of the agency head, who may have many different titles (to include director, supervisor, secretary, chief, etc.) depending on the structure within the agency itself. The level of support that is needed will also be directly correlated to the size and scope of the project. If the project is large, it may behoove project managers to form a steering committee of upper-level management to help ensure agency goals are met and any obstacles are removed expediently.[3]

Next, the daily activities will be handled by the project manager. This individual is responsible for ensuring that proper planning is conducted, all stakeholders are updated, tasks are conducted, deliverables are submitted, and all activities are completed on time, within budget, and of a high quality. Needless to say, this is an extremely important individual in the overall quality and effectiveness of the project. An agency has the option to appoint an existing employee to be the project manager or contract with an outside individual to carry out the necessary responsibilities. This decision may depend on existing employee skill levels on the topic, project complexity, availability of existing employees, and available budget allocations.

The last piece of the decision-making structure is the formation of a project team. The team will consist of both users and technical support staff to ensure that system operational requirements are paired with the current technical environment. In addition to this group of individuals, the advice and support of other subject matter experts will be sought depending on current discussion points within the team. Other members of this team may include representatives from various departments including, but not limited to, purchasing, budgets, and legal counsel. It should be noted that some groups will be smaller than others, depending on the complexity of the project.

Following the development of the decision-making structure, the planning process should commence. One effective way to begin a technology project is through the implementation of strategic planning. Strategic planning is an organizational management activity used to set priorities by focusing energy and resources in an effort to strengthen operations.[4] While various strategic planning methodologies exist, many will start with an environmental scan noting strengths, weaknesses, opportunities, and threats (SWOT analysis). The SWOT analysis identifies the internal and external factors that are favorable and unfavorable to achieving the specified objective. Various inputs should be taken into consideration within all levels of the planning process that will help develop the project scope. This scope or charter will help plan the high-level components of the upcoming project and outline the planning methodology (to include a needs assessment) that will be utilized during the course of the project.

Assess Agency Needs

As noted by the National Center for Education Statistics (2016), "a needs assessment is a comprehensive evaluation of the existing environment and capabilities of an organization relative to their preferred environment and capabilities. The gap that exists between the current and preferred conditions can be defined as the organization's needs."[5]

One key consideration in the needs assessment process is the definition of the agency's overall vision for technology; this documentation was started in the technology initiation step. In an effort to realize efficiencies in a comprehensive planning process, all long-range planning should be coordinated as opposed to a number of individualized, siloed projects. The needs assessment is not as much about the actual functionality of the technology as it is about the identification of how the implementation of technology can help the organization achieve its goals and objectives. The process of benchmarking may also be useful at this phase. Benchmarking includes finding, adapting, and implementing best practices in relationship to the problem/process/strategy under consideration.

There are three primary steps that must be taken for a comprehensive needs assessment. First, all needs-related information must be gathered through a variety of techniques to obtain information from all types of potential users. Methods include interviews (group and individual), questionnaires, and focus groups. Following the acquisition of data, the team should conduct content analysis looking for patterns in the listed needs using the assumption that respondents will share common viewpoints.

Finally, the team must document the prioritized findings. There is no single correct way to document the results of the needs assessment process. However, documentation should be clear and concise and require no agency knowledge in order to understand the findings. For example, to facilitate readability and organization, needs may be categorized under the headings of environmental, operational, and administrative. This step will likely result in the development of a technology requirements document outlining current capabilities, desired capabilities, functional requirements, user impacts, performance requirements, required hardware and software, and security and system requirements.

After the needs assessment is completed, the team should work to identify technologies to fill the identified specifications. It is important to note that some needs may be filled with nontechnology solutions such as changes in policies and procedures. However, for technology-related gaps, the process of technology identification and evaluation should begin.

Create Project Plan/Timeline

The statesman Benjamin Franklin is credited with the quote, "If you fail to plan, plan to fail."[6] Planning is an essential component in project management and in any technology implementation process and should be given adequate amounts of time and attention. This section in and of itself will not provide adequate information on all aspects of creating a project plan and timeline. However, there are a plethora of guides and resources available if necessary. A quality program manager will likely possess these skill sets or the ability to reach out to someone in another government office for assistance.

While many different resources exist, a common set of components required for a project plan include:

- **Scope:** Listing of specific project goals, deliverables, tasks, costs, and deadlines.
- **Tasks:** Activities that need to be accomplished within a defined period or by a deadline to accomplish work-related goals.
- **Deliverables:** Tangible or intangible objects produced because of the project that are intended to be delivered to a customer/agency.
- **Resources:** People, equipment, facilities, funding, or anything else required for the completion of a project activity.
- **Schedule/Timeline:** A list of project tasks and deliverables and the deadlines associated with their completion.
- **Quality Assurance:** Strategies/procedures to obtain a desired level of quality in a service or product.

A key attribute of effective project planning is the ability to set realistic times and levels of effort for the tasks identified. Additionally, the plan should be capable of displaying the various stages of the project and provide estimates on the likely amount of time remaining. While detailed software suites exist to assist with this process, some project managers may find a simple table structure adequate for planning.

Ensure/Obtain Financial Resources

As many agencies are painfully aware, scarce resources make budgeting for technology difficult. Difficult decisions are required on a daily basis regarding an agency's budget allocations, and technology may be a last consideration behind personnel and other operating costs. However, it should be emphasized that some technologies can serve as a force multiplier and alleviate tasks and activities that free up employees to conduct other work. If an agency does not have in-house or internal budget resources to fund technology procurement, attempts should be made to obtain funds through outside sources such as grants.

According to the Business Dictionary, grants are "contributions, gifts, or subsidies (in cash or kind) bestowed by a government or other organization

Table 3.1 Example Grant Funding Web Sites

Agency	Description	URL
Grants.Gov	Funding opportunities from the 26 federal agencies that award grants	http://www.grants.gov
U.S. Department of Homeland Security	List of available grant opportunities	http://www.dhs.gov/how-do-i/find-and-apply-grants
U.S. Fire Administration	Fire service grants and funding	http://www.usfa.fema.gov/grants/index.html
Federal Emergency Management Agency	Nondisaster preparedness grants	http://www.fema.gov/grants
National Institute of Justice	Justice-related funding opportunities	http://www.nij.gov/funding
Center for Disease Control	Public health-related funding	http://www.cdc.gov/grants/index.html
U.S. Department of Health and Human Services	Health and human services-related funding	http://www.hhs.gov/grants/grants/funding
U.S. Department of Transportation	Transportation-related funding	https://www.transportation.gov/grants

for a specified purpose to an eligible recipient."[7] Agencies can contact state and federal resources for grant opportunities or peruse Web sites such as those listed in Table 3.1.

After locating a potential grant, applicants should carefully examine the requirements for grant eligibility, the types of eligible expenses under the funding, and whether there are any potential limitations to the agency, such as cost-sharing. Next, a necessity for a competitive grant application is the development of a well-written narrative. Peer reviewers carefully examine proposal narratives so it is the agency's opportunity to describe the project, providing an explanation of the financial need (with accompanying budget), a description of the cost-benefit of the proposed project, and an explanation of how the project will improve daily operations.[8] The information collected in the needs assessment phase of the process will be a sound addition to any grant application. Lastly, agencies are encouraged to reach out to other agencies in their government structure who may have proven success with grant application development and could serve as a resource. There are several government publications available to assist agencies in the development of grant applications, such as the 2012 U.S. Fire Administration's (USFA) *Funding Alternatives for Emergency Medical and Fire Services.*

Next, it is important to understand that government grants, which will also depend on the types of technology that the agency desires to procure, will not always be readily accessible. When this occurs, agencies are encouraged to look at other funding alternatives. In the USFA guide previously mentioned, the authors provide a variety of alternative funding suggestions (in addition to federal and state mechanisms):

- Local Sources
  - Taxes
  - Development Impact and User Fees
  - Fines, Forfeitures, and Citations
  - Enterprise Funds and Utility Rates
  - Sales of Assets
  - Borrowing
- Private Sector Sources
  - Foundations
  - Corporate Giving
  - Program-Related Investments

Identify/Evaluate Existing Technologies

An assessment is used to conduct an impartial, practitioner-relevant, and operationally oriented assessment and validation of the technology under question. Simply stated, does it work like the company purports and will it improve the organization? A comprehensive assessment may take a great deal of time and resources to carefully consider the various options available on the market. If an agency has these resources, technology evaluations can be very informative regarding the technology selection phase. However, agencies should first determine if evaluations have been previously conducted by an outside agency. While these evaluations may not provide answers to every question/scenario an agency may have, they will provide a great foundation from which to build upon. One example of an outside evaluation agency is the U.S. Department of Homeland Security (DHS) System Assessment and Validation for Emergency Responders (SAVER) Program.

The SAVER Program, located within the DHS Science and Technology (S&T) Directorate, assists emergency responders with making procurement decisions. It conducts objective assessments and validations on commercial equipment and systems and provides those results, along with other relevant equipment information, to the emergency responder community. Results can be obtained at www.firstresponder.gov. SAVER implements a multistep process to determine "what equipment is available" and "how does it perform" in order to provide those results to the homeland security community.

As reprinted from the 2009 DHS *SAVER Program Assessment Process* document, there are five attributes that must be considered when evaluating technology:

- **Affordability:** This category groups criteria related to life-cycle costs of a piece of equipment or system.
- **Capability:** This category groups criteria related to the power, capacity, or features available for a piece of equipment or system to perform or assist the responder in performing one or more responder-relevant tasks.
- **Deployability:** This category groups criteria related to the movement, installation, or implementation of a piece of equipment or system by responders at the site of its intended use.
- **Maintainability:** This category groups criteria related to the maintenance and restoration of a piece of equipment or system to operational conditions by responders.
- **Usability:** This category groups criteria related to the quality of the responders' experience with the operational employment of a piece of equipment or system. This includes the relative ease of use, efficiency, and overall satisfaction of the responders with the equipment or system.[9]

However, it is feasible that a federal/outside evaluation has not been conducted on the specific technology that an agency is researching. There are still viable options for an agency without resources to conduct their own comprehensive evaluation instead of making an uninformed procurement decision.

First, an agency should schedule a variety of vendor demonstrations for stakeholders in the technology procurement. Stakeholders should be encouraged to ask any questions they may have and utilize the technology (if possible) during the demonstration. Follow-up surveys or interviews with the stakeholders should be scheduled after each demonstration to obtain their opinions.

Next, existing users of the technology should be contacted to obtain their opinions. A variety of questions should be developed prior to the correspondence, and if funds are available, a small project team could schedule a visit to see the technology in use by the agency. After the number of potential products has been narrowed down, the agency should request a trial period with the technology prior to procurement. The pilot project is designed to evaluate how the technology performs in the field and provides rapid results. These small assessments help agencies develop policies and procedures in advance of large-scale procurements. While this may not be possible with customized technologies, the ability for practitioners in the field to use the product in a real-world setting may be advantageous.

Finally, agencies should determine if any standards exist regarding the functionality of the technology. Due to the diversity of technologies, there are no universal standards to cover all technologies. However, agencies should examine various Standards Development Organizations (SDOs), such as those listed below, to determine the existence of applicable standards.

- American Society for Testing and Materials (ASTM)
- Institute of Electrical and Electronics Engineers (IEEE)
- International Security Committee (ISC)
- International Standards Organization (ISO)
- National Electrical Manufacturers Association (NEMA)
- National Fire Protection Association (NFPA)
- National Institute of Standards and Technology (NIST)
- U.S. Department of Defense (DoD) Military Standards

Additionally, the American National Standards Institute (ANSI) operates a homeland security standards database at http://www.hssd.us. The site provides access to standards critical to the jobs of responders, code officials, and others charged with keeping America safe.

It should be noted that if the technology is procured with grant funding, there may be specific parameters applied to permissible equipment. For example, the Authorized Equipment List (AEL) is produced by the Federal

Emergency Management Agency (FEMA) and is used to determine which types of equipment can be purchased under FEMA's major homeland security grants. The information found within the AEL will usually be limited to broad equipment descriptions and grant information.[10] Related, the Standardized Equipment List (SEL) is "maintained by Inter Agency Board (IAB), a group of senior-level first responders and federal government representatives from all disciplines who meet three times a year to update and consider additions to the list. Since the IAB is not part of DHS, the SEL does not contain any policy or grant eligibility information. Nevertheless, it does contain the IAB's suggestions of items to consider when purchasing each type of equipment." These suggestions are listed under the headings "Important Features," "Operating Considerations," and "Training Considerations."[11]

Procure Technology

After financial resources are obtained, an agency can then begin the process of procuring the technology. Procurement is a process that allows agencies the opportunity to create functional requirements and seek qualified providers.[12] Federal, state, and local laws, guidelines, and regulations should be consulted in this step. Issues such as state price contracts, bid processes, and requests for proposals from vendors, are better handled by those trained in, and responsible for, these practices. Additionally, there will be legalities surrounding the procurement process that should be handled by the appropriate offices.

The agency's budget and pricing agreements with the vendor are often cited as one of the most important factors in selecting a technology, especially at the local community level. As a result, the ability to negotiate pricing with vendors to acceptable levels becomes important. The benefit of bulk purchases is the opportunity to negotiate discounted pricing. At the state and local levels, purchasing officials at the county or city levels often have the expertise to conduct the negotiations.

Bulk purchases also provide agencies with greater bargaining power to negotiate the terms of their warranties beyond the standard one-, two-, or three-year warranty and the type of coverage included in the purchase. One agency interviewed for a recent project on the procurement of ruggedized computers noted they were able to negotiate for a five-year warranty that included coverage for both defective parts and repairs needed because of accidents. Note that bulk purchases may not be feasible or necessary for many agencies.

When purchasing, it is common for agencies to first consider vendors listed on a General Services Administration (GSA) Schedule or state-level system of vendor agreements and contracts often managed by a state

Table 3.2 Sample DHS Authorized Equipment List Technology Listing

AEL/ SEL Number	01AR-04-SCER
Title	Respirator, Escape, Self-Contained, Single-Use, CBRN
Description	CBRN Self-Contained Escape Respirator (SCER) designed for escape from hazardous and oxygen-deficient environments (certified by NIOSH as compliant with the CBRN approval criteria)
FEMA Grant Programs	Port Security Grant Program (PSGP), Homeland Security Grant Program (HSGP), Transit Security Grant Program (TSGP), Urban Areas Security Initiative Program (UASI), Amtrak (IPR-Amtrak), Tribal Homeland Security Grant Program (THSGP), Operation Stonegarden (OPSG), State Homeland Security Program (SHSP)
Grant Notes	DHS has adopted the NIOSH Standard for Chemical, Biological, Radiological, and Nuclear (CBRN) Air-Purifying Escape Respirator and CBRN Self-Contained Escape Respirator. Although SCER manufacturers may have conducted self-testing of their products, NIOSH testing of equipment against these standards is not yet complete. Following completion of these tests, FEMA anticipates limiting allowable equipment under this standard to items that successfully meet test requirements. As a result, grantees should consider delaying procurement of SCERs covered by the above-referenced standards until testing is complete and the results are published.

purchasing authority. These lists provide many benefits and are often the first stop for many agencies procuring equipment. For example, government contracts often provide agencies with prenegotiated discounted pricing, which would save the agency the administrative burden of negotiating with the vendor. In some states, the selection of a listed vendor and costs under a specified dollar amount exempts agencies from having to solicit bids in a competitive and open manner, therefore reducing administrative costs and delays. Note that the list of vendors on government contracts may be limited, so agencies should be cautious they are not settling for a product that fails to address their operational needs. Several concepts regarding technology procurement include:

- **Advertising Requirements:** Governments are often required to advertise procurements for a specified period.
- **Functional Specifications:** Detailed, technical descriptions of the tasks the desired technology will be able to perform.
- **Preproposal Conferences:** Allotment of time to respond to questions submitted by the vendor regarding the request for proposals document. This may also be handled via the solicitation Web page.
- **Procurement Thresholds:** Ordinance that requires competitive procurement if the value of the purchase exceeds a certain dollar amount.
- **Request for Information:** Process to collect written information about the capabilities of various technologies or suppliers.
- **Request for Proposals:** A bidding solicitation to potential suppliers announcing the procurement specifications of a commodity procurement or a requested service to be provided.
- **Sole Source Justification:** Vendor chosen is the only one capable of supplying the requested goods or services; generally involves upgrades of existing equipment or procurement of a unique technology.

Install Technology and Train Personnel

As previously stated, just because the technology is received and installed does not mean the implementation process is over. Staff who will be using the technologies should be adequately trained on functional operations, or there could be associated negative consequences. First, the user may never fully understand the full features of the procured technology and may end up never using it to its fullest capability. A significant amount of money was likely spent on the procurement, so agencies need to make sure they are utilizing all technology features. Second, a more serious consequence is that users may not feel comfortable with the technology and may simply put it on a shelf or never use it. As discussed, implementation is a long and arduous process, so a seemingly simple task such as the provision of training should not be overlooked.

Training is generally available from the vendor and should be written into the procurement contract as a term of the sale. Additionally, a train-the-trainer method may be used whereby an agency representative is trained and then comes back to the other staff and trains them on the technology's operation and maintenance. In either scenario, the trainer should ensure that an acceptable comfort level is obtained by the technology users.

Manage Change

The last step in the implementation process is one that can be conducted throughout the entire process. Even before procurement is conducted, agencies must review their current policies and procedures and ensure they enable the full use of the technology. This may require revisions to the way things have always been done at the agency. It is difficult to integrate a technology into a daily routine if the agency's own standard operating procedures do not allow for the activity.

In addition to managing the human aspect of change, agencies must ensure that maintenance is scheduled so that the system is able to continue functioning properly. The impact of not following manufacturer recommendations for maintenance could shorten the product's life cycle, void the existing warranty, and cause undue hardship on the agency as a determination is made on how to replace the nonworking technology. Agencies must also ensure that adequate funding is allocated each year to pay for any costs associated with maintenance.

Conclusion

In closing, agencies should be vigilant for technologies that will assist in personnel safety and improve the overall effectiveness of their staff's ability to perform their mission and the citizens they serve. As such, each step of the technology assessment and implementation process should be carefully followed to ensure the maximum return on the technology investment. Throughout the process identified in the chapter, users should ensure they incorporate a continuous improvement loop that measures technology performance. The establishment and utilization of performance indicators are helpful in diagnosing problems and will help stakeholders reconcile any identified deficiencies. Further, performance measurement helps justify the technology and the investment made with taxpayer resources.[13] As noted in COPS Tech Guide:

> Whether you buy an off-the-shelf solution or build a custom system in-house, it is essential that certain steps be taken to ensure that the project has the proper user support, is clearly defined, stays on track and within budget, is designed to meet specific business needs or solve a particular problem, and can operate within the constraints of a new or existing technical environment.[14]

Discussion Questions

1. As the operations officer for a county emergency management agency, you have been encouraged to write grants to obtain additional funds for

your agency. Describe where you would begin with the grant development process.

2. For many years, you have worked as an intelligence analyst within the state homeland security office. While the current analysis software is usable, you have seen various demonstrations of a new software tool that you believe would make the office more effective. How would you convince the administration of the need to procure it using a needs assessment process?

3. As the lieutenant assigned to supervise the city police department's homeland security unit, many vendors have been calling and e-mailing, and a few have even stopped by the office. Each promise the latest and greatest technology that will revolutionize your agency's mission. How can you use the five technology evaluation considerations to analyze the technologies?

4. The regional administrator of your FEMA region has asked you to procure various technologies for your seven-state region. Describe your first steps and initial contacts.

5. As a county emergency management director in a rural county, there are only two staff members in your agency (including yourself)! Despite the small human resources on hand, your agency still has needs for technology like your larger counterparts. How could a small agency obtain technology with a limited tax revenue source and operating budget?

Notes

1. David Brower Center, "Welcome."
2. Harris and Romesburg, *Law Enforcement Tech Guide*, vi.
3. Ibid.
4. Balanced Scorecard Institute, "Strategic Planning Basics."
5. National Center for Education Statistics, "Determining Your Technology Needs."
6. Franklin, *GoodReads*.
7. Business Dictionary, "Grant."
8. U.S. Fire Administration, *Funding Alternatives for Emergency Medical and Fire Services.*
9. Reprinted from U.S. Department of Homeland Security, *SAVER Program Assessment Process.*
10. U.S. Department of Homeland Security, "DHS Authorized Equipment List."
11. Interagency Board, "Standardized Equipment List."
12. Harris and Romesburg, *Law Enforcement Tech Guide.*
13. Roberts, *Law Enforcement Tech Guide for Creating Performance Measures That Work.*
14. Harris and Romesburg, *Law Enforcement Tech Guide.*

Bibliography

Balanced Scorecard Institute. "Strategic Planning Basics." Balanced Scorecard Institute. Accessed February 16, 2016. http://balancedscorecard.org/Resources/Strategic-Planning-Basics.

Business Dictionary. "Grant." *Business Dictionary.* Accessed September 5, 2015. www.businessdictionary.com.

David Brower Center. "Welcome." David Brower Center. Accessed September 6, 2015. www.browercenter.org.

Franklin, B. *GoodReads.* Accessed September 6, 2015. www.goodreads.com.

Harris, K., and W. Romesburg. *Law Enforcement Tech Guide: How to Plan, Purchase and Manage Technology (Successfully).* Washington, DC: U.S. Department of Justice. 2002.

Interagency Board. "Standardized Equipment List." *Interagency Board.* Accessed September 7, 2015. https://iab.gov/SEL.aspx.

National Center for Education Statistics. "Determining Your Technology Needs." Accessed November 8, 2016. http://nces.ed.gov/pubs2005/tech_suite/part_2.asp?nav=2.

Roberts, D. *Law Enforcement Tech Guide for Creating Performance Measures that Work.* Washington, DC: U.S. Department of Justice. 2006.

U.S. Department of Homeland Security. "DHS Authorized Equipment List." U.S. Department of Homeland Security. Accessed September 7, 2015. https://www.fema.gov/media-library/assets/documents/101566.

U.S. Department of Homeland Security. (Reprinted from *SAVER Program Assessment Process.* Washington, DC: U.S. Department of Homeland Security. 2009.)

U.S. Fire Administration. *Funding Alternatives for Emergency Medical and Fire Services.* Washington, DC: Federal Emergency Management Administration. 2012.

CHAPTER FOUR

Perspectives in Homeland Security Training

Enhancing Training Access and Delivery through Technology

Brian K. Simpkins

Learning Objectives

After reading this chapter, readers should be able to:

- Describe the various training delivery methods beyond traditional class-room- and lecture-based training.
- Summarize the various technology-based training solutions that are currently available and utilized within the homeland security community.
- Describe the barriers related to traditional classroom- and lecture-based training.
- Recognize implementation barriers and organizational impacts of technology-based training solutions.
- Evaluate the effectiveness of technology-based training solutions as compared to traditional classroom- and lecture-based training.
- Analyze how the implementation of technology-based training solutions beyond traditional classroom- and lecture-based training can overcome training barriers.

- Analyze why there is a push to make training more interactive and technology driven.
- Apply knowledge obtained through chapter to discussion questions.

Key Terms

Adaptive Training
Augmented Reality
Distance Learning
E-learning
5Is Framework
Gaming
M-learning
PADDIE Framework
Tactical Barriers
Traditional Training
Transfer
Transfer Barriers
Virtual Reality

Introduction and Overview

FOLLOWING THE TRAGIC EVENTS OF September 11, 2001, and the hurricane season of 2005, preparedness, response, and recovery training within the homeland security community became a significant national priority at the federal, state, and local levels. Training within the homeland security community is unique because emergency response occurs in a complex and dynamic environment in which critical decisions must be made with the knowledge that there is no single correct answer, action, and/or solution.[1] Ultimately, the provision of relevant, timely, and effective emergency preparedness and response training to individuals within the homeland security partners is a critical issue because they protect and save lives and property through action, which is the main objective of any emergency response.[2] Further, their actions, judgments, and behaviors are a result of the training they have received (and their inherent intuition developed through training and experience) that is subsequently utilized in emergency situations, which is especially true for very low-frequency, high-consequence events (e.g., major earthquakes).[3]

Homeland security partners are currently facing difficulties related to expanding training requirements that are pitted against limitations in agency financial and human resources. Complicating this fact is that a one-size-fits-all approach cannot be applied to homeland security partners due to different disciplines across the community (e.g., fire, law enforcement, and emergency management), different roles across and within disciplines and individual agencies, and different backgrounds, experiences, and skills within individuals. Further, training must now be modernizing in terms of development and delivery in order to motivate and be applicable to the new generation of digital learners that are entering the homeland security workforce.[4]

Presently, there are various ways for individuals within homeland security partners to receive needed training, which includes the traditional training methods (e.g., classroom-based training, exercises, computer-based training, etc.). The current trend, however, is the integration of technology-based training solutions to increase effectiveness and efficiency. These solutions include greater use of online skill training and assessment, virtual reality simulation technologies, and training based on popular gaming formats. Although some of these technology-based training solutions are not new (e.g., Internet-based training), technology accessibility has greatly expanded within homeland security training over the past several years, which is buoyed by the fact that individuals who grew up with technology and the Internet are now entering the homeland security workforce.[5]

Therefore, in order to effectively and efficiently do more with less related to emergency preparedness and response training, homeland security partners are recognizing significant savings by integrating training technologies beyond the traditional classroom setting.[6] These technologies range from e-learning to m-learning, different realities (augmented and virtual), and everything in between. Although the implementation of these technologies does not change the need to achieve training objectives, training programs are now being greatly influenced by technology.[7] The traditional classroom- and lecture-based training model is being forced out in preference for a model that is more interactive and driven by technology.[8] The remainder of this chapter will provide an overview of training technologies within the homeland security community that reduce training barriers and allow state and local agencies to do more with less in terms of emergency preparedness and response training. Within the discussion, effectiveness and considerations involving implementation and impacts are detailed as well. Overall, this chapter will provide basic information to aid in the decision process to implement technology-based training solutions within the homeland security community.

The 5Is Model

To provide structure to the information presented within the chapter, Ekblom's 5Is framework is utilized to effectively organize and present the content. The 5Is framework is a knowledge management framework that acts as a tool to transfer and share knowledge through a standardized format.[9] In essence, the 5Is framework provides an information process model through the utilization of five top-level tasks.[10] Based on the 5Is framework, this chapter is organized into four sections covering all five tasks: (1) Intelligence, (2) Intervention, (3) Implementation and Involvement, and (4) Impact.

Intelligence

Overcoming Traditional Training Barriers

To fully understand how technology can overcome training barriers within homeland security partners, an understanding of the barriers related to traditional training must be achieved. These barriers can be grouped into two categories: tactical barriers and transfer barriers. Tactical barriers are "logistical challenges that make it difficult for trainees to attend and complete training programs."[11] Examples of common tactical barriers faced by homeland security partners are listed below:

- **Limited Staffing Resources:** Many agencies face difficulties in providing time for officers to attend training because it results in pulling them away from their daily responsibilities. This is especially true in agencies that rely on volunteers who have other day jobs that limit their ability to attend training.
- **Limited Organizational Resources:** Training is a huge financial, time, and personnel investment. However, increasing economic pressure and fewer organizational resources often means that training budgets are tight and there is a push to do more with less.
- **Geographic Location of the Officers:** Traditional training occurs in a classroom setting, requiring trainees to be physically present in one location for the duration of the training. Due to the nature of working in the homeland security field, coordinating a time and place for employees to jointly participate in training can be challenging with a traditional training approach.
- **Retention Issues:** Some agencies have issues with officer turnover in the line staff. Therefore, it becomes difficult to maintain complete knowledge transfer when there is an ever-changing blend of new hires and tenured workers.

As for transfer barriers, these "include the failure to use and apply the knowledge and skills learned in training after returning to the job," which can be compounded by tactical barriers.[12] Common transfer barriers are

(a) lack of relevance / perceived value of the training (to trainee's job) and (b) lack of authenticity. An example would be a rural emergency responder participating in a training designed for major metropolitan areas or vice versa. Transfer barriers are extremely important because knowledge transfer is considered the ultimate aim/goal of training.

Currently available and utilized technology-based training solutions offer content and delivery methods that decrease the tactical and transfer barriers of traditional training. In addition, technology-based training solutions can address, reduce, and/or eliminate organizational, social, cultural, psychological, and other training barriers.[13] In fact, training and staff development have been heavily influenced by technology over the years as agencies have recognized the savings and cost-effectiveness that technology-based training solutions provide in achieving training objectives.[14] The advancement and implementation of technology, however, can be considered asymmetrical.[15] This can be somewhat explained due to today's information age in which teaching and learning methods range from studying printed materials alone to training via online gaming systems.[16] Therefore, there are many ways in which technology-based training solutions can assist in training individuals within homeland security partners.[17] Despite the availability of technology-based training solutions, one of the largest issues that remains is that many homeland security partners do not fully understand how to effectively and efficiently leverage technology to support training.[18]

Technology-based training solutions continue to evolve every year, much like consumer technologies. Despite the constant evolution, there are general technologies that are currently being utilized within the homeland security training community (e.g., e-learning) as well as others that are gaining more acceptance due to their inherent promise to overcome training barriers (e.g., augmented reality). The remainder of this chapter focuses on these general technologies rather than specific products. Understanding technology is key because homeland security partners must find the right balance of technology that (a) best satisfies the needs of their employees and (b) is effective in transferring knowledge, skills, and abilities. Regardless of the training or the technology utilized, all "learning requires at least two types of actors, the person who will be instructed and the content of learning itself."[19] The successful interplay between these two actors is of utmost importance.

Technology Explosion: No Longer Simply Butts in the Seats

Although forms of training and education beyond traditional training have been around for over 100 years, the inventions and omnipresence of today's technologies, like the Internet, has fundamentally changed training and learning.[20] For example, no longer are so-called distance learning courses comprised of the postal mail correspondence courses of yesteryear,[21] but rather a variety of formats that include live virtual classrooms; individualistic, self-paced courses; immersive role-playing/gaming simulations; and smaller-scale, rapid/on-demand courses.[22] This change is also a pressure felt within homeland security partners by which professional training is migrating from unstructured on-the-job training systems to solutions that provide structure and formal assessments.[23] Therefore, it is no surprise that technology-based training solutions are now an accepted and favored training delivery method within government, higher education, and even the military.[24] For example, Dr. Denis Onieal, current superintendent of the U.S. Fire Academy, has been quoted as stating, "Now is the time for us to embrace the future and improve our education through distance learning."[25] Further, the U.S. Army recently released a new training vision that calls for a reduction in traditional training and a switch to technology-based instruction and training.[26] Some even insist that technology-based training is considered to be consistent with the way individuals in this digital age now prefer to learn and incorporates modern learning pedagogy.[27] Therefore, it is no surprise that training programs are moving away from traditional classrooms and to solutions that are technology-driven and provide more interactivity.

Intervention

The Rise of E-learning and Distance Learning

Marking 25 years of change associated with the Internet, the Pew Research Center released a report in February 2014 declaring that the "Internet has been a plus for society and an especially good thing for individual users."[28] Many have also considered the advancement of online training and education as part of the telecom revolution that has been caused by the Internet boom over the past few decades.[29] The telecom revolution has also had profound and transformative impacts beyond just individual trainees to institutions, including homeland security partners, which have been forced to adjust to the revolution in the span of just a few years. In fact, the impact of the telecom revolution on homeland security partners has been quite possibly more significant than in other public sectors, as it presents not only new opportunities to achieve greater efficiencies in some areas such as training, but also new threats enabled through use of the Internet (e.g., fraud and theft, conspiracy, crimes against children).

The so-called telecom revolution is not a figurative term but rather an appropriate adjective for how distance learning is changing training and education. Current statistics on the continual rise of distance learning illustrate its growth and breadth in a relatively short amount of time (less than 30 years) in both industry and higher education. For example, industry statistics illustrate that the percentage of companies utilizing distance-learning technology to facilitate training has increased from 8 percent in 1999 to 30 percent in 2012.[30] Further, the distance-learning industry revenues, which were projected to increase by 100 percent between 2007 and 2014 ($12 billion to $24 billion), have continued to expand immensely.[31] In addition to industry, higher education has felt the pressure to move to and offer education online in order to be more cost effective in light of shrinking public funding, reach new student populations to increase enrollments, improve access for nontraditional students, and ultimately increase profits for the institution.[32] Further, a survey of chief academic leaders from over 2,800 higher education institutions across the United States revealed that close to 70 percent agreed that "online learning is critical to their long-term strategy."[33]

Training Delivery Technologies beyond E-learning and Distance Learning

Although the general distance-learning classifications of e-learning and computer-based learning receive much attention (and are the most common), there are other technology-based training solutions available that can enhance training. The degree of development of these solutions is mixed, with some more advanced and widely accessible than others. The variety of these solutions, however, provides the homeland security community options to ensure training objectives are met effectively and efficiently. Further, although some of these solutions are achieved using a computer, they go beyond the simple accessing of static training material (e.g., PowerPoints) commonly found within computer-based training programs. Further, some of these solutions support current training systems or other training technologies. Although not an exhaustive list, examples of commonly utilized solutions, as well as others that are gaining more acceptance due to their inherent promise to overcome training barriers, are detailed in the following sections.

Adaptive Training

Adaptive training supports technology-based training solutions by allowing the instruction to dynamically change/adapt based on individual trainee characteristics, such as performance, skill level, experiences, etc. Adaptive training utilizes artificial intelligence to adapt/tailor the training to an individual, which is a form of an intelligent tutor. For example, students could receive individualized versions of a training based on current knowledge or ability level (i.e., obtained via a pretest) and be allowed to progress through the training at an individualized pace based on the speed at which the individual illustrates mastery of training content, concepts, principles, and/or skills. This is also considered micro–adaptive training because the training content adapts in real time through continual assessment of the trainee's performance against training objectives and knowledge/skill checks in order to target trainee strengths and weaknesses. Although adaptive technologies enable a training to support individual trainee needs, it is also very costly to implement and provide. Despite the cost, adaptive training technologies have the promise to improve training on an individual level by assisting with subject understanding, reducing the overall time needed to train, and saving training resources. Presently, the U.S. Department of Defense is currently incorporating adaptive training technologies in order to develop sustainable training platforms that can effectively and efficiently meet training objectives, because adaptive technologies have proven to be flexible enough to meet individual training needs across the department.[34]

Augmented Reality

Augmented reality technology provides the ability to extend the physical world by applying virtual objects and/or information over an individual's view of the physical world.[35] A simple and crude example of augmented reality is a heads-up display (HUD) found in military applications (e.g., fighter jets), civilian applications (e.g., speedometer and other information projected on a vehicle's windshield), and wearable products (e.g., Google Glass). In essence, an individual's view of the physical world is augmented by computer-generated sensory inputs (graphical, visual, auditory, etc.) that are superimposed with a person's field of view.[36] Described in another way, augmented reality enables an individual to "bridge the gap between the real and the virtual in a seamless way."[37]

The continued development of augmented reality training technologies has been supported by the need for flexible and realistic training simulations for homeland security partners.[38] For example, while simulators (e.g., firearms) can be placed within a mobile apparatus (e.g., trailers), augmented reality extends this approach by allowing trainees to take physical action in tangible settings.[39] The advantage of augmented reality is that it enhances a trainee's perception of reality and transforms how information is utilized and shared, which has the potential to revolutionize training.[40] For example, augmented reality can enable the training content to utilize local information based on the location of the trainee(s) due to the ability of augmented reality technologies to integrate global positioning system (GPS) data, which is an ability not available with traditional paper-based training materials.[41] The abilities also allow augmented reality to have numerous benefits, such as the ability to be easily updated, less reliance on traditional classroom-based training, and an increase in motivation to train by trainees due to realism-based training.[42]

Gaming

It is obvious that the current generation has embraced and relies on technology and gaming.[43] Therefore, it is no surprise that game-based training technologies are gaining ground within homeland security partners as they are looking for new ways to train employees.[44] Gaming technology has continued to significantly expand as computers and smartphones have become necessary equipment for individuals within homeland security partners as fully digital learners are entering the homeland security field.[45] Further, advances in gaming technology have illustrated the ability to effectively replicate environments found in actual crisis situations in a digital format.[46] Therefore, training has begun to utilize gaming technology (via serious games) to provide affordable and accessible solutions that support training objectives through the provision of realistic and repeatable training scenarios.[47] Specifically, most gaming systems can provide a multitude of repeatable scenarios that enable the trainee to act in different roles that may be needed within an emergency response, which is a benefit that live exercises cannot provide.[48] Further, the gaming solutions can range from single-player or small-group games up to large multiplayer Internet-based games.[49] Most importantly, gaming technology is advanced enough to allow a trainee to effectively simulate task performance with the right amount of realism to enable learning, practicing, improving, and transfer of necessary knowledge and skills.[50]

As interest in game-based learning continues to grow, so does the research that illustrates the learning effectiveness of gaming. While a serious (training) game has the same mental contest aspect as entertainment games, serious (training) games also have additional pedagogical functionality and allow teachers to adapt the game scenario according to the learning objectives.[51] Despite the research supporting gaming as an effective form of training, most are also quick to point out that gaming is not a replacement for traditional training methods or a panacea for traditional training barriers.[52] Rather, gaming is viewed as a supportive and/or complementary training format to traditional training methods, especially for lower-level officers, as live exercises are viewed as critical for training upper-level officials.[53]

M-learning

The proliferation of broadband-enabled mobile devices (e.g., smartphones) is causing a shift in the thinking regarding training delivery methods and formats.[54] Some even say that mobile and microtraining is the next logical step in knowledge delivery because mobile devices are considered an untapped resource for training and learning.[55] By using ubiquitous and inexpensive smartphones, tablets, and other mobile devices, trainees and their respective agencies are provided with a low-cost training device that can be utilized to access training anywhere, anytime.[56]

By definition, mobile learning (m-learning) is "an extension of distance education, supported by mobile devices equipped with wireless technologies."[57] In today's constantly connected world, m-learning is a new learning model and delivery format.[58] M-learning allows for easily distributed training that can be delivered in a microtraining fashion (e.g., small portions of information that can be immediately accessed and applied by the individual user).[59] Further, since individuals are spending more and more time on mobile devices, some see m-learning is where training needs to go.[60]

While m-learning provides advantages related to availability, there are concerns related to scope due to the limits of content that can be provided via a mobile device with a small screen.[61] Further, some training programs that were developed for personal computers may not transfer well to mobile devices without significant redesign efforts, which is an issue apparent in private businesses transitioning to m-learning.[62] There are also security issues related to m-learning, especially when accessing sensitive information via wireless connectivity.[63] This is of particular concern to homeland security partners. Despite the concerns, m-learning is positioned to expand its reach in both the public and private sectors in the near future.

Simulation-Based / Virtual Reality Training

Common across all homeland security partners is the cost (financial and human resources) associated with training, especially related to live, large-scale simulated exercises. Further, some state there is little evidence that live exercises improve the preparedness or response capabilities of agencies in response to major incidents.[64] Of particular concern is the low frequency of live exercises and the fact that there may or may not be a sufficient number of players (e.g., responders, role players, etc.) for an effective exercise.[65] Further, live training exercises place officers and other participants at risk during the events in which injuries or other accidents can occur, such as with live burn exercises within the fire service.

To overcome this, virtual reality training technologies (a.k.a. immersive training or simulation-based training) provide an accessible, effective, and cost-effective alternative to live exercises to achieve training objectives.[66] Virtual reality is "human interaction technology that allows actual users to participate in a virtual world reproduced by computers."[67] Virtual reality enables a trainee to be immersed within and interact with 3-dimensional (3-D) environments that are artificial/simulated.[68] Virtual reality utilizes the simulated environment to enable the trainee to demonstrate procedural techniques, decision making, and critical thinking in a real-world environment to achieve specific training objectives.[69] Therefore, virtual reality can provide an engaging, interactive, and collaborative virtual experience that can lead to higher levels of training motivation and learning performance.[70]

One of the greatest advantages of virtual reality simulation training is the ability to repeatedly place trainees in situations without associated risks.[71] This is valuable for any situation, but especially for low-frequency, high-consequence events where virtual training may be the only option.[72] For example, civil support teams within the United States utilize virtual reality technology to train for radiological disaster response, and law enforcement has been utilizing firearm simulators for many years.[73] Further, the U.S. Department of Homeland Security is using virtual reality training technology to provide training for first responders in response to terrorist attacks.[74] As a result of its success, virtual reality training technology is increasingly being utilized to support various forms of training, such as crime scene investigation, disaster management, and eyewitness identification.[75] Further, recent events illustrate that civil disobedience is becoming a common issue across the United States, but the ability to gain experience through training in the field is time-consuming and dangerous.[76] Virtual reality training technology can provide "a safe and controlled environment to assist police officer training in simulated urban environments."[77] Further, virtual reality training technologies can also support disaster/fatality management where responders are exposed to uncommon and disturbing situations and sights to better prepare them when responding to actual events.[78]

As Walsh explains in "Using a Simulated Learning Environment," virtual reality simulations are ideal in emergency response training because they can enable trainees to:

- practice skills in safe settings where they can make and learn from mistakes;
- critically analyze and reflect on their performance and that of others;
- repeat activities until they are confident in undertaking them;
- engage in active learning so that what has been learned can be retained longer;
- access situations that are rarely encountered in real-world practice;
- encounter traumatic situations in a safe environment before they are experienced in the real world;
- learn from, and solve problems in, realistic, complex situations;
- take part in multiprofessional learning;
- encounter the same experiences that other trainees encounter, which standardizes the learning experience;
- practice history-taking skills in difficult situations;
- reassess narratives until they are sure they have learned their objectives fully;
- assess trainee performance; and
- discuss the ethical and professional dilemmas raised in the narratives.[79]

Despite the elements above, virtual reality training technology continues to be a niche technology that is primarily used by research universities, large corporations, and the military.[80] Wider acceptance and use of virtual reality training technology is limited by associated high costs and the requirement for a dedicated space and support infrastructure.[81] Even if wider use is achieved, some express caution that virtual reality training should be viewed and utilized as a supportive learning environment to more traditional suit-on, boots-on training.[82]

Implementation and Involvement

Due to the sheer number of training technologies today and their continual fast-paced evolution, leaders within homeland security partners may quickly feel overwhelmed when looking to incorporate technology-based training solutions. This is not an uncommon feeling, as the private industry and education communities have encountered the same conditions. To help those within homeland security partners responsible for training, the following section will provide information that can assist in making informed decisions. This is achieved by discussing the advantages and disadvantages of technology-based training, followed by specific implementation guidance based on lessons learned and best practices within the field. While this information does not provide a specific implementation plan for an individual agency, the presented information will arm decision makers with the necessary evaluation points needed in order to make the most efficient and effective use of training funds.

Before moving on, a discussion of the effectiveness of technology-based training solutions is warranted. This is important because the learning (ability to acquire new or transform existing knowledge, skills, or behaviors) and transfer (applying learning to daily job setting) of concepts is the ultimate goal of any training. However, the growing diffusion of technology-based training solutions has not only improved the quality and flexibility of training but also led to new paradigms in learning (e.g., m-learning).[83] As for effectiveness, it is impossible to generalize a whole swath of technologies in terms of effectiveness, and especially for an expansive and complex community like homeland security. Much of the transfer-specific comparative research between various forms of technology-based training (such as e-learning) and traditional training, however, results in the *no significant difference* phenomenon that is commonly found. Despite the usefulness and applicability of technology-based training solutions, some feel a gap still exists between training objectives/requirements and what can ultimately be provided by technology-based training solutions.[84] Even if this and other barriers (tactical and transfer) are overcome, some feel that the most significant problem still remains, which is the fact that agencies simply do not fully understand how to leverage technology to support training.[85]

Advantages and Disadvantages Comparison

Despite its growth, use, and acceptance, there are well-known and significant advantages and disadvantages to technology-based training and education. Although the current literature that highlights and provides deep analysis into these advantages and disadvantages is voluminous, Table 4.1 attempts to provide a summary of some of the research.[86]

One of the main advantages of technology-based training solutions is the fact that they provide a safe environment in which repetitive training can occur.[87] For example, full-scale, live exercises where actual situations are replicated, while very beneficial, require significant financial and human resources and have the risk of injuries to trainees and/or role players.[88] Therefore, technology-based training solutions, such as virtual reality simulations, have the ability to provide an effective secondhand experience that can achieve training objectives in a more affordable and adaptable fashion.[89] Further, some technology-based training solutions have

Table 4.1 Technology-Based Training Advantages and Disadvantages

Advantages	Disadvantages
Anytime and anywhere learning	Computer literacy issues
Automated record keeping and tracking	Failure to communicate expectations
Consistent learning environment	
Develop problem-solving, critical thinking, and team collaboration skills	Higher levels of frustration, anxiety, and confusion
Diminish student inhibitions regarding communication by removing psychological and social barriers to student-teacher and student-student interactions	Ineffective hands-on practices
	Internet connectivity issues
	Lack of and/or delayed instructor feedback
	Lack of human interaction
Exposure to low occurrence, high consequence events, disturbing events and sights	Lack of nonverbal cues
Flexibility in delivery formats	Longer timeframe to develop and/or update curriculum
Higher enrollments per session	Maintenance costs and/or technologies fees (e.g., service accounts)
Interactive learning to promote learner interest	
Learner-centered environment	Many accepted advantages have not been empirically tested
Meet the needs of nontraditional students as well as technology-driven students	Privacy and computer security issues
More autonomous (e.g., less dependent on teacher's approval and instruction)	Requires self-motivation for learning
Multimedia content	Student feelings of isolation
Reduced occurrence of training related injuries, accidents, or equipment breakage	Supplements real/live training (not a direct replacement); not the same
Reduced training costs (e.g., delivery, trainee attendance, etc.)	Technology-focus instead on content-focus
Reduced training time	Upfront costs to acquire needed technology and/or access specialized training facilities
Repeatable training	
Self-paced learning	
Sophisticated interactions that incorporate game-based activities and business simulations	
Wider access to wide range of populations	

shown to offer a more engaging and collaborative training experience, which can lead to higher rates of learning and transfer.[90]

Despite their promise, technology-based training tools and systems are plagued by the thought (either real or imagined) that they generally cannot replicate traditional training or field training.[91] Further, technology-based training solutions based on the usage of scenarios is further limited because the development and updating of scenarios is a very resource-heavy process (in both human and financial resources).[92] Additionally, due to the numerous possibilities within technology-based training solutions, the simple management of the various approaches to technology-based training becomes a difficult task.[93] For example, a training administrator must keep pace with and match employee requirements in order to find the appropriate technology-based training solutions that best meet the needs of employees but at the same time effectively transmit knowledge, skills, and abilities.[94] Therefore, training administrators within homeland security partners must rely on guidance, lessons learned, and best practices when implementing technology-based training solutions.

Training Technology Implementation Guidance

Despite the inherent advantages of technology-based training solutions, the efficiencies and effectiveness offered by technology can be severely diminished if they are not properly implemented. For example, many training technology implementation projects fail to fully achieve potential benefits due to factors such as poor strategy, leadership, and/or engagement.[95] Despite the difficulties, training technology implementation is an area where homeland security partners need to adapt despite the fact that "there is a lack of guidance for *how* to adapt."[96] Therefore, how should a homeland security partner proceed with implementing a technology-based training solution? In order to provide specific implementation guidance, the PADDIE framework will be utilized to segment and present information in a more orderly and comprehendible fashion. PADDIE is an instructional design model that can help an agency select the right technology for the right training and includes the following processes: Planning, Analysis, Design, Development, Implementation, and Evaluation.[97] The remainder of this section will be organized around these processes.

Planning

Although it seems like common sense, it is worth noting that a successful project will devote necessary time and attention to the planning stage.[98]

When looking to implement and/or utilize a technology-based training solution, homeland security partners should include all necessary stakeholders as early as possible, which will help to obtain critical buy-in.[99] Most importantly, support is needed for leadership, who must adequately convey the message that the technology is needed.[100] This is extremely important for those individuals who have aversions to technology and have desires to continue doing things the old way (e.g., traditional training). In essence, technology champions must be identified and allowed to help push the technology.[101] Overall, homeland security partners need to properly plan when looking to implement technology-based training solutions. This planning must also include budget planning if necessary, which will help to ensure that adequate resources are available.[102] Once all necessary and appropriate planning has occurred, a homeland security partner can move on to the analysis phase.

Analysis

During the analysis phase, a homeland security partner will identify the specific technology-based training solutions that will support training objectives. Within this step, homeland security partners must be careful to let the training objectives drive the technology, rather than the other way around.[103] Therefore, homeland security partners must clearly understand the training objectives that must be achieved.[104] Homeland security partners must also understand their employees' preferred learning types.[105] Specifically, individuals utilize three main types of learning—auditory, visual, and kinesthetic.[106] Although most individuals use a combination of learning styles, they typically have a clear preference for one style.[107] Knowing employees' learning styles will assist in achieving greater knowledge obtainment and transfer by helping to identify proper technology-based training solutions.[108] Therefore, homeland security partners must be deliberate in identifying technology-based training solutions that will be implemented to ensure that they will support training objectives and the learning styles of employees.

Design and Development

When agencies are identifying technology-based training solutions for possible implementation, additional considerations must be noted during the process that deal with design and development. Training design, whether technology-supported or not, is very important in determining whether training objectives are meet. For example, although a training may incorporate a desired technology, if it is poorly designed/developed, it will not enable achievement of training objectives. Further, homeland security partners must ensure that implemented technology-based training solutions are not too easy or too hard for trainees based on their existing skill level.[109] In essence, there might be some trial and error involved with some agencies until they find the right fit. Therefore, it is wise for homeland security partners to implement technology-based training solutions that have low failure consequences and/or where failure can be acceptable.[110] Lastly, it is important that the technology-based training solution incorporates some level of learner control.[111] This is especially true within training that is completed by an individual anytime/anywhere. This enables a learner to access the most pertinent materials, even in a nonlinear fashion.[112] However, appropriate feedback and knowledge assessments are required to help ensure learning.[113] As stated above, homeland security partners must be careful not to let the technology drive the training objectives.[114]

Implementation

When implementing technology-based training solutions, whether within training or other operations (e.g., communications), it is good practice to start small. Conducting a pilot before full-scale implementation can help identify issues, address contingencies, and devise larger implementation strategies without the costs of fixes during full implementation. Again, there might be some trial and error involved with some agencies until they find the right fit. Therefore, it is wise for agencies to implement technologies that have acceptable failure consequences.[115] Therefore, is may be wise to select a few officers to participate in an experimental group to experience the new training technology. If the pilot is successful, these officers then in turn become the necessary technology champions. Homeland security partners must be careful if the pilot training is considered successful. Rather than turning the faucet completely on, an agency should utilize a slow-drip methodology to extend the technology out to the agency (i.e., the process is a marathon not a sprint).[116] Lastly, the slow-drip methodology will allow for so-called technology champions to help pull, not push, other individuals and leadership to fully utilize the identified technology.

Evaluation

One of the most important but often overlooked elements of the PADDIE process is evaluation. When implementing technology-based training solutions, homeland security partners need to determine whether the solutions are effectively achieving training objectives. Determining efficiencies with technology-based training solutions is also important, as technology is viewed as a force multiplier. Before the use of a technology-based training solution, an agency needs to decide how it will evaluate the technology and interpret the results.[117] Determining these two important data points after the fact will result in invalid and unreliable data. It is important that evaluations include performance-based assessments that evaluate learning and, if possible, transfer.[118] Relying simply on pre- and post-test scores will not provide a true picture of the technology. Further, a homeland security partner should not rely on easily obtainable quantitative data; rather, evaluations should include feedback strategies to capture more detailed information that can provide a more comprehensive view of the technology.[119] Overall, it is imperative that homeland security partners fully evaluate technology-based training solutions to determine if the technologies can provide highly effective training that can also provide needed efficiencies.

Impact

Implementation of new ideas, procedures, equipment, technology, etc. will have specific impacts. Implementing technology-based training solutions is no different and will primarily affect (a) agency individuals and (b) the agency itself. Individual impacts are assumed since trainees are one of the two actors that are required for learning (the other being the learning content).[120] Ultimately, the impacts on individuals are the most important, because if they are unfavorable, learning and transfer will fail, regardless of the type of instruction (traditional or technology-based). Individual impacts, however, may vary based on the characteristics of the individuals. Characteristics to consider include type of learning style (e.g., auditory, visual, kinesthetic); acceptance versus aversion to technology; preference of new ways (e.g., technology-based training) versus desires to continue the old way (e.g., classroom-based training); etc. Therefore, a homeland security partner needs to determine how the implementation of a technology-based training solution will affect individuals within their agency and how to manage, reduce, and/or eliminate any possible unfavorable impacts to ensure effective and efficient learning and transfer.[121]

In addition to managing individual impacts, agency leadership must also manage impacts to the agency itself. Of upmost concern to homeland security partners today in light of strained budgets is costs associated with implementing new technology-based training solutions. Typically, training budgets are the first to be reallocated when budget constraints dictate more money is needed for other organizational needs (e.g., personnel and/or equipment). Therefore, when an agency decides to implement a technology-based training solution or direct employees to technology-based training, any additional costs associated with the technology must be accounted for. While one of the benefits of technology is reduced training costs, homeland security partners must still perform a cost–benefit analysis to ensure that training is effective and efficient. A homeland security partner must also be concerned with agency personnel perspectives. In addition to a possible preference for the old way of doing things (e.g., traditional training), if new technologies are perceived as not working, then homeland security partner personnel may be less likely to support other technology-based enhancements. Again, a homeland security partner must balance costs and benefits to help ensure that their personnel are provided the most relevant, timely, effective, and efficient training as possible that achieves training objectives. Lastly, as technologies continue to expand and become more ubiquitous, homeland security partners may find difficulty in managing the diversity of technology-based training solutions while at the same time ensuring they keep pace with employee requirements and preferences.[122]

Conclusion

Technology has been rapidly evolving since the Industrial Revolution. Even though the homeland security field is relatively young in comparison, it continues to be greatly influenced by technology, especially in terms of equipment and communications. Training is no different, as those technology-based training solutions discussed in this chapter have illustrated. Again, training can no longer be envisioned as butts in the seats, but rather must be seen as a large tree in which each branch represents a different technology or delivery method that can help in achieving training objectives. It is obvious that technology has helped to create a new training paradigm, and technology-based training solutions are now considered compatible with the way individuals prefer to learn and incorporate modern learning pedagogy.[123] Overall, there is a noticeable push to provide training in more intuitive and interactive ways to increase leaning and transfer.[124] To achieve this, the relationship between training and technology has become one of necessity:

> There is no doubt that successful training currently exist[s] as a result of a partnership with new and developing technology. Despite the challenges of the economy, this condition has become the new reality for leaders at every level. It is their responsibility to remain aware and to leverage the advantages.[125]

Discussion Questions

1. Define tactical barriers and transfer barriers and explain how technology-based training solutions can overcome these barriers.
2. Identify and explain the influences behind the push to make training more interactive and technology driven.
3. Explain the difference between augmented reality and virtual reality as it pertains to training.
4. Explain how technology-based training solutions can address individual learning styles (auditory, visual, and kinesthetic).
5. Identify the individual PADDIE process that you feel is the most important when implementing technology-based training solutions, and explain your reasoning.

Case Study Analysis

Background: You are the director of the County Emergency Management Agency (EMA). Facts about the county include:

- Square Miles: 443
- Population: 83,000
- Number of Municipalities: 2 incorporated, 4 unincorporated
- Number of Colleges/Universities: 1 public, 1 private
- Major Highways: 1 interstate, 2 U.S. highways
- Major Rivers: 1 (northern border)
- Natural Hazards: tornadoes, flooding, and severe weather
- Technological Hazards: U.S. military storage facility for conventional munitions and chemical weapons
- Hospitals: 2
- Law Enforcement: college/university departments, municipal departments, county sheriff, and state police post
- Fire Services: municipal departments, county department, and volunteer departments
- Emergency Medical Services: county department
- Emergency Management: county department

Grant: The county has just received a large multimillion dollar training grant from the U.S. Department of Homeland Security (DHS). You have been assigned as the county's grant coordinator, meaning you are in charge of the grant and all training activities that will be funded through the grant. The grant totals $5 million. The amount spent each year is up to the county, but all funding must be spent within a five-year timeframe. The grant is restricted to implementing technology-based training solutions into training programs for the county's first responder agencies (career and volunteer). The grant provides funding for training solutions to address needs beyond yearly certification training prescribed by federal, state, and local mandates. Therefore, the grant will be utilized to implement countywide technology-based training solutions that can increase capability in all mission areas (planning, prevention, response, recovery, and mitigation).

Training Solution: The training solution you decide to implement must be technology-based, per the grant restrictions. Your selected solution should be realistic in terms of funding and the ability to implement the solution. Remember that a one-size-fits-all approach cannot be applied to the first responder community due to different disciplines across the community (e.g., fire, law enforcement, and emergency management), different roles across and within disciplines and individual agencies, and different backgrounds, experiences, and skills within individuals. Further, training must be modernized in terms of development and delivery in order to motivate and be applicable to the new generation of digital learners that are entering the first responder community workforce. Therefore, you must focus on current employees as well as future employees.

Training Implementation Plan: This case study requires you to develop a training implementation plan for your selected technology-based training solution. To develop your training implementation plan, the PADDIE framework must be utilized. Therefore, you must detail what you will do within each element of the PADDIE framework. Also, think about how you are going to identify the training needs the training solution will address, as well as how the training solution can be maintained and sustained after the grant funding ends.

Notes

1. Moskaliuk, Bertram, and Cress, "Impact of Virtual Training Environments on the Acquisition and Transfer of Knowledge."

2. Mendonca et al., "Designing Gaming Simulations for the Assessment of Group Decision Support Systems in Emergency Response."

3. Atherton and Sheldon, "Correctional Training and Technology"; Mendonca et al., "Designing Gaming Simulations for the Assessment of Group Decision Support Systems in Emergency Response."

4. Spain, Priest, and Murphy, "Current Trends in Adaptive Training with Military Applications."

5. Jarventaus, "Virtual Threat, Real Sweat."

6. Atherton and Sheldon, "Correctional Training and Technology."

7. Ibid.

8. Kranz, "Learning Gets a Higher Degree of Attention at Workplaces."

9. Ibid.

10. Berlusconi, "Paul Ekblom."

11. Stober and Putter, "Going Mobile and Micro," 41.

12. Ibid.

13. Targamadze and Petrauskiene, "The Use of Information Technology Tools to Reduce Barriers of Distance Learning."

14. Atherton and Sheldon, "Correctional Training and Technology."

15. Ibid.

16. Andronie, "Distance Learning Management Based on Information Technology."

17. Ibid.

18. Jass, "Take the Mobile Learning Plunge."

19. Pereira and Rodrigues, "Survey and Analysis of Current Mobile Learning Applications and Technologies," 2.

20. Shachar and Neumann, "Twenty Years of Research on the Academic Performance Differences between Traditional and Distance Learning"; Howell, Williams, and Lindsay, "Thirty-Two Trends Affecting Distance Education"; Thirunarayanan and Perez-Prado, "Comparing Web-Based and Classroom-Based Learning"; Galusha, "Barriers to Learning in Distance Education."

21. Ibid.

22. Blanchard, *E-learning.*

23. Ford et al., "Factors Affecting the Opportunity to Perform Trained Tasks on the Job."

24. Martin, "Final Comparison Study of Teaching Blended In-Class Courses vs. Teaching Distance Education Courses."

25. American Society of Safety Engineers, "Industry Notes," 20.

26. Spain, Priest, and Murphy, "Current Trends in Adaptive Training with Military Applications."

27. Thirunarayanan and Perez-Prado, "Comparing Web-Based and Classroom-Based Learning"; Tucker, "Distance Education."

28. Fox and Rainie, *The Web at 25 in the U.S.,* 25.

29. Martin, "Final Comparison Study of Teaching Blended In-Class Courses vs. Teaching Distance Education Courses"; Shachar and Neumann, "Twenty Years of Research on the Academic Performance Differences between Traditional and Distance Learning"; Shachar and Neumann, "Differences between Traditional and Distance Education Academic Performances"; Schmeeckle, "Online Training"; Bell, "The Third Technological Revolution and Its Possible Socioeconomic Consequences."

30. Peters et al., "Learning and Motivation to Transfer after an E-learning Program"; Sitzmann et al., "The Comparative Effectiveness of Web-based and Classroom Instruction."

31. Peters et al., "Learning and Motivation to Transfer after an E-learning Program."

32. Martin, "Final Comparison Study of Teaching Blended In-Class Courses vs. Teaching Distance Education Courses"; Motteram and Forrester, "Becoming an Online Distance Learner"; Thirunarayanan and Perez-Prado, "Comparing Web-Based and Classroom-Based Learning"; Tucker, "Distance Education."

33. Allen and Seaman, *Changing Course*, 4.

34. Spain, Priest, and Murphy, "Current Trends in Adaptive Training with Military Applications."

35. Nam, "Designing Interactive Narratives for Mobile Augmented Reality"; Diaz, "Augmented Reality"; Tsai, Liu, and Yau, "Using Electronic Maps and Augmented Reality-Based Training Materials as Escape Guidelines for Nuclear Accidents."

36. Diaz, "Augmented Reality"; Antal, "Augmented Reality for the Soldier."

37. Kangdon, "Augmented Reality in Education and Training," 13.

38. Krum, Suma, and Bolas, "Augmented Reality Using Personal Projection and Retroreflection."

39. Ibid.

40. Antal, "Augmented Reality for the Soldier."

41. Tsai, Liu, and Yau, "Using Electronic Maps and Augmented Reality-Based Training Materials as Escape Guidelines for Nuclear Accidents."

42. Diaz, "Augmented Reality"; Kangdon, "Augmented Reality in Education and Training."

43. Friedl and O'Neil, "Designing and Using Computer Simulations in Medical Education and Training."

44. Jarventaus, "Virtual Threat, Real Sweat."

45. Ibid.

46. Mendonca et al., "Designing Gaming Simulations for the Assessment of Group Decision Support Systems in Emergency Response."

47. Knight et al., "Serious Gaming Technology in Major Incident Triage Training."

48. Ibid.; Jarventaus, "Virtual Threat, Real Sweat."

49. "Technologies to Watch."

50. Serge et al., "The Effects of Static and Adaptive Performance Feedback in Game-Based Training"; Taylor and Barnett, "Evaluation of Wearable Simulation Interface for Military Training"; Mendonca et al., "Designing Gaming Simulations for the Assessment of Group Decision Support Systems in Emergency Response."

51. Simic, "Constructive Simulation as a Collaborative Learning Tool in Education and Training of Crisis Staff."

52. Jarventaus, "Virtual Threat, Real Sweat."

53. Ibid.

54. Stober and Putter, "Going Mobile and Micro."

55. Ibid.; "Technologies to Watch."

56. Antal, "Augmented Reality for the Soldier."
57. Pereira and Rodrigues, "Survey and Analysis of Current Mobile Learning Applications and Technologies," 1.
58. Ibid.
59. Stober and Putter, "Going Mobile and Micro"; Webel et al., "An Augmented Reality Training Platform for Assembly and Maintenance Skills."
60. Cone, "Look before You Leap into Mobile Learning."
61. Ibid.
62. Jass, "Take the Mobile Learning Plunge."
63. Ibid.
64. Cohen et al., "Emergency Preparedness in the 21st Century."
65. Ibid.
66. Heinrichs et al., "Simulation for Team Training and Assessment."
67. Cha et al., "A Virtual Reality Based Fire Training Simulator Integrated with Fire Dynamics Data," 12.
68. Cohen et al., "Emergency Preparedness in the 21st Century"; Hoang et al., "VFire."
69. Farra et al., "Improved Training for Disasters Using 3-D Virtual Reality Simulation."
70. Luo et al., "A Review of Interactive Narrative Systems and Technologies."
71. Cha et al., "A Virtual Reality Based Fire Training Simulator Integrated with Fire Dynamics Data"; Farra et al., "Improved Training for Disasters Using 3-D Virtual Reality Simulation."
72. Bertram, Moskaliuk, and Cress, "Virtual Training."
73. Hoang et al., "VFire."
74. Smith and Carter, "A Virtual Environment to Test Police and Public Awareness of Anti-social Behavior Indicators."
75. Ibid.
76. Ibid.
77. Ibid., 548.
78. Ibid.
79. Reprinted from Walsh, "Using a Simulated Learning Environment," 12, 14.
80. Hodgson et al., "WeaVR."
81. Ibid.
82. Smith and Carter, "A Virtual Environment to Test Police and Public Awareness of Anti-social Behavior Indicators."
83. Pereira and Rodrigues, "Survey and Analysis of Current Mobile Learning Applications and Technologies."
84. Luo et al., "A Review of Interactive Narrative Systems and Technologies."
85. Jass, "Take the Mobile Learning Plunge."
86. Hoyt, "Predicting Training Transfer of New Computer Software Skills"; Mugford, Corey, and Bennell, "Improving Police Training from a Cognitive Load Perspective"; Cha et al., "A Virtual Reality Based Fire Training Simulator Integrated with Fire Dynamics Data"; Emerson and MacKay, "A Comparison between

Paper-Based and Online Learning in Higher Education"; Kaynar and Sumerli, "A Meta-analysis of Comparison between Traditional and Web-Based Instruction"; Blanchard, *E-learning*; Dykman and Davis, "Online Education Forum"; Petty, Lim, and Zulauf, "Training Transfer between CD-ROM Based Instruction and Traditional Classroom Instruction"; Fenrich, "Getting Practical with Learning Styles in Live and Computer-Based Training Settings"; Harris and Gibson, "Distance Education vs Face-to-Face Classes"; Beard, Harper, and Riley, "Online Versus On-Campus Instruction"; Piccoli, Ahmad, and Ives, "Web-Based Virtual Learning Environments"; Tucker, "Distance Education"; Galusha, "Barriers to Learning in Distance Education"; Wehr, "Instructor-Led or Computer-Based."

87. Cha et al., "A Virtual Reality Based Fire Training Simulator Integrated with Fire Dynamics Data."

88. Ibid.

89. Luo et al., "A Review of Interactive Narrative Systems and Technologies."

90. Ibid.

91. Cha et al., "A Virtual Reality Based Fire Training Simulator Integrated with Fire Dynamics Data."

92. Luo et al., "A Review of Interactive Narrative Systems and Technologies."

93. Andronie, "Distance Learning Management Based on Information Technology."

94. Ibid.

95. Andison et al., "Transformation and Training for a Mobile Workforce."

96. Spain, Priest, and Murphy, "Current Trends in Adaptive Training with Military Applications," 89 (emphasis is original).

97. Porter, Weisenford, and Smith, "A Journey through the Design of a Virtual Learning Environment."

98. Ibid.

99. Ibid.

100. Jass, "Take the Mobile Learning Plunge."

101. Ibid.

102. Ibid.

103. Porter, Weisenford, and Smith, "A Journey through the Design of a Virtual Learning Environment."

104. Cone, "Look Before You Leap into Mobile Learning."

105. Ibid.

106. Pereira and Rodrigues, "Survey and Analysis of Current Mobile Learning Applications and Technologies."

107. Ibid.

108. Ibid.

109. Luo et al., "A Review of Interactive Narrative Systems and Technologies."

110. Cone, "Look Before You Leap into Mobile Learning."

111. Ibid.

112. Ibid.

113. Ibid.

114. Porter, Weisenford, and Smith, "A Journey through the Design of a Virtual Learning Environment."

115. Cone, "Look Before You Leap into Mobile Learning."

116. Jass, "Take the Mobile Learning Plunge."

117. Cone, "Look Before You Leap into Mobile Learning."

118. Porter, Weisenford, and Smith, "A Journey through the Design of a Virtual Learning Environment."

119. Ibid.

120. Pereira and Rodrigues, "Survey and Analysis of Current Mobile Learning Applications and Technologies."

121. Ibid.

122. Andronie, "Distance Learning Management Based on Information Technology."

123. Pereira and Rodrigues, "Survey and Analysis of Current Mobile Learning Applications and Technologies"; Thirunarayanan and Perez-Prado, "Comparing Web-Based and Classroom-Based Learning"; Tucker, "Distance Education."

124. Luo et al., "A Review of Interactive Narrative Systems and Technologies."

125. Atherton and Sheldon, "Correctional Training and Technology," 33.

Bibliography

Allen, I., and J. Seaman. *Changing Course: Ten Years of Tracking Online Education in the United States.* Babson Park, MA: Babson Survey Research Group and Quahog Research Group, LLC. 2013.

American Society of Safety Engineers. "Industry Notes: Professional Development—USFA Announces New Online Training System." *Professional Safety* 52, no. 12 (2007): 20.

Andison, M., S. Benge, N. Miller, L. Francis, and H. Cherry. "Transformation and Training for a Mobile Workforce: Sharing Lessons Learnt." *International Journal of Integrated Care* 14, no. 8 (2014). Retrieved from http://www.ijic.org/index.php/ijic/article/viewFile/1746/2573.

Andronie, M. "Distance Learning Management Based on Information Technology." *Contemporary Readings in Law and Social Justice* 6, no. 1 (2014): 350–361.

Antal, J. "Augmented Reality for the Soldier." *Military Technology* 37, no. 7 (2013): 27–30.

Atherton, E., and P. Sheldon. "Correctional Training and Technology: Keys to the Future." *Corrections Today* 73, no. 6 (2012): 28–33.

Baggett, R. "The Effectiveness of Homeland Security Training for Rural Communities: A Comparative Analysis of Web-Based and Instructor-Led Training Delivery." PhD Dissertation, Eastern Kentucky University. 2012.

Baldwin, T., and J. Ford. "Transfer of Training: A Review and Directions for Future Research." *Personnel Psychology* 41, no. 1 (1988): 63–105.

Beard, L., C. Harper, and G. Riley. "Online Versus On-Campus Instruction: Student Attitudes and Perceptions." *TechTrends* 48, no. 6 (2004): 29–31.

Bell, D. "The Third Technological Revolution and Its Possible Socioeconomic Consequences." In *Industrialization: Critical Perspectives on the World Economy*, ed. P. O'Brien. New York, NY: Routledge. 1988.

Berlusconi, G. "Paul Ekblom: Crime Prevention, Security and Community Safety Using the 5Is Framework." *European Journal of Criminal Policy and Research* 17 (2011): 249–251.

Bertram, J., J. Moskaliuk, and U. Cress. "Virtual Training: Making Reality Work." *Computers in Human Behavior* 43 (2015): 284–292.

Blanchard, K. *E-learning: An Effective, Engaging Solution for Boosting Training Participation and Completion.* Escondido, CA: The Ken Blanchard Companies. 2009.

Cha, M., S. Han, J. Lee, and B. Choi. "A Virtual Reality Based Fire Training Simulator Integrated with Fire Dynamics Data." *Fire Safety Journal* 50 (2012): 12–24.

Cohen, D., N. Sevdalis, D. Taylor, K. Kerr, M. Heys, K. Willett, A. Batrick, and A. Darzi. "Emergency Preparedness in the 21st Century: Training and Preparation Modules in Virtual Environments." *Resuscitation* 84, no. 1 (2013): 78–84.

Cone, J. "Look Before You Leap into Mobile Learning." *T+D* 67, no. 6 (2013): 40–45.

Diaz, O. "Augmented Reality: Merging the Real and Digital World." *Occupational Health & Safety.* July 1, 2014. http://ohsonline.com/Articles/2014/07/01/Rich -New-Training-Technologies-for-Professional-Development.aspx.

Dykman, C., and C. Davis. "Online Education Forum: Part Two—Teaching Online Versus Teaching Conventionally." *Journal of Information Systems Education* 19, no. 2 (2008): 157–164.

Ekblom, P. *The 5Is Framework: A Practical Tool for Transfer and Sharing of Crime Prevention and Community Safety Knowledge.* London, UK: Design against Crime Research Center. 2008.

Emerson, L., and B. MacKay. "A Comparison between Paper-Based and Online Learning in Higher Education: A Comparison of Paper-Based and Online Learning." *British Journal of Educational Technology* 42, no. 5 (2011): 727–735.

Farra, S., E. Miller, N. Timm, and J. Schafer. "Improved Training for Disasters Using 3-D Virtual Reality Simulation." *Western Journal of Nursing Research* 35, no. 5 (2013): 655–671.

Federal Emergency Management Agency. *National Training and Education Division (NTED) Condensed Course Development Specifications Guide.* Washington, DC: Federal Emergency Management Agency, National Training and Education Division. 2014.

Federal Emergency Management Agency. "Who Do We Serve?" Federal Emergency Management Agency. 2014. https://www.firstrespondertraining.gov/content.do ?page=serve.

Fenrich, P. "Getting Practical with Learning Styles in Live and Computer-Based Training Settings." *Issues in Informing Science & Information Technology* 3 (2006): 233–242.

Ford, J., M. Quinones, D. Sego, and J. Sorra. "Factors Affecting the Opportunity to Perform Trained Tasks on the Job." *Personnel Psychology* 45, no. 3 (1992): 511–527.

Fox, L., and S. Rainie. *The Web at 25 in the U.S.* Washington, DC: Pew Research Center. 2014.

Friedl, K., and H. O'Neil. "Designing and Using Computer Simulations in Medical Education and Training: An Introduction." *Military Medicine* 178, no. 10S (2013): 1–6.

Galusha, J. "Barriers to Learning in Distance Education." *Educational Resources Information Center*. 1998. http://eric.ed.gov/?id=ED416377.

Harris, M., and S. Gibson. "Distance Education vs Face-to-Face Classes: Individual Differences, Course Preferences, and Enrollment." *Psychological Reports* 98, no. 3 (2006): 756–764.

Heinrichs, W., P. Youngblood, P. Harter, and P. Dev. "Simulation for Team Training and Assessment: Case Studies of Online Training with Virtual Worlds." *World Journal of Surgery* 32, no. 2 (2008): 161–170.

Hoang, R., M. Sgambati, T. Brown, D. Coming, and F. Harris. "VFire: Immersive Wildfire Simulation and Visualization." *Computers & Graphics* 34, no. 6 (2010): 655–664.

Hodgson, E., E. Bachmann, D. Vincent, M. Zmuda, D. Waller, and J. Calusdian. "WeaVR: A Self-Contained and Wearable Immersive Virtual Environment Simulation System." *Behavior Research Methods* 47, no. 1 (2015): 296–307.

Howell, S., P. Williams, and N. Lindsay. "Thirty-Two Trends Affecting Distance Education: An Informed Foundation for Strategic Planning." *Online Journal of Distance Learning Administration* 6, no. 3 (2003).

Hoyt, B. "Predicting Training Transfer of New Computer Software Skills: A Research Study Comparing E-learning and In-Class Delivery." *Association for University Regional Campuses of Ohio (AURCO) Journal* 19 (2013): 83–111.

Jarventaus, J. "Virtual Threat, Real Sweat." *T+D* 61, no. 5 (2007): 72–78.

Jass, B. "Take the Mobile Learning Plunge." *T+D* 67, no. 2 (2013): 29–31.

Kangdon, L. "Augmented Reality in Education and Training." *TechTrends* 56, no. 2 (2012): 13–21.

Kaynar, B., and G. Sumerli. "A Meta-analysis of Comparison between Traditional and Web-Based Instruction." *Ekev Academic Review* 14, no. 43 (2010): 153–164.

Knight, J., S. Carley, B. Tregunna, S. Jarvis, R. Smithies, S. Freitas, A. Dunwell, and K. Jones. "Serious Gaming Technology in Major Incident Triage Training: A Pragmatic Controlled Trial." *Resuscitation* 81, no. 9 (2010): 1175–1179.

Kranz, G. "Learning Gets a Higher Degree of Attention at Workplaces." *Workforce* 93, no. 1 (2014): 44–47.

Krum, D., E. Suma, and M. Bolas. "Augmented Reality Using Personal Projection and Retroreflection." *Personal and Ubiquitous Computing* 16, no. 1 (2012): 17–26.

Luo, L., W. Cai, S. Zhou, M. Lees, and H. Yin. "A Review of Interactive Narrative Systems and Technologies: A Training Perspective." *Simulation* 91, no. 2 (2015): 126–147.

Martin, S. "Final Comparison Study of Teaching Blended In-Class Courses vs. Teaching Distance Education Courses." *Journal of Systemics, Cybernetics & Informatics* 10, no. 6 (2012): 40–46.

Mendonca, D., G. Beroggi, D. Gent, and W. Wallace. "Designing Gaming Simulations for the Assessment of Group Decision Support Systems in Emergency Response." *Safety Science* 44, no. 6 (2006): 523–535.

Moskaliuk, J., J. Bertram, and U. Cress. "Impact of Virtual Training Environments on the Acquisition and Transfer af Knowledge." *Cyberpsychology, Behavior, and Social Networking* 16, no. 3 (2013): 210–214.

Motteram, G., and G. Forrester. "Becoming an Online Distance Learner: What Can Be Learned from Students' Experiences of Induction to Distance Programs?" *Distance Education* 26, no. 3 (2005): 281–298.

Mugford, R., S. Corey, and C. Bennell. "Improving Police Training from a Cognitive Load Perspective." *Policing: An International Journal of Police Strategies & Management* 36, no. 2 (2013): 312–337.

Nam, Y. "Designing Interactive Narratives for Mobile Augmented Reality." *Cluster Computing* 18, no. 1 (2015): 309–320.

Pereira, O., and J. Rodrigues. "Survey and Analysis of Current Mobile Learning Applications and Technologies." *ACM Computing Surveys* 46, no. 2 (2013): 1–35.

Peters, S., M. Barbier, D. Faulx, and I. Hansez. "Learning and Motivation to Transfer after an E-learning Program: Impact of Trainees' Motivation to Train, Personal Interaction, and Satisfaction." *Innovations in Education and Teaching International* 49, no. 4 (2012): 375–387.

Petty, G., D. Lim, and J. Zulauf. "Training Transfer between CD-ROM Based Instruction and Traditional Classroom Instruction." *Journal on Technology Studies* 33, no. 1 (2007): 48–56.

Piccoli, G., R. Ahmad, and B. Ives. "Web-Based Virtual Learning Environments: A Research Framework and a Preliminary Assessment of Effectiveness in Basic IT Skills Training." *MIS Quarterly* 25, no. 4 (2001): 401.

Porter, E., J. Weisenford, and R. Smith. "A Journey through the Design of a Virtual Learning Environment." *Public Manager Summer* (2012): 64–68.

Schmeeckle, J. "Online Training: An Evaluation of the Effectiveness and Efficiency of Training Law Enforcement Personnel over the Internet." *Journal of Science Education and Technology* 12, no. 3 (2003): 205–260.

Serge, S., H. Priest, H. Durlach, and C. Johnson. "The Effects of Static and Adaptive Performance Feedback in Game-Based Training." *Computers in Human Behavior* 29 (2013): 1150–1158.

Shachar, M., and Y. Neumann. "Differences between Traditional and Distance Education Academic Performances: A Meta-analytic Approach." *The International Review of Research in Open and Distance Learning* 4, no. 2 (2003): 1–20.

Shachar, M., and Y. Neumann. "Twenty Years of Research on the Academic Performance Differences between Traditional and Distance Learning: Summative Meta-analysis and Trend Examination." *Journal of Online Learning and Teaching* 6, no. 2 (2010): 318–334.

Simic, G. "Constructive Simulation as a Collaborative Learning Tool in Education and Training of Crisis Staff." *Interdisciplinary Journal of Information, Knowledge, and Management* 7 (2012): 221–236.

Sitzmann, T., K. Kraiger, D. Stewart, and R. Wisher. "The Comparative Effectiveness of Web-Based and Classroom Instruction: A Meta-analysis." *Personnel Psychology* 59, no. 3 (2006): 623–664.

Smith, S., and T. Carter. "A Virtual Environment to Test Police and Public Awareness of Anti-social Behavior Indicators." *International Journal of Police Science & Management* 12, no. 4 (2010): 548–566.

Spain, R., H. Priest, and J. Murphy. "Current Trends in Adaptive Training with Military Applications: An Introduction." *Military Psychology* 24 (2012): 87–95.

Stober, D., and S. Putter. "Going Mobile and Micro." *Professional Safety* 58, no. 2 (2013): 41–43.

Targamadze, A., and R. Petrauskiene. "The Use of Information Technology Tools to Reduce Barriers of Distance Learning." *Vocational Education: Research & Reality* 23 (2012): 64–75.

Taylor, G., and J. Barnett. "Evaluation of Wearable Simulation Interface for Military Training." *Human Factors* 55, no. 3 (2013): 672–690.

"Technologies to Watch." *Tech & Learning* 31, no. 1 (2010): 14.

Thirunarayanan, M., and A. Perez-Prado. "Comparing Web-Based and Classroom-Based Learning: A Quantitative Study." *Journal of Research on Technology in Education* 34, no. 2 (2001): 131–137.

Tsai, M., P. Liu, and N. Yau. "Using Electronic Maps and Augmented Reality-Based Training Materials as Escape Guidelines for Nuclear Accidents: An Explorative Case Study in Taiwan." *British Journal of Educational Technology* 44, no. 1 (2013): 18–21.

Tucker, S. "Distance Education: Better, Worse, or as Good as Traditional Education?" *Online Journal of Distance Learning Administration* 4, no. 4 (2001).

Walsh, M. "Using a Simulated Learning Environment." *Emergency Nurse* 18, no. 2 (2010): 12–16.

Webel, S., U. Bockholt, T. Engelke, N. Gavish, M. Olbrich, and C. Preusche. "An Augmented Reality Training Platform for Assembly and Maintenance Skills." *Robotics and Autonomous Systems* 61 (2013): 398–403.

Wehr, J. "Instructor-Led or Computer-Based: Which Will Work Best for You?" *Training and Development Journal* 42, no. 6 (1988): 18–21.

CHAPTER FIVE

Social Media's Role in Supporting the Homeland Security Mission

Ryan K. Baggett

Learning Objectives

After reading this chapter, readers should be able to:

- Identify, compare, and contrast the six identified categories of social media applications.
- Apply social media applications to various situations that homeland security partners may encounter.
- Explain the seven social media benefits and their usefulness for homeland security agencies.
- Summarize the potential challenges that may be experienced when implementing social media.
- Identify considerations that should be made by homeland security partners when implementing social media campaigns.

Key Terms

Crowdsourcing
Implementation
Information Dissemination
Magnitude
Microblogging

Mobile Applications
Monitoring
Photo Sharing
Short Message Service (SMS)
Situational Awareness
Social Media
Social Media Engagement
Social Networking
Strategy Considerations
Sustainability
Video Sharing

Introduction

IN AN ERA DEFINED AS THE GREATEST revolution in communications and citizen empowerment since the rise of print, the start of the 21st century witnessed the significant dawn of social networking.[1] Not only do private citizens benefit from this advancement, but also homeland security partners in an effort to fulfill their mission areas. This vast array of technologies hanging on the backbone of the Internet gave rise to the capabilities of Web 2.0 technologies, providing a platform for collaboration and interactivity. One key tool that utilizes the Web 2.0 platform is social media. Specifically, Kaplan and Haenlein defined social media as "a group of Internet-based applications that build on the ideological and technological foundations of Web 2.0, and that allow the creation and exchange of user-generated content."[2] Social media tools allow individuals or groups to create, organize, edit, comment on, and share information. Additionally, the amount of information available increases as the number of adults using social media networking sites has jumped nearly tenfold in the past decade, according to a 2015 Pew Research Center report.[3] As indicated in Figure 5.1, "nearly two-thirds of American adults (65 percent) use social networking sites, up from 7 percent when Pew Research Center began systematically tracking social media usage in 2005."[4]

These social media users have demonstrated the benefits of the various tools in natural disasters, missing person events, and even small situations that may impact only a specific group of citizens. These events have been mitigated with various social media applications that have been created, with more likely to surface in coming years. These applications have served

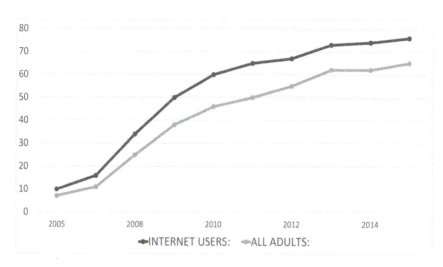

Figure 5.1 Percentage of American Adults and Internet Using Adults Who Use at Least One Social Networking Site (Source: Adapted from Pew Research Center).

many purposes for homeland security partners, with the Department of Homeland Security (DHS) Social Media Strategy providing specific categories including: information sharing and dissemination, overall situational awareness, requests for assistance, decision making, employee accountability, misinformation management, donation solicitation, and volunteer management.[5] The following chapter will identify several common applications for social media use by homeland security partners, identify benefits and challenges, and provide implementation considerations.

Social Media Applications

Although a plethora of social media applications exist throughout the world (with new applications being released regularly), this chapter will focus on six well-known categories: social networking, microblogging, video sharing, photo sharing, mobile applications, and short message service (SMS).

Social Networking

Social networking sites allow for the dissemination of information to a myriad of individuals. In fact, Facebook announced in 2014 that "its monthly active users cleared 1.35 billion individuals, roughly equal to the population of China and 9 percent larger than that of India."[6] A significant advantage of social networking is the ability to follow specific profiles and subsequently receive notifications when new information is released. Homeland security officials can leverage this feature to share information and engage citizens from their specific jurisdictions.

From a historical perspective, the majority of social media development occurred after the tragic events of September 11, 2001. It was in 2002 and 2003 that the networking sites Friendster and Myspace were created. Although these sites, especially Myspace, were very popular in the first five years of operation, the site Facebook was created in 2008. After Facebook's introduction, the two other sites quickly waned, and after Google, Facebook now holds the distinction of being the second most visited Web site.[7]

One example of effective Facebook utilization is by the Kentucky State Police (KSP). In October 2014, KSP held the record for the second largest Facebook following among state police agencies. In February 2016, the agency had over 126,000 followers. The KSP media coordinator reported that the site started small with press releases, current events, and fundraisers, but quickly saw its followers increase by the thousands each week of operation. Further, the coordinator noted that other law enforcement agencies with successful social networking sites were contacted for smart practices and lessons learned. The KSP social media portfolio has quickly added applications such as a commissioner's blog, a mobile application, Twitter, YouTube, and Instagram.[8]

Microblogging

A blog is a chronological online diary that allows visitors to post responses to a discussion thread on a particular topic.[9] As noted in the DHS Social Media Strategy, "Twitter (a microblogging application) enables users to send and received shortened messages (commonly known as tweets, comprised of less than 140 characters) through a variety of electronic methods. Users can send a message to a group of users or a single user, or communicate directly with an individual/organization they have followed."[10] Another feature of Twitter is the ability to search for specific topics by using keywords or hashtags.

Twitter was launched in 2006 and in 2016 reported more than 320 million active users each month.[11] One example of the effective uses of Twitter can be seen in response to Hurricane Isaac (2012) in the city of New Orleans. After a less than impressive response to Hurricane Katrina in 2005,

New Orleans looked to improve their preparation, response, and recovery to natural disasters. Due to the city's geographic location, the question was not if another hurricane would hit but rather when it would occur.

Seven years after Katrina, government officials used collaborative communications during Hurricane Isaac. Using the hashtag Isaac (#Isaac), users (to include government, nongovernment, the public, and the news media) shared information about the storm. In fact, the mayor of New Orleans Twitter account and a city of New Orleans account (@NOLAready) was used to respond directly to community members and to correct misinformation that was circulating throughout the area. The strategy was described as a coordinated and powerful method of distributing information throughout the community.[12]

Video Sharing

The increased ability to capture, edit, store, and share video has resulted in the growth of video-sharing sites such as YouTube. Video sharing sites allow users to post videos quickly, which allows for situational awareness for those in the field. YouTube was launched in 2005 to upload, share, and view videos.[13] Since that time, various homeland security partners (to include the U.S. Department of Homeland Security) have launched YouTube channels.

The DHS YouTube channel allows the agency to use video to highlight events, speeches, public service announcements, and other related content. DHS's emphasis on Web 2.0 tools such as YouTube allows the department to provide greater transparency and access to public, state, local, territorial, tribal, private sector, and international partner sites. The department believes that YouTube (and other social media sites) will build community engagement through transparency and provide timely, accurate information.[14]

Photo Sharing

Many homeland security agencies are beginning to understand the utility of agency profiles on photo-sharing sites. These sites encourage the public to post photos from the field. Like other forms of social media, these images provide situational awareness for homeland security partners as well as the public.[15]

One popular example of a photo- and video-sharing site is Instagram, which allows users to take pictures and videos and share them on a variety of social networking platforms. Like Twitter, Instagram utilizes hashtags;

however, unlike YouTube, Instagram limits video duration to 15 seconds or less. The site launched in October 2010 and was acquired by Facebook in April 2012.[16] Since that time, over 40 billion photos have been shared, with 80 million photos shared on a daily basis.[17]

Several agencies have noted the Instagram audience is generally younger than that of other social media sites. For example, a Virginia Commonwealth University Police representative noted, "We recognize that the vast majority of our audience are students who use Instagram more so than Facebook or Twitter. We use the site to connect to our young and ever-changing community."[18] As noted by the American Red Cross, Instagram is just one additional tool in the social media toolbox.

Mobile Applications

According to a 2015 Pew Research Center report, "nearly two-thirds of Americans are now smartphone owners, and for many these devices are a key entry point to the online world."[19] In fact, Americans now own more mobile phones than landline phones. Regardless of whether the application is on the iPhone or Android platform, the development and rollout of mobile applications is nevertheless a wise strategy to reach many Americans.

One example of a homeland security mobile application is the preparedness application developed by the Federal Emergency Management Agency (FEMA). The application, available for Apple, Android, and Blackberry mobile devices, provides many features for the user: "First, the application will receive alerts from the National Weather Service, allowing severe weather alerts for up to five locations across the United States. Additionally, the application will link to the FEMA Disaster Reporter, which is an application to crowdsource and share disaster-related information for events occurring within the United States, allowing citizens, first responders, emergency managers, community response and recovery teams, and others to view and contribute information on a publicly accessible map. In addition to safety tips, the application provides maps and driving directions to open shelters and disaster recovery centers. Last, the application will allow users easy access to DisasterAssistance.gov to apply for federal disaster assistance."[20]

Short Message Service

While SMS, or texting, is very popular for personal uses, the ability for information sharing and donation solicitation can be very useful for homeland security partners. With regard to information sharing, many universities and colleges use SMS to send alerts and instructions to students regarding emergencies and important messages. For example, Eastern Kentucky University (EKU) utilizes a multimodal emergency notification system to inform the community about incidents and emergencies affecting campus. Realizing that message redundancy is a necessity, EKU has seven primary notification systems available for the community. Any one, or a combination, of the alert methods may be used depending on the nature and severity of the event. In addition to Twitter and Facebook, which were previously explored, EKU utilizes text messaging as one of the seven modalities for notifications.

With regard to donation acquisitions, the American Red Cross (ARC) has launched several successful text campaigns to assist with disaster relief. For example, a 2010 SMS campaign to raise money for relief efforts in Haiti resulted in the collection of more than $21 million. The worldwide fundraiser, completed through electronic mechanisms, was enhanced using social media and exceeded the ARC's expectations.[21]

Social Media Benefits for Homeland Security Partners

As reprinted from the DHS *Social Media Strategy*, social media provides many benefits for homeland security partners. Specifically, the strategy outlines seven benefits:

1. Facilitating direct agency engagement within a community
2. Creating trust, credibility, and relationships within the community
3. Providing situational awareness about emergency events and partnership opportunities
4. Providing an additional method to disseminate emergency public information
5. Providing evaluation of public information
6. Allowing communities to engage in problem solving
7. Using social media to meet public expectations[22]

The following section will outline each of those benefits while providing additional context.

Facilitating Direct Agency Engagement within a Community

Community engagement is certainly not a concept that is unique to homeland security practitioners. In fact, all organizations serving the public should seek to learn smart practices in engaging communities and learn from strategies that have been utilized. One example is the following excerpt from the Clinical and Translational Science Awards Consortium:

> Building and sustaining networks of individuals and entities for community engagement includes establishing and maintaining communication channels, exchanging resources, and coordinating collaborative activities. Existing social networks can be effective and efficient platforms for efforts in community engagement if they reach people who are central to these efforts and if their members share the goals of the engagement efforts. Through the community engagement process, new networks can also be developed. Social media applications can provide a mechanism for engaging large and diverse groups of users, including individuals or groups that might otherwise be hard to reach or to bring together. Social media also provides a forum for discussion that has important differences from face-to-face interactions. With social media, all participants have an opportunity to contribute to the discussion, responses need not be immediate, and time can be taken to review the thread of a discussion.[23]

As noted above, the ability to establish these relationships will lead to other advantages. Social media has enabled individuals who may have never communicated to interact in near real time.

Creating Trust, Credibility, and Relationships within the Community

Trust in social media engagement is built over time, with an essential need for transparency in communications. Both trust and credibility are built on consistency and on follow-through. Timely and accurate advice and information is fundamental in establishing an effective network with attentiveness and responsiveness. Sincerity and the human touch go a long way toward building trust and credibility and toward laying the foundation of social media engagement.

Providing Situational Awareness about Emergency Events and Partnership Opportunities

Situational awareness can be defined as the ability to understand the current environment and utilize current information to make informed decisions about future occurrences. The DHS report *Using Social Media for Enhanced Situational Awareness and Decision Support* notes that social networking situational awareness activities can fall into two areas: monitoring and crowdsourcing. As defined, "monitoring encompasses a passive information search based on varying degrees of specificity, depending on a mission or goals. Crowdsourcing, or active 'listening,' leverages the crowd in various ways to provide, find, and produce new information. Finally, on-going monitoring may help to identify baseline trends to detect events quickly. Additionally, a lack of noise, when abnormal, may also signify points for further consideration, verification, or follow-up."[24]

Providing an Additional Method to Disseminate Emergency Public Information

As explored in the previous section of this chapter, there are many applications of social media that can be used to disseminate information by homeland security partners. As indicated with previous identified statistics, most Americans now have access to the Internet through smartphones or other devices. Homeland security partners can now capitalize on this connectedness in order to reach the community and provide warnings at a moment's notice in multiple modalities.[25]

Providing Evaluation of Public Information

It goes without saying that all information is not good information. The Internet, and social media by default, is a channel for free speech and unfortunately erroneous information. While the effects of quality information on social media have been identified in the previous sections, the converse is the fact that misinformation must be identified and corrected whenever possible. As DHS notes, "Misinformation may lead to ineffective decision making, hazardous actions, and inaccurate directions. Although homeland security partners will never completely stop misinformation, they can often correct the information through timely engagement with the community."[26]

Allowing Communities to Engage in Problem Solving

Communities consist of diverse individuals from a variety of careers with differing resources. Homeland security partners should actively seek opportunities to engage in whole-community problem solving through social media. Inviting the community to collectively solve problems and seek opportunities is an effective strategy for social media engagement. As described by FEMA, "Whole Community is an approach to emergency management that reinforces the fact that FEMA is only one part of our nation's emergency management team; that we must leverage all of the resources of our collective team to meet the needs of the entire community in each of these areas."[27] As identified by Gouillart and Billings, homeland security partners should start with identifying a large problem that needs the help of many people with various backgrounds to solve. Next, what platform should be used to engage the community so that they may connect for problem solving? Further, what valuable experiences will the users receive from these interactions? Finally, what value will the interactions generate for the homeland security partner and the problem identified? The authors note that the idea is to attract people onto platforms that the agency provides, get users to "start exploring new ways to connect and generate new experiences, and let the system grow organically."[28]

Using Social Media to Meet Public Expectations

It is highly unlikely that homeland security organizations will have a dedicated staff member whose sole job responsibility is to monitor social media. In a time of limited resources, most practitioners must wear multiple "hats" and perform a variety of different job functions. Another product of the information age is the tendency for the public to use social media to request help instead of utilizing traditional methods such as the telephone.[29] For example, one report notes that "a University of San Francisco Masters of Public Administration program found that 80 percent of Americans expect homeland security partners to monitor social media sites, with one out of three citizens expecting help to arrive within an hour of posting a request online."[30] In order to stay relevant to the communities they serve, it appears that homeland security partners must engage in social media while also setting realistic expectations for the communities they serve.

Social Media Challenges for Homeland Security Partners

Homeland security partners are under continuous pressure to expand or improve services and reduce costs while achieving the same or better results, and to protect equity while expanding representation and participation. In September 2013, the DHS Office of Inspector General issued a report that stated:

> DHS and its operational components have recognized the value of using social media to gain situational awareness and support mission operations, including law enforcement and intelligence-gathering efforts. However, additional oversight and guidance are needed to ensure that employees use technologies appropriately. In addition, improvements are needed for centralized oversight to ensure that leadership is aware of how social media are being used and for better coordination to share best practices. Until improvements are made, the Department is hindered in its ability to

assess all the benefits and risks of using social media to support mission operations.[31]

While DHS addressed these comments through various policies and operational changes, it does point to the fact that social media can be associated with challenges that homeland security partners should fully understand prior to implementation. One effective way to ensure visibility into issues regarding social media implementation is through capacity building and professional development. While many courses exist, one example is the *IS-42: Social Media in Emergency Management*. The purpose of the Web-based course "is to provide the participants with best practices including tools, techniques and a basic roadmap to build capabilities in the use of social media technologies in their own emergency management organizations in order to further their emergency response missions."[32] The following section will elaborate on many of the challenges identified in the FEMA training course.

Leadership Support

Homeland security partners must obtain leadership support for social media implementation. Depending on agency leadership's technology aptitude level, there could be an initial distrust of the technology and the implications for use. Administrators may question the reliability of information and the possibility of misuse or abuse. Further, command structures (generally very structured and controlled) may be uneasy that social media is decentralized and nonhierarchical. Essentially anyone with access (any Web-enabled device) and minimal skills can post and view. These concerns can be lessened through discussion with other administrators who have effective social media campaigns and through the analysis of smart practices reports on the topic.

Organizational Deployment Capabilities

Homeland security partners must consider the organizational capability for the deployment of social media and the infrastructure that may be necessary to accommodate its implementation. There may be associated costs to successful social media deployment, such as support staff and platforms that may require licensing with specific enterprise solutions. Additionally, as noted throughout this textbook, training is essential in any technology deployment to ensure effective use of social media. Progressive agencies should investigate the use of grant funds for acquisition of technologies and work with private sector developers to negotiate terms and conditions with homeland security users.[33]

Campaign Sustainability

Related to cost, homeland security partners are already working with limited resources and expected to do more with less. Homeland security partners should be creative when considering the sustainability of social media campaigns. Effectiveness will not be obtained when overburdening an existing staff member who is already overloaded with daily responsibilities. As noted before, homeland security partners should explore external funding opportunities or look within their state, county, or city structure to determine if there is an existing office that could be collaborated with (at least initially) to explore agency social media strategies.

Security Policies

Security policies and restrictions related to social media should be considered. Some technology representatives may believe that social media platforms are potential security risks. This opinion will generally be found in homeland security partners who have not kept pace with the current state of Web technology. However, the installation of basic information security principles (firewalls, etc.) can be utilized to ensure sensitive computer systems are not connected to social media sites. Additionally, homeland security partners must ensure that they consider requirements associated with records retention, sunshine laws, records requests (Freedom of Information Act requests) and the distribution and retention of Personally Identifiable Information (PII).

Social Media Implementation Considerations

After the evaluation of potential applications and potential benefits and challenges, homeland security partners should ensure that several considerations are made in implementing their social media campaign. This section will outline various considerations for homeland security agencies embarking upon social media engagement.

Magnitude

Many have likely heard of the "crawl, walk, run" analogy when discussing a new skill or program. However, homeland security partners must decide the magnitude of their social media campaign based upon their resources and skill set. In *Disasters 2.0*, Adam Crowe notes that the consideration of implementing "social media systems is divided into three categories: active, passive and stationary. [The] difference between these models is related to the degree of social media monitoring, analysis, and validation as well as [information] dissemination applied by the [agency]. The active model of social media involves the routine utilization of social media for dissemination and vigorous monitoring." On the other hand, passive application does not support the robustness of the active model and either disseminates information or monitors information, but not both. The stationary model includes no social media application by agencies and may be considered careless to use due to the responsibility that homeland security partners have been granted by the communities they serve.[34]

Strategy Development

As with any program, strategic planning is essential to ensure that specific goals and objectives are obtained by the program in question. Further, implementation procedures and strategy should also be clearly identified so that stakeholders may understand the details behind the program. A social media strategy should be a component of a homeland security partner's all-hazards communications plan. However, it should be emphasized that when developing policies, all applicable departments (Information Technology, Legal, Human Resources, etc.) should be involved to ensure effectiveness. In the January 2012 DHS report, *Next Steps: Social Media for Emergency Response*, several strategy considerations are reprinted below.

- **Human Resources**
  - Resources required
  - Training and education required
  - Job descriptions
  - Liability
  - Ethical conduct and accountability to an agency's rules of conduct (personal versus professional use of social media tools and techniques)

- **Operational and Communications Security (OPSEC and COMSEC)**
  - Classification and handling guidelines (e.g., For Official Use Only, Sensitive but Unclassified, Classified, etc.)
  - Training and education
  - Devices (e.g., personal versus agency provided, etc.)
  - Interaction with existing tools and processes

- **Legal and Compliance**
  - Copyright laws
  - Records retention requirements
  - Endorsement of products, services, and postings
  - Public disclosure and sunshine laws
  - Privacy

- **Business Continuity**
  - Necessary access rights and password policies
  - Redundancies

- **Information Technology**
  - Bandwidth and other resources (servers, etc.)
  - Training and education
  - Integration

- **Communications and Engagement**
  - Messaging
  - Metrics and measuring success
  - Outreach[35]

While other topics will be necessary (based on function and jurisdiction), this list provides a foundation on which to build.

Technology Selection

In the first section of this chapter, several categories of social media applications were presented. As noted, other categories exist and thousands of specific tools exist within those categories. Technology is a dynamic, ever-changing area, which equates to the fact that homeland security partners that implement social media must be flexible and be prepared to use new tools that meet the needs of the communities that they serve. To ensure the appropriate tools are being implemented, homeland security partners must consider the communication plan goals and objectives, audience, available resources, timeline with close attention to changing trends and advancements.[36] Each tool category has various limitations, messaging types, and associated audiences. Before time and effort is expended on one specific tool, due diligence must be conducted to ensure the right fit for the agency's purposes.

Engaging the Community

An effective social media strategy must contain a plan for regular and timely messaging in order to establish their campaign as a credible and reliable source for important information. It is important for homeland security partners to let their communities know what social media will and will not be used for. For example, users should understand that 9-1-1 is still the primary communication channel for emergencies and that social media will not be monitored 24 hours a day. Further, social media must be monitored to ensure unsolicited assistance (donations, volunteering, etc.) is controlled through established protocols.

Next, on many social media applications, the homeland security partner will be limited in the number of characters that they may use to communicate. Therefore, it is imperative that appropriate and effective messaging be developed to maximize effectiveness. Establish the authorized individuals who can release social media messaging (and their backups) and ensure that an approval process is discussed.

Last, ensure protocols are in place that encourage interaction and participation. This two-way communication will empower community members to provide information with benefits as previously identified in this chapter. However, if a homeland security partner requests two-way communications, they must have procedures in place to monitor and respond to the correspondence to ensure that the user is satisfied that the message has been received and the agency receives the valuable information so that an informed decision can be made.[37]

Address Challenges: Adoption, Privacy, Records, Information Technology and Security

The last section in implementation considerations is a reminder to address several of the challenges previously noted. As identified by the Virtual Social Media Working Group and DHS First Responders Group, the following considerations are reprinted below:

- Discourage users from disclosing personal information.
- Content should not be restricted unless restriction is narrowly tailored to achieve compelling government interest or public quality.
- Ensure training and education programs/policies are in place within the agency to encourage safe use of social media by government officials.
- Staff-assigned social media responsibilities may require additional or specific skills—consider including characteristics in future job descriptions to ensure appropriate staff hiring.
- Consider existing information technology guidelines or restrictions within the agency to ensure compliance and how social media technologies may affect compliance.
- Establish operational security (OPSEC) procedures and communications security (COMSEC) protocols dictating staff behavior with social media technologies.[38]

Conclusion

Information sharing is vital during disasters and emergencies and the ability to disseminate information about threats and the subsequent emergency response will determine the difference between effective and ineffective responses. A successful response will require a Whole Community effort with the highest level of situational awareness available. FEMA Director Craig Fugate notes, "Social media provides the tools needed to minimize the communication gap and participate effectively in an active, ongoing dialogue."[39]

The reality is that social media has changed mass communications. As David Kaufman explains, "We have shifted from large organizations as authorities to an authority within a network, whether that person is a legitimate authority or not. The public will not fit into the plan. Instead, the emergency plan needs to fit the public."[40]

This chapter has outlined several categories of social media applications and benefits to their implementation. However, it should be noted that technology can be an enabler of improved communications only if it is coordinated and deployed effectively. Along with the benefits, several challenges were identified that must be handled by homeland security partners to ensure that social media can continue to be a viable tool for homeland security officials. The challenges can be mitigated through many of the considerations noted in the last section of the chapter with the understanding that social media can be leveraged in a powerful way as a critical tool for preventing and responding to natural, man-made, and technological threats.

Discussion Questions

1. Recently, you have been hired as a Public Information Officer (PIO) for a county emergency management agency. The agency has limited resources and no visible social media presence. The director has asked you to begin the agency's first social media campaign, where would you begin?

2. As an analyst for the state office of homeland security, you have been tasked with handling the agency's short messaging service application, Twitter. According to weather reports, it appears that an F3 tornado is heading toward part of the state. What would your 120-character message say?

3. As a FEMA region representative, you have been called to testify in front of Congress on the benefits of social media to your six-state region. How would you summarize these benefits in a concise, logical manner?

4. As a shift captain for a county law enforcement agency, you have been actively crowdsourcing social media regarding the county fair that is cur-

rently under way in your jurisdiction. Explain what you are doing and why.

5. A recent local newspaper article has shed negative publicity on your city fire department. The battalion chief has asked you to use video and photo-sharing sites to improve the department's overall image to the community. What would you feature on the sites and why?

Notes

1. Flynn and Bates, *Connecting America*.
2. Kaplan and Haenlein, "Users of the World, Unite!"
3. Perrin, "Social Media Usage: 2005–2015."
4. Ibid.
5. U.S. Department of Homeland Security, *Social Media Strategy*.
6. Dewey, "Almost as Many People Use Facebook as Live in the Entire Country of China."
7. Flynn and Bates, *Connecting America*.
8. Foreman, "Getting the Word Out."
9. U.S. Department of Homeland Security, *Innovative Uses of Social Media in Emergency Management*.
10. U.S. Department of Homeland Security, *Social Media Strategy*.
11. Twitter, "Twitter Company Facts."
12. U.S. Department of Homeland Security, *Innovative Uses of Social Media in Emergency Management*.
13. Hopkins, "Surprise!"
14. U.S. Department of Homeland Security, "DHS Launches YouTube Channel and Redesigns DHS.gov."
15. U.S. Department of Homeland Security, *Social Media Strategy*.
16. Frommer, "Here's How to Use Instagram."
17. Instagram, "Instagram Press."
18. Waugh, "Why Law Enforcement Should Be Using Instagram."
19. Smith, "U.S. Smartphone Use in 2015."
20. Federal Emergency Management Agency, "FEMA Mobile Applications."
21. Gross, "Red Cross Text Donations Pass $21 million."
22. Reprinted from U.S. Department of Homeland Security, *Social Media Strategy*.
23. National Institutes of Health, *Principles of Community Engagement*.
24. U.S. Department of Homeland Security, *Using Social Media for Enhanced Situational Awareness and Decision Support*.
25. U.S. Department of Homeland Security, *Social Media Strategy*.
26. U.S. Department of Homeland Security, *Using Social Media for Enhanced Situational Awareness and Decision Support*.

27. U.S. Department of Homeland Security, *Whole Community*.
28. Gouillart and Billings, "Community-Powered Problem Solving."
29. Mazmanian, "Twitter for Disaster Responders."
30. Thomas, "Social Media Changing the Way FEMA Responds to Disasters."
31. U.S. Department of Homeland Security, Office of Inspector General, *DHS Uses Social Media to Enhance Information Sharing and Mission Operations, but Additional Oversight and Guidance Are Needed (OIG-13-115)*, 1.
32. Federal Emergency Management Agency, "IS-42: Social Media in Emergency Management."
33. U.S. Department of Homeland Security, *Using Social Media for Enhanced Situational Awareness and Decision Support*.
34. Crowe, *Disasters 2.0*.
35. Reprinted from U.S. Department of Homeland Security, *Next Steps: Social Media for Emergency Response*.
36. Ibid.
37. Ibid.
38. Ibid.
39. *Understanding the Power of Social Media as a Communication Tool in the Aftermath of Disasters: Hearing before the Ad Hoc Subcommittee on Disaster Recovery and Intergovernmental Affairs of the Committee on Homeland Security and Governmental Affairs, U.S. Senate*. 112th Cong. 2011.
40. West, *A Vision for Homeland Security in the Year 2025*.

Bibliography

Bacon, J. *The Art of Community: Building the New Age of Participation*. Boston, MA: O'Reilly Media. 2009.
Crowe, A. *Disasters 2.0: The Application of Social Media Systems for Modern Emergency Management*. Boca Raton, FL: CRC Press. 2012.
Dewey, C. "Almost as Many People Use Facebook as Live in the Entire Country of China." *The Washington Post*. Last modified October 29, 2014. https://www.washingtonpost.com/news/the-intersect/wp/2014/10/29/almost-as-many-people-use-facebook-as-live-in-the-entire-country-of-china/.
Federal Emergency Management Agency. "FEMA Mobile Applications." *Federal Emergency Management Agency*. Last modified May 21, 2015. http://www.fema.gov/mobile-app.
Federal Emergency Management Agency. "IS-42: Social Media in Emergency Management." *Federal Emergency Management Agency, Emergency Management Institute*. Last modified October 31, 2013. http://www.training.fema.gov/is/courseoverview.aspx?code=IS-42.
Flynn, S., and S. Bates. *Connecting America: Building Resilience with Social Media*. Washington, DC: Center for National Policy. 2014.
Foreman, K. "Getting the Word Out: Effectively Using Social Media in Kentucky Law Enforcement." *Kentucky Law Enforcement Magazine* 14, no. 4 (2014): 38–43.

Frommer, D. "Here's How to Use Instagram." *Business Insider.* Last modified November 1, 2010. http://www.businessinsider.com/instagram-2010-11.

Gouillart, F., and D. Billings. "Community-Powered Problem Solving." *Harvard Business Review.* Accessed February 2016. https://hbr.org/2013/04/community-powered-problem-solving.

Gross, D. "Red Cross Text Donations Pass $21 million." *CNN.* Last modified January 18, 2010. http://www.cnn.com/2010/TECH/01/18/redcross.texts/.

Hopkins, J. "Surprise! There's a Third YouTube Co-Founder." *USA Today.* Last modified October 11, 2006. http://usatoday30.usatoday.com/tech/news/2006-10-11-youtube-karim_x.htm.

Instagram. "Instagram Press." Instagram. Accessed February 2016. https://www.instagram.com/press/.

Kaplan, A., and M. Haenlein. "Users of the World, Unite! The Challenges and Opportunities of Social Media." *Business Horizons* 53, no. 1 (2010): 61.

Mazmanian, A. "Twitter for Disaster Responders." *Federal Computer Weekly.* Last modified July 7, 2013. https://fcw.com/articles/2013/07/09/fema-social-media.aspx.

National Institutes of Health. *Principles of Community Engagement.* (2nd ed.) Bethesda, MD: National Institutes of Health.

Perrin, A. "Social Media Usage: 2005–2015." Pew Research Center. Last Modified October 8, 2015. http://www.pewinternet.org/2015/10/08/social-networking-usage-2005-2015/.

Smith, A. "U.S. Smartphone Use in 2015." Pew Research Center. Last modified April 1, 2015. http://www.pewinternet.org/2015/04/01/us-smartphone-use-in-2015/.

Thomas, S. "Social Media Changing the Way FEMA Responds to Disasters." *National Defense Magazine.* Last modified September 2013. http://www.nationaldefensemagazine.org/archive/2013/September/Pages/SocialMediaChangingtheWayFEMARespondstoDisasters.aspx.

Twitter. "Twitter Company Facts." *Twitter.* Last modified December 31, 2015. https://about.twitter.com/company.

Understanding the Power of Social Media as a Communication Tool in the Aftermath of Disasters: Hearing before the Ad Hoc Subcommittee on Disaster Recovery and Intergovernmental Affairs of the Committee on Homeland Security and Governmental Affairs, U.S. Senate. 112th Cong. 2011. https://www.gpo.gov/fdsys/pkg/CHRG-112shrg67635/pdf/CHRG-112shrg67635.pdf.

U.S. Department of Homeland Security, Office of Inspector General. *DHS Uses Social Media to Enhance Information Sharing and Mission Operations, but Additional Oversight and Guidance Are Needed (OIG-13-115).* Washington, DC: U.S. Department of Homeland Security, Office of Inspector General. 2013.

U.S. Department of Homeland Security, Office of Inspector General. "DHS Launches YouTube Channel and Redesigns DHS.gov." U.S. Department of Homeland Security. Last modified July 22, 2009. http://www.dhs.gov/news/2009/07/22/dhs-launches-youtube-channel-and-redesigns-dhsgov.

U.S. Department of Homeland Security, Office of Inspector General. *Innovative Uses of Social Media in Emergency Management.* Washington, DC: U.S. Department of

Homeland Security, System Assessment and Validation for Emergency Responders (SAVER). 2013.

U.S. Department of Homeland Security, Office of Inspector General. *Next Steps:
Social Media for Emergency Response*. Washington, DC: U.S. Department of
Homeland Security. 2012.

U.S. Department of Homeland Security, Office of Inspector General. *Social Media
Strategy*. Washington, DC: U.S. Department of Homeland Security. 2012.

U.S. Department of Homeland Security, Office of Inspector General. *Using Social
Media for Enhanced Situational Awareness and Decision Support*. Washington, DC:
U.S. Department of Homeland Security. 2014.

U.S. Department of Homeland Security. *Whole Community*. Last modified June 10,
2016. https://www.fema.gov/whole-community.

Waugh, D. "Why Law Enforcement Should Be Using Instagram." *International
Association of Chiefs of Police Center for Social Media*. Last modified September
10, 2014. http://blog.iacpsocialmedia.org/Home/tabid/142/entryid/395/Default
.aspx.

West, D. *A Vision for Homeland Security in the Year 2025*. Washington, DC: The
Brookings Institute, 2012.

CHAPTER SIX

Physical Security Technologies

Protecting Assets and Critical Infrastructure through Technology

Brian K. Simpkins

Learning Objectives

After reading this chapter, readers should be able to:

- Define the fundamental concept of physical security.
- Describe the approach to physical security through layers and levels.
- Summarize the various physical security technologies that are currently available.
- Analyze how the implementation of technology-based physical security solutions can overcome barriers related to traditional physical security methods.
- Analyze why there is a push to make physical security more intelligent and proactive (rather and passive) and more information driven.
- Apply knowledge obtained through chapter to discussion questions.

Key Terms

Access Card
Access Control
Asset
Barriers

Cloud Storage
Critical Infrastructure
Edge Storage
Immersive Surveillance
Internet of Things (IoT)
Intrusion Detection
Physical Security
Security Layers
Security Levels
Smart Light Emitting Diode (LED)
Video Analytics
Video Surveillance

Introduction and Overview

THE PROTECTION OF ASSETS, BOTH tangible and intangible, has long been a focus of individuals, private businesses, and governmental entities. There is a natural and universal need to protect physical items and intellectual property from others. Unfortunately, criminal and terroristic elements continuously attempt to obtain assets no matter the level of protection. Items of value create motivations and intentions within individuals and groups to procure items of want through any means necessary. Although no asset is 100 percent secure (any security system can be defeated), technological advances within the physical security realm have created new methods to protect assets as well as strengthened traditional protective measures. Further, technological advances continue to influence future trends within the physical security field similar to other professional communities.

The shear expanse of the physical security field and the countless technologies that are currently available (and those that continue to be developed) can result in cognitive overload to those who are entering the field and/or are assigned to develop or significantly update physical security for a facility. Further, what were once disparate systems (e.g., video surveillance system independent of access control system) are now morphing into integrative systems that enable individuals, critical infrastructure owners/operators, and other security elements to do more with less related to physical security. Although the implementation of these technologies does not change the need to achieve security objectives, the ability to achieve those objectives is being greatly influenced by technology. The traditional image of a security guard viewing multiple static surveillance camera monitors is being replaced by physical security systems and models that are more interactive and driven by information and technology. The remainder of this chapter will help to provide a general overview of physical security technologies to enable a general understanding. Within the discussion, appropriate background information is detailed along with a discussion on future trends within physical security technologies. Overall, this chapter will provide basic information to aid in the decision process to implement technology-based security solutions.

What Is Physical Security?

Before discussing physical security technologies, a basic understanding of physical security and its concepts is warranted. Physical security entails much more than a security guard walking around a facility ensuring all doors are locked. To aid in the understanding of the concept of physical security, it can be boiled down to two important elements: measures and guidance. Specifically, physical security can be defined as "*measures* that are designed to deny access to unauthorized personnel (including attackers or even accidental intruders) from physically accessing a building, facility, resource, or stored information; and *guidance* on how to design structures to resist a potentially hostile act."[1] From a theoretical perspective, physical security can be viewed as a guardian of items of value (i.e., assets) from motivated offenders (i.e., criminals, terrorists).[2]

The most fundamental aspect of protection continues to be physical security as it includes the use of physical controls to protect a facility, its perimeter, interior assets, and people.[3] Therefore, physical security is a major element and is the first line of defense of a facility's security envelope.[4] Physical security measures are also the security baseline from which all additional security measures are built.[5] Despite the generality of the physical security concepts, individuals must keep two elements in mind. First, physical security measures cannot be viewed as one size fits all.[6] Characteristics related to type of facility, location, assets (contained within the facility), risks, and vulnerabilities affect the overall physical security envelope. Second, regardless of the facility, the most important asset is and will always be people. Based on these two elements, how should physical security and associated technologies be approached?

The Physical Security Approach

In a basic sense, the physical security approach is developing a satisfactory level of physical security through layering to prevent unauthorized access as a single physical security control cannot achieve all security needs.[7] This general approach begins with assessments (to identify and analyze risks, threats, and vulnerabilities) and audits/surveys (to identify security strengths, weaknesses, and opportunities). Although assessments and audits/surveys are very important to overall physical security, they are beyond the scope of this chapter. However, individuals are encouraged to obtain a fundamental knowledge of assessments and audits/surveys as they help to influence the selection and implementation of physical security technologies to meet defined security objectives.[8]

Returning to the security layering concept, layering security controls from the outer boundaries to the inner boundaries enables the development of an adequate security envelope to achieve security requirements as well as to identify specific technologies to implement.[9] Physical security can be consolidated into two specific layers: outer layer and inner layer (see Figure 6.1: Security Layers). The outer layer is the first layer of control and can take many forms based on the facility characteristics.[10] Outer layer protective elements are typically utilized up to the facility walls.[11] Example outer layers can include expansive areas such as site perimeter, barriers

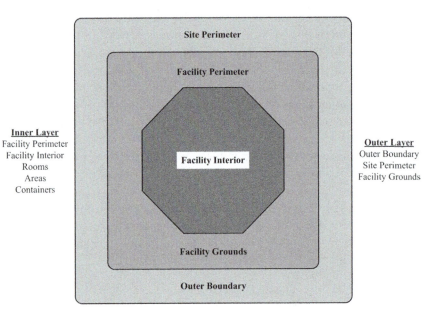

Figure 6.1 Security Layers (Source: Adapted from Kovacich and Halibozek, "Physical Security," p. 341).

(e.g., fences), parking lots, roads, and site grounds for some facilities such as a manufacturing facility.[12] Conversely, a city office building may only have the walls of the building as its outer layer.[13] As for the inner layer, this includes facility perimeter (e.g., doors, windows, and roof) and facility interior (e.g., individual rooms, areas, and containers such as safes). Breaking down facilities into layers enables more detailed analysis into the determination of the necessary security envelope and helps identify possible physical security technologies that can be implemented to achieve security objectives.

Lastly, security analysis through assessments, audits/surveys, and layering can also help to determine the overall level of physical security and necessary physical security methods and technologies that are needed. Although there is a lack of standards by which a physical security system can be classified into a specific level, a commonly accepted model includes five levels and associated objectives, which is presented in Table 6.1. In order to upgrade a physical security system to another level, all stated criterion for that level must be achieved.[14] Similar to the aforementioned layers, assessments, and audits/surveys, this model provides information that can help to determine adequate security objectives and possible technologies to achieve stated objectives.

Importance to the Homeland Security Enterprise

Physical security and related technologies generally do not receive as much attention as other homeland security topics, technologies, and strategies. This in no way diminishes its overall importance to homeland security enterprise. In fact, physical security and related technologies play a major role in protecting the nation's critical infrastructure by providing necessary protection and response elements against human-caused incidents, which result from the intentional actions of an adversary, such as a threatened or actual criminal or terrorist attack.[15] This is extremely important as critical infrastructure represents those "systems and assets, whether physical or virtual, so vital to the United States that the incapacity or destruction of such systems and assets would have a debilitating impact on security, national economic security, national public health or safety, or any combination of those matters."[16] Complicating the protection of U.S. critical infrastructure is that it (a) is largely owned and operated by the private sector (approximately 85 percent), (b) is extremely diverse and complex, and (c) includes interdependencies across the 16 critical infrastructure sectors.[17] Therefore, the first line of defense for U.S. critical infrastructure is largely the responsibility of the private sector in an ever-changing and

Table 6.1 Security Levels, Layers, Objectives, and Methods Crosswalk

Security Level	Security Objective	Activity	Layer	Facility Example	Physical Security Methods
Minimum	Impede	External	Outer	Private residence	Simple Physical Barriers Simple Locks
Low-Level	Impede Detect	External	Outer Inner	Small Retail Stores Storage Warehouses	Basic Local Alarm System Simple Security Lighting Basic Security Physical Barriers High-Security Locks
Medium	Impede Detect Assess	External Internal	Outer Inner	Large Industrial and Manufacturing Plants Large Retail Outlets National Guard Armories	Advanced Remote Alarm System High-Security Physical Barriers Unarmed Guard Force Basic Communications
High-Level	Impede Detect Assess	External Internal	Outer Inner	Prisons Defense Contractors Pharmaceutical Companies Sophisticated Electronic Manufacturers	Video Surveillance Perimeter Alarm System Armed Guard Force Advanced Communications Access Control System High-Security Lighting Local Police Coordination Formal Contingency Plans

Maximum	Impede Detect Assess Neutralize	External Internal	Outer Inner	Nuclear Facilities Federal Prisons Military Bases Certain Federal Government Research Sites	On-Response Force Sophisticated Alarm System

Source: Adapted from Gigliotti, Jason, and Cogan, "What Is Your Level of Physical Security?"

Activity: External activity is defined as activity that "originates outside the scope of the security system and could range from simple intrusion to armed attack" (p. 78). Internal activity can "range from simple shoplifting to conspiracy to commit sabotage" (p. 79).

evolving risk environment.[18] The importance of protecting U.S. critical infrastructure and physical security's role is based in national strategies and doctrine as detailed in the *National Strategy for Homeland Security, National Strategy for the Physical Protection of Critical Infrastructures and Key Assets*, and the *National Infrastructure Protection Plan*, which aim to protect U.S. critical infrastructure from physical attack by reducing their vulnerability to criminal and terrorist acts.[19] The implementation and use of physical security technologies (by both the private and public sector) and the continued research and development of new physical protective technologies are important elements in achieving the defined goals within the aforementioned strategies and doctrine. The next section continues this discussion by detailing example technologies that are being utilized by physical security professionals.

Physical Security Technologies

No single chapter could feasibly cover all physical security technologies that are being utilized to secure facilities. Therefore, the intent of this section is to provide a general understanding of physical security technologies one may experience while working in the public safety and security community. Understanding these technologies is crucial for public safety and security professionals to create and maintain an adequate security posture regardless of facility type and/or location. The technologies that are discussed should not be considered an exhaustive list, but rather a sampling of some of the commonly utilized physical security technologies. Further, the fact that technology rapidly advances must also be kept in mind, which applies to the technologies discussed below. Lastly, although cybersecurity and drones have become major elements of the security profession, they fall outside the scope of this chapter. (For more information on drones and cybersecurity, please see Chapter 7: Cybersecurity Threats and Technology Applications in Homeland Security and Chapter 8: Unmanned Aircraft Systems in Homeland Security.)

Structural Protective Barriers

Protective barriers are used to define the territoriality and/or defensible space of a facility.[20] Barriers act to restrict as well as direct access to a facility and form a continuous line of defense around a facility.[21] Structural barriers are utilized for perimeter protection and are human-made devices (opposite from natural barriers such as cliffs, water obstacles, and other terrain features) and include fences, walls, grills, bars, roadblocks, and other construction (e.g., bollards) to prohibit or inhibit access.[22] One must remember, however, that while no barrier can completely prevent access, they make unauthorized access more difficult, especially when used with other layers of physical control.[23]

Protective barriers were once simple, low-tech, static, and passive security elements that were routinely comprised of simple chain-link fences, masonry walls, jersey barriers, and gates. However, technological advances have fundamentally changed these barriers and what can be achieved with them. For example, fencing is now transforming into a pseudo security network in which signals are sent through wires embedded within the fence to detect fence cutting, disruption of electrified fencing current, and possible scaling/climbing of the fence by individuals. When these types of activities are sensed, alarms and notifications can be automatically activated so security personnel can assess the situation and make appropriate responses. Therefore, the integration of sensors is allowing what were traditionally passive protective barriers to transition to active security elements.

This transition is important as protective barriers serve as the first line of defense and provide a psychological deterrent to criminal and terroristic elements. This illustrates that technological innovations have enabled barriers to evolve to meet the new requirements of physical security.[24] In addition to the networked fencing mentioned above, perimeters are now being physically secured through the use of technologies in the areas of bollards and wedges (e.g., retractable, mobile, high-ram/crash resistance), anti-climb barriers based on construction, anti-ram/crash fencing, open-area sensors (e.g., microwave, infrared, ground-based radar) for large area perimeter security or where barriers are not existing, and buried sensors (fiber optic, leaky coaxial, geophone) that can detect footprints indicating the presence of an individual.[25] These technology-based barriers enable security professionals to create multiple internal perimeters for a single facility that allows for protective layers against intrusion and multiple opportunities for deterrence and detection.[26]

Windows, Doors, and Locks

Despite their simplicity, doors and windows are very important physical security elements (and are the most important within facilities with a minimum level of security such as private residences). For example, both commercial and domestic burglars commonly force open a door or window as their entry technique.[27] In fact, over 80 percent of all break-ins occur through openings such as doors, windows, vents, and skylights.[28] Therefore, there is a large array of available technologies to enhance a facility's security profile when it comes to doors and windows. Beginning with windows (specifically the types of glass), there are multiple choices security professionals can make. Basic decisions evolve around the incorporation of laminated, tempered, and/or bullet-resistant glass. However, even this simple decision can be enhanced by special coatings and films that provide anti-shatter (i.e., designed to withstand certain bomb blast forces and other kinetic energy) and anti-graffiti properties; provide one-way or two-way privacy without affecting environmental lighting; or even can detect movement.[29]

Doors can incorporate the same technologies when they contain sections of glass. Aside from glass, doors have also benefited from advances in bullet-resistant materials, thereby increasing their protection level in certain situations (protection can be further expanded through the availability of bullet-resistant fiberglass wall panels that can be installed within interior and exterior wall cavities). Additional door technologies include systems that can detect and prevent an unauthorized individual from tailgating or piggybacking behind an authorized individual through an opened door. A door, however, is only as secure as its locking mechanism. Over the years, the fundamental design and operations of door locks and their internal mechanisms have remained constant. However, locking mechanisms continue to be paired with access control, biometrics, and badging technologies (discussed in later sections) to provide additional functionality. Today's locks can also incorporate stand-alone technologies for the purposes of protection such as keypads (e.g., enter a PIN instead of using keys) and wireless communications to enable the ability to communicate with a smartphone for locking/unlocking. Despite the lock and associated technology, one must remember that no lock is completely tamper proof, but how long it resists an intruder determines its effectiveness.[30]

Video Surveillance

Similar to consumer electronics, video surveillance continues to rapidly evolve. No longer does the term video surveillance conjure up images of a security guard intently (or unintently) watching a bank of video screens showing grainy, black and white feeds from security cameras. Since the early mid-2000s, video surveillance has transitioned to the digital age in which technological advances are helping security officials to do more with less. The best example of this transition is the switch to Internet Protocol (IP)-based cameras and systems (or networked systems) from analog systems that are reaching their end of life.[31] Although analog systems were once the workhorses of the surveillance community, they are now considered obsolete when compared with the abilities, scalability, and cost effectiveness of IP-based systems. One of the major advances related to the digitalization of video surveillance is the ability to capture up to full high-definition (HD) quality (1080p) video even with wireless cameras that are quickly becoming more commonly utilized. HD video is only one of the major advantages of IP-based video surveillance systems. Another important advantage is that IP-based systems provide synergies and force multipliers with other resources through communication on a common network.[32] Not only can IP-based video surveillance systems be installed on and greatly expanded by the use of existing network infrastructure, they also provide new functionality to professionals.[33] For example, IP-based video surveillance systems support expanded content distribution in which video can be easily shared via networks and accessed through devices that are able to connect to the network (e.g., desktop computers, smartphones, laptops, tablets).[34] This type of connectivity also allows security professionals to access video data in real time, which greatly aids mobile security professionals.[35]

What this means is that video surveillance is slowly migrating to the cloud similar to other industries. Some perceive this as the most exciting advancement within video surveillance and its natural progression.[36] The benefit of this migration is that it enables access to video anywhere in the world through an Internet-connected device. It also significantly reduces and/or eliminates the costs that are associated with video recorders utilized in non-cloud-based video surveillance systems.[37] Further, the ability to pair cloud video management with the continued advancement of edge storage devices (i.e., a distributed/decentralized approach to data storage where video is stored at the device/camera and accessed when needed) enables security professionals to create a powerful, custom solution that fits their specific needs and is easily managed.[38]

Another major advancement in video surveillance coupled with the move to IP-based systems, networked video recording, and HD-quality video capture is the ability to run (intelligent) video analytics, which is the "convergence of physical security and logical (data-based) security."[39] Video analytics (or automated video surveillance) is a subdivision of video surveillance[40] that analyzes, in real time, video footage to detect abnormal or threatening activity.[41] Simply stated, video analytics "learns" what is normal and identifies unusual or threatening behavior (e.g., loitering, someone moving in an unauthorized or unusual direction) that may be missed by security personal monitoring numerous camera feeds.[42] The push behind video analytics is to eliminate human error and to increase operational efficiency by reducing the sole dependence on human monitoring.[43] Whereas a security professional has a limited attention span (which is further limited when performing multiple tasks), video analytics is always watching and ready to notify security personnel of potential threats in real time.[44] HD cameras with analytics capabilities are an efficient and effective option for monitoring facilities with large and/or open spaces (e.g., airports, warehouses, and public transit terminals).[45] Further, video analytics has advanced to point that it can even be effectively run on in-motion point-tilt-zoom (PTZ) cameras, which is referred to as motion detection while scanning.[46]

Presently, video analytics is being done either at the edge (via the camera itself) or at the server level, which integrates information from a large number of cameras.[47] Further, video analytics are now transitioning into a third generation. The first generation focused on providing real-time alerts (e.g., someone entering an unauthorized area) and reducing false alarms.[48] The second generation improved those abilities while adding forensic tools to search and analyze captured video post-event.[49] The third generation consists of purpose-built systems to provide situational awareness through real-time insight through analytics that can identify, track, and/or search for someone or something across multiple cameras and perform detailed analysis before, during, and after events.[50] As video surveillance evolves, new technological advancements will continue to make video surveillance more efficient and effective.

Intrusion Detection Systems

The basic purpose of an intrusion detection system is to alert security personnel about the presence of an unauthorized individual.[51] Although they enhance the detection process, they may also serve as a deterrent to would-be intruders. Therefore, intrusion detection systems augment barriers, guards, and other technical systems. By calling attention to immediate problems, intrusion detection systems can greatly enhance a facility's security envelope as they can be used in both the outer and inner layers and be connected/integrated with other systems such as video surveillance systems. They also provide cost efficiencies as they can help to reduce and/or eliminate the need for a large stationary guard force. While there is a wide array of possible detection methods, this section discusses the intrusion detection technologies that are commonly utilized in three specific areas/functions: perimeter/outer layer protection, interior space/inner layer protection, and single object/spot protection.

It is appropriate to begin with perimeter/outer layer protection as it acts as the first line of a facility's defense and serves as the first point in which an intruder can be detected.[52] This protection is also important since approximately 80 percent of all break-ins occur through perimeter openings (e.g., doors, windows, skylights, vents). Further, depending on the type and location of a facility, its outer layer may in fact consist solely of the exterior walls. Despite the facility, common technologies are being utilized to secure facility perimeters. These include, but are not limited to, door and window switches (sensors that activate an alarm when a door or window is opened to gain entry), glass break detectors (sensors that detect glass breakage by either shock [on-glass installation] or by sound [off-glass installation] to activate an alarm), and foil and wire sensors (utilize thin/fine/brittle wire or foil material that will break during unlawful entry thereby activating an alarm).[53]

Moving to interior space/inner layer protection, these systems protect against unauthorized access regardless of if and/or how the perimeter/outer layer was breached (e.g., a stay-behind intruder).[54] Although these systems provide an invisible means of detection that are highly sensitive, they should not be solely relied on and should be paired with adequate perimeter/outer layer protection.[55] The most common technology utilized for interior intrusion detection is passive infrared detectors (PIRs). PIRs do not transmit a signal (hence "passive") but rather detect movement through thermal changes within the field view that is caused by an intruder.[56] Other commonly utilized technologies include pressure mats and sound sensors, and to a lesser degree photoelectric eye (beams), ultrasonic, and microwave sensors.[57] As part of interior space/inner layer protection, there may be objects or specific spots of extreme importance/value that require additional protection (e.g., items on display in museums). Protection in this instance requires technologies such as capacitance/proximity detectors (detects changes in the electrostatic field of the object when touched) and/or electronic vibration detectors (specialized, adjustable microphones that detect the delicate penetration of glass or even a sledgehammer hitting a concrete barrier).[58]

Throughout this chapter, physical security technologies have been discussed that help to keep unauthorized individuals away and out of facilities. However, physical security systems and utilized technologies must also enable effective and efficient access to authorized individuals in a secure manner. The following sections discuss this aspect.

Access Cards

An important element of inner layer security is access control (which can also be utilized in outer layer security elements). Access control consists of numerous elements to preclude unauthorized access to facilities, areas within facilities, specific assets, and even people. This section will focus on technologies that are utilized in the most common form of access control, which is badging and access cards. Once only found in highly secure facilities, access control through badging is now utilized in every critical infrastructure sector. The simplicity of these systems, ease of use, and cost effectiveness has enabled access control through badging to become a preferred way to control facility access both externally (outer layer) and internally (inner layer). Although there are multitudes of access cards, their functionality is consistent. The access card is read by the card reader (either physically or wirelessly), which then compares the information/signal to a database to confirm or deny entry authorization. Further, access cards typically fall into one of the following categories: proximity, magnetic stripe, Wiegand, smart card, and radio frequency identification (RFID). All of these remain popular and effective despite magnetic strip and Wiegand cards giving way to proximity cards, which are now giving way to smart and RFID cards.[59] One of the main benefits in the expansion of technology in all physical security areas is that access control systems are no longer a separate system. Today's electronic access control (EAC) systems are now becoming an important part of fully integrated facility management systems.[60] Where once a security manager could only pull audit trails through access control systems, these systems are now linked with such other security elements as video surveillance and intrusion detection systems.

Despite the long-standing use, effectiveness, and low costs of typical access cards, there are new developments that will help shift access cards to new arenas. Although new access card technology remains contactless, the card itself is fundamentally changing. With the ubiquity of smartphones globally, it is no surprise that they have become an access card itself. Today's card readers and smartphones can take advantage of Bluetooth and near field communication (NFC) to enable access control that is considered more convenient, less expensive, and more secure than previous access card technologies.[61] Further, smartphone access control is now being considered the new biometric because smartphones seem to be permanently attached to individuals in this day and age.[62] The application of smartphone-based access control is even expanding beyond physical security. For example, major hotel chains are now offering services that allow guests to unlock their hotel rooms with their smartphones. Further, numerous universities across the United States are implementing programs that utilize smartphones for services to students, facility, and staff. As with other physical security technologies, access control will continue to evolve in the future.

Future Trends and Technology

Throughout the preceding sections, various physical security technologies were discussed. This was not meant to be an exhaustive list of physical security methods or the technologies utilized within each. Physical security is a broad and complex mission that must manage tangible and intangible assets, evolve with changing risk and threats, and remain vigilant in the face of competing priorities. Despite the complexity, technology-based physical security solutions can act as force multipliers to increase the security envelope (the critical aspects of deterrence, detection, delay, assessment, and response) while at the same time creating efficiencies and reductions in cost. The remainder of this section will provide an overview of some of the future trends within physical security as they relate to technology.

Smart LEDs

One of the more interesting emerging technologies, but at the same time very controversial, is the growing use of smart light emitting diodes (LEDs). Municipalities and private businesses have been switching to LEDs from conventional lighting sources (e.g., high-intensity discharge lights) due to costs savings. However, technological advances have allowed the simple LED bulb to do much more. Namely, individual bulbs can now be fitted with sensors and cameras that are part of a larger network.[63] This network has the ability to monitor and record activities around connected fixtures, which can be data mined through cloud-based services.[64] Based on the type of sensors installed, smart LEDs can monitor weather, pollution, seismic activity, and traffic and can even pinpoint gunshots.[65] Physical security-related monitoring abilities include cameras that can monitor foot traffic in certain areas, spot unattended items, read license places, record video footage, identify suspicious activity, and possibly detect a dirty bomb prior to detonation.[66] Presently, smart LEDs are being tested in major cities across the United States in both critical infrastructure sites (e.g., airports) and open public areas.

Due to the inherent abilities of smart LEDs, there are limitless types of information and data that can be gathered.[67] Once collected, the data can be mined and analyzed for a broad range of needs.[68] However, some see this as a major problem and a threat to privacy. In essence, a network of smart LEDs could continuously record and track everywhere people go, everything they buy, and everything they do, and analyze the collected data on an ad hoc basis.[69] This very real possibility has led some to state that the potential for misuse of smart LED technology is terrifying.[70] These concerns will continue to grow as the public and private sectors continue to take advantage of cost efficiencies provided by LEDs and consider the implementation of sensors and cameras within LEDs for public safety and security purposes.

Robots

Robots already have a long history within the public safety and security field. Most notably, robots have been utilized by explosive ordinance disposal (EOD) teams, hazardous materials (hazmat) teams, Special Weapons and Tactics (SWAT) teams, Civil Support Teams (CST), and other specialized response units at the local, state, and federal levels. Therefore, it is no surprise that robots are now beginning to supplement security personnel in the physical security context. Today, robots are commonly outfitted with cameras, lights, infrared sensors, two-way communications equipment, extinguishers (for fire suppression), and nonlethal responses (e.g., piercing sirens and bright/flight lights to stun an intruder).[71] Obviously, robots have the potential to provide cost savings in terms of personnel (over an extended period of time), but their greatest asset is that they can be deployed to areas/environments hazardous to humans, whether it be an active shooter situation, fire, hazmat incident, or bomb threat.[72]

It is expected that the use of robots within the physical security context will continue to increase in the future as production and operational costs continue to decrease.[73] An example of their use can be found at the National Nuclear Security Administration (NNSA), Nevada National Security Site (NNSS), which is located roughly 65 miles outside of Las Vegas, Nevada. Three robots, currently being utilized to help monitor the perimeter of the 1,360-square-mile facility, have been described as a camera on a mini-Hummer.[74] The robots are semiautonomous in that they complete random surveillance routes, but transition all high-level decision making to a human operator located in a central command center once a target or other unusual activity is detected.[75] The robots feed real-time data to human operators through various mounted sensors and cameras, which can patrol for up to 16 hours before refueling.[76] Human operators can even communicate with individuals encountered by the robots through mounted microphones and speakers.[77] Through the use of the robots, security personnel are able to monitor a much larger area than a single person could physically patrol on his or her own.[78] In addition to the perimeter patrol capabilities shown at the NNSS, it is expected in the near future that robots will be utilized to support a wide range of other physical security activities.[79]

Immersive Surveillance

A conventional surveillance camera can offer a single, limited view of a scene from its point of view. Utilizing multiple cameras can provide different viewing angles of the same scene or their view can be dispersed across a scene. This is especially true with static cameras. Even PTZ cameras can only allow security personnel to see a single point of view because when the camera pans, tilts, or zooms, the camera and security personnel lose visual contact with the scene that is not within the field of view. Further, security personnel must routinely balance the scales between high resolution/small field of view and wide field of view/low resolution.[80] This is in addition to the proliferation of the use of surveillance cameras due to their low cost, which has increased the demand on security personnel who must monitor numerous cameras at once (even though video analytics have helped this to some degree). In order to overcome the limitations of conventional cameras and surveillance systems, immersive surveillance systems are being developed that can bring the so-called perfect security camera system closer to reality, which can "see everything all the time."[81]

In order to "immerse" security personnel into the monitored environment, immersive surveillance systems provide a continuous 360-degree field of view through the use of multiple video cameras and new video-stitching technology.[82] Unlike a typical fish-eye lens that distorts the image, immersive surveillance systems create high-resolution, perfect edge-to-edge detailed video created through the use of multiple cameras that stitch the real-time video feed together—like a high-resolution video quilt.[83] Panomersive systems achieve the same results, but through the use of panoramic cameras.[84] Although still image stitching has been around for a very long time, immersive surveillance systems stiches or quilts real-time video through an advanced interface that can maintain a full 360-degree field of view while at the same time zooming to a preferred point of interest.[85] The huge advantage to this ability is that it enables "multiple operators to scan and zoom to different regions of the scene with digital analytics optimized for high resolution video, including the ability to track individuals and objects forward and backward in time."[86] Immersive surveillance can also be paired with video analytics to, among other things, define exclusion zones (send an alert when the zone is breached) and to track/follow a target (an individual, a package, or a vehicle) even against cluttered backgrounds.[87] Another major benefit of immersive surveillance is the ability to review footage after the event. This is because security personnel or other investigators can view recorded video using PTZ controls to help reconstruct what happened, when it happened, and who made it happen.[88] Further, multiple individuals can simultaneously analyze the recorded video and view different regions of the field of view due to the virtual controls.[89] Presently, immersive surveillance systems are in the beginning stages and the U.S. Department of Homeland Security (DHS) is testing a current system at the Logan International Airport in Boston, Massachusetts.[90] The pilot system at Logan International Airport was built with commercial off-the-shelf equipment, including cameras, computers, and image processing software.[91] However, future developments will integrate additional sensors, more powerful video analytics, and advanced cameras with higher resolution, longer ranges, and infrared capability.[92] Overall, immersive surveillance can help address common surveillance issues by enabling more effective and efficient video surveillance for larger areas utilizing fewer security personnel.[93] Further, this can be achieved through a basketball-sized enclosed system that can be mounted virtually anywhere (e.g., ceiling, exterior wall, roof, truck-mounted telescoping mast, etc.).[94]

System Integration and the Internet of Things

Physical security systems are often comprised of disparate systems that control a single function. For example, an individual system would administer access control through badging while another individual system would handle video surveillance. Therefore, security personnel would have to monitor various systems and pour over nonstandardized data from multiple systems post-incident. This undesirable situation creates both cost and performance inefficiencies for both personnel and utilized systems. However, physical security systems are beginning to fundamentally change. Going beyond digital door locks, IP-based camera systems, and cloud- and edge-based data storage, new physical security systems are leveraging these technological advances and others to integrate systems. Physical security is no longer disparate systems, but rather interconnected systems that are turning physical security to digital security.

The push toward physical security system integration is partly due to the Internet of Things (IoT). In essence, today's physical security systems are networks of physical objects and devices (e.g., cameras, badge readers, digital locks) embedded with electronics, software, sensors, and network connectivity, which enables the objects and devices to collect and exchange data via a network. Further, data retrieval and analysis does not have to be done at a central station. Rather, cloud-based networks and services enable security personnel to view and analyze data anywhere, anytime. This is especially true with regard to the mobilizing of physical security through security-linked mobile devices (e.g., smartphones, tablets) that are being used more every day for security activities. The push for further integration and interconnectivity does not focus solely on physical security systems. Rather, there are cost and efficiency benefits when physical security systems are integrated with other building functions (e.g., heating, ventilation, and air conditioning systems; elevator controls) to create enterprise-level Building Automation Systems (BAS). A BAS provides a proactive system of interconnected systems that helps entities, businesses, critical infrastructure owners/operators, and the like save money and reduce consumption (e.g., energy) while at the same time keeping facilities secure. Utilizing the data from an all-systems analysis enables U.S. critical infrastructure owners /operators "to better understand how their facility functions as a whole and lets them make informed operational changes."[95] In essence, new interconnected technologies are allowing security personnel to transition from the passive monitoring of yesteryear to proactive control in today's digital age.[96]

Conclusion

Physical security has been fundamentally changed by technological advances over the years. No longer is physical security comprised of a single security guard conducting rounds and making sure all doors are locked. Rather, physical security has transitioned to the digital age and includes immersive surveillance, robots, smart LEDs, video analytics, and a host of other technologies that are developed and implemented on a continuous basis. Further, much like society, the IoT has enabled what once were disparate systems (e.g., access control, video surveillance) to be interconnected to provide a proactive stance against risks and threats. Overall, continued technological advances within the physical security realm create performance and cost efficiencies while at the same time provide a more enhanced security envelope. This is important as the risks and threats faced by critical infrastructure owners/operators continue to evolve.

Discussion Questions

1. Define physical security and explain its relation to security layers and levels.
2. Explain the advantages of IP-Based Camera Systems over Analog Camera Systems.
3. Explain how Video Analytics can increase security personnel performance effectiveness while at the same time providing cost efficiencies.

4. Explain how ethical and privacy concerns of smart LEDs can be addressed.
5. Define Storage and Analysis at the Edge and its associated benefits.
6. List advantages and disadvantages of using smartphones as security-linked mobile devices as part of an access control system.

Case Study Analysis

The U.S. federal government has approved the building of a new facility to review requests for citizenship in the Unites States. The high-level logistics for the new facility include the following:

- 30,000 square foot facility
- Located in a rural area
- Housed data includes those classified as secret and confidential
- Approximately 60 on-site federal employees ranging from custodial to executive levels
- Requirements for secured areas as well as lines for secured communications (both voice and data)
- Normal business hours from 7:00 a.m. to 6:00 p.m.

Based on the stated facility logistics, identify and explain the reason behind answers to the following questions (see Table 6.1 for reference):

1. What security level is warranted?
2. What are the security objectives?
3. What activities must be protected against?
4. What outer layer physical security technologies should be implemented?
5. What inner layer physical security technologies should be implemented?

Notes

1. Dempsey, *Introduction to Private Security*.
2. Felson, *Crime and Everyday Life*.
3. Kovacich and Halibozek, "Physical Security."
4. Ibid.
5. Ibid.
6. Ibid.
7. Ibid.
8. See Fennelly, *Effective Physical Security* and Broder, *Risk Analysis and the Security Survey* for more information.

9. Kovacich and Halibozek, "Physical Security."

10. Ibid.

11. Ibid.

12. Ibid.

13. Ibid.

14. Gigliotti and Jason, "Approaches to Physical Security."

15. U.S. Department of Homeland Security, *Comprehensive Preparedness Guide*.

16. U.S. Department of Homeland Security, *National Infrastructure Protection Plan*, 7.

17. The White House, *The National Strategy for the Physical Protection of Critical Infrastructures and Key Assets*; The White House, *Presidential Policy Directive 21*.

18. The White House, *The National Strategy for the Physical Protection of Critical Infrastructures and Key Assets*; U.S. Department of Homeland Security, *National Infrastructure Protection Plan*.

19. The White House, *The National Strategy for the Physical Protection of Critical Infrastructures and Key Assets*; U.S. Department of Homeland Security, *National Infrastructure Protection Plan*.

20. Fennelly, *Effective Physical Security*.

21. Ibid.

22. Ibid.; Kovacich and Halibozek, "Physical Security."

23. Ibid.

24. Goudlock, "First Line of Defense."

25. Ibid.

26. Ibid.

27. Prenzler, *Preventing Burglary in Commercial and Institutional Settings*.

28. McKinnon, "Alarms."

29. Advanced Glass Technology, "Advanced Glass Technology"; Barnard, "High Tech Security Glass."

30. Edgar et al., "Use of Locks in Physical Crime Prevention."

31. Krone, "Guest Column."

32. Tyco, "IP."

33. Ibid.

34. Ibid.

35. Ibid.

36. Colombo, "Checking Out the Latest Surveillance Technologies."

37. Ibid.

38. Ibid.

39. Tyco, "The New Age of Video Surveillance," para. 11.

40. Ibid.

41. Saptharishi, "The New Eyes of Surveillance."

42. Ibid.; McCready, "Growing the Role of Analytics in Video Surveillance."

43. Saptharishi, "The New Eyes of Surveillance."

44. Ibid.

45. McCready, "Growing the Role of Analytics in Video Surveillance."

46. Olson, "Using Video Analytics with Pan-Tilt-Zoom Cameras."

47. Banerjee, "The Evolution of Video Analytics."

48. Ibid.

49. Ibid.

50. Ibid.

51. McKinnon, "Alarms."

52. Ibid.

53. Ibid.

54. Ibid.

55. Ibid.

56. Ibid.

57. Ibid.

58. Ibid.

59. HID Corporation, *Smart Cards for Access Control.*

60. Nelson, "Access Control and Badges."

61. Bodell, "Communications."

62. Ibid.

63. Newcombe, "Are Smart Street Lights the Future of Security Tech?"

64. Ibid.; Cardwell, "At Newark Airport, the Lights Are On, and They're Watching You."

65. Ibid.; Newcombe, "Are Smart Street Lights the Future of Security Tech?"

66. Ibid.; Cardwell, "At Newark Airport, the Lights Are On, and They're Watching You"; CBS News, "These LED Smart Lights Are Tracking Your Moves."; Newcombe, "Are Smart Street Lights the Future of Security Tech?"

67. CBS News, "These LED Smart Lights Are Tracking Your Moves."

68. Cardwell, "At Newark Airport, the Lights Are On, and They're Watching You."

69. CBS News, "These LED Smart Lights Are Tracking Your Moves."

70. Cardwell, "At Newark Airport, the Lights Are On, and They're Watching You."

71. Fennelly, *Effective Physical Security.*

72. Ibid.

73. Ibid.

74. Hickey, "Robots Guard Nuclear Test Site"; Homeland Security News Wire, "Barrier Systems, Robots Reduce Security Costs"; Saenez, "Robots Guarding U.S. Nuclear Stockpile."

75. Saenez, "Robots Guarding U.S. Nuclear Stockpile."

76. Ibid.

77. Ibid.

78. Hickey, "Robots Guard Nuclear Test Site"; Homeland Security News Wire, "Barrier Systems, Robots Reduce Security Costs"; Saenez, "Robots Guarding U.S. Nuclear Stockpile."

79. Fennelly, *Effective Physical Security.*

80. U.S. Department of Homeland Security, *Imaging System for Immersive Surveillance.*

81. Ibid., 1.
82. U.S. Department of Homeland Security, "Imaging System for Immersive Surveillance."
83. Ibid.
84. Coulombe, "New Technology Fashions."
85. U.S. Department of Homeland Security, "Imaging System for Immersive Surveillance."
86. U.S. Department of Homeland Security, *Imaging System for Immersive Surveillance*, 1.
87. U.S. Department of Homeland Security, "Imaging System for Immersive Surveillance."
88. Ibid.
89. Ibid.
90. Ibid.
91. Ibid.
92. Ibid.
93. U.S. Department of Homeland Security, *Imaging System for Immersive Surveillance*.
94. U.S. Department of Homeland Security, "Imaging System for Immersive Surveillance."
95. Strohm, "Enterprise Level Systems Integration Delivers ROI," 17.
96. Ibid.

Bibliography

Advanced Glass Technology. "Advanced Glass Technology: Advanced Glass Protection Systems." Advanced Glass Technology. Accessed January 2016. http://www.agtwindowfilm.com/.

Advanced Perimeter Systems. "Security Systems and Detection Products." Advanced Perimeter Systems. Accessed January 2016. http://www.aps-perimeter-security.com/products/.

Ameristar Security Products. "High Security Perimeter Fences." Ameristar Security Products. Accessed January 2016. http://www.ameristarsecurity.com/perimeter-fence/.

Banerjee, B. "The Evolution of Video Analytics." *Security Technology Executive* 25, no. 4 (2015): 30–33.

Barnard, J. "High Tech Security Glass." *Popular Science.* Last modified March 23, 2009. http://www.popsci.com/scitech/article/2009-03/high-tech-security-glass.

Bauer, L., L. Cranor, M. Reiter, and K. Vaniea. *Lessons Learned from the Deployment of a Smartphone-Based Access-Control System.* Pittsburg, PA: Carnegie Mellon University, School of Computer Science, Institute for Software Research. 2007.

Bennett, B. *Understanding, Assessing, and Responding to Terrorism: Protecting Critical Infrastructure and Personnel.* Hoboken, NJ: John Wiley and Sons. 2007.

Bodell, P. "Communications: Bluetooth vs. NFC." *Security Info Watch*. Last modified August 9, 2013. http://www.securityinfowatch.com/article/11034554 /smartphone-access-control.

Broder, J. *Risk Analysis and the Security Survey* (3rd ed.). New York, NY: Butterworth-Heinemann. 2006.

Burrus, D. "The Internet of Things Is Far Bigger Than Anyone Realizes." *Wired*. Last modified in November 2014. http://www.wired.com/insights/2014/11 /the-internet-of-things-bigger/.

Cardwell, D. "At Newark Airport, the Lights Are On, and They're Watching You." *The New York Times*. Last modified on February 17, 2014. http://www.nytimes .com/2014/02/18/business/at-newark-airport-the-lights-are-on-and-theyre -watching-you.html?_r=0.

CBS News. "These LED Smart Lights Are Tracking Your Moves." *CBS News*. Last modified June 30, 2014. http://www.cbsnews.com/news/technology-in-led -smart-lights-raises-privacy-concerns/.

Cisco Systems, Inc. *Simplifying Physical Access Control with Cisco UPOE: Unleash the Power of Your Network*. San Jose, CA: Cisco Systems, Inc. 2011.

Colombo, A. "Checking Out the Latest Surveillance Technologies." *Campus Safety Magazine*. Last modified April 21, 2015. http://www.campussafetymagazine .com/article/checking_out_the_latest_surveillance_technologies.

Coulombe, R. "New Technology Fashions: What's Hot on the Trade Show Floor." *Security Technology Executive* 25, no. 4 (2015): 10, 35.

CS Staff. "What's Next for Physical Security Information Management Systems?" *Campus Safety Magazine*. Last modified January 11, 2016. http://www .campussafetymagazine.com/article/an_expert_gives_reflections_and _predictions_on_the_psim_world.

Dempsey, J. *Introduction to Private Security* (2nd ed.). Belmont, CA: Wadsworth. 2010.

Edgar, J., W. McInerney, E. Finneran, and J. Hunter. "Use of Locks in Physical Crime Prevention." In *Effective Physical Security* (4th ed.), ed. L. Fennelly, 117–168. New York, NY: Butterworth-Heinemann. 2013.

Felson, M. *Crime and Everyday Life: Insight and Implications for Society*. Thousand Oaks, CA: Pine Forge Press. 1994.

Fennelly, L. *Effective Physical Security* (4th ed.). New York, NY: Butterworth-Heinemann. 2013.

Fitchard, K. "One Day You Won't Need a Badge to Enter Your Building, Just a SIM Card." *Gigaom*. Last modified February 7, 2014. https://gigaom.com/2014 /02/07/one-day-you-wont-need-a-badge-to-enter-your-building-just-a-sim -card/.

Gigliotti, R., and R. Jason. "Approaches to Physical Security." In *Effective Physical Security* (4th ed.), ed. L. Fennelly, 77–92. New York, NY: Butterworth-Heinemann. 2013.

Gigliotti, R., R. Jason, and N. Cogan. "What Is Your Level of Physical Security?" *Security Management* (1980): 46–50.

Goudlock, J. "First Line of Defense: New Technologies Help Meet the Demand to Ward Off Strangers." *Security Today*. Last modified April 1, 2013. https://security-today.com/Articles/2013/04/01/First-Line-of-Defense.aspx.

Hickey, K. "Robots Guard Nuclear Test Site." *GCN*. Last modified October 14, 2010. https://gcn.com/Articles/2010/10/14/robots-guard-nuclear-test-site.aspx?Page=2.

HID Corporation. *Smart Cards for Access Control; Advantages and Technology Choices*. Austin, TX: HID Corporation. 2005.

HID Global Innovation Team. "2016 Trends." *Security Today*. Last modified January 25, 2016. https://security-today.com/Articles/2016/01/25/2016-Trends.aspx?Page=1.

Homeland Security News Wire. "Barrier Systems, Robots Reduce Security Costs." *Homeland Security News Wire*. Last modified December 20, 2013. http://www.homelandsecuritynewswire.com/barrier-systems-robots-reduce-security-costs.

Homeland Security News Wire. "Sensor Cable Monitors Fences—and Can Even Detect Low-Level Drones." *Homeland Security News Wire*. Last modified March 27, 2015. http://www.homelandsecuritynewswire.com/dr20150327-sensor-cable-monitors-fences-and-can-even-detect-lowlevel-drones.

Hsieh, M., S. Chen, Y. Cai, Y. Chen, and J. Chiang. "Immersive Surveillance for Total Situational Awareness." In *2010 International Computer Symposium*: 300–305. 2010. doi:10.1109/COMPSYM.2010.5685499.

Kovacich, G., and E. Halibozek. "Physical Security." In *Effective Physical Security* (4th ed.), ed. L. Fennelly, 339–354. New York, NY: Butterworth-Heinemann. 2013.

Krone, J. "Guest Column: 10 Reasons to Switch from Analog Cameras and DVRs to IP Cameras and NVRs." *Business Solutions*. Last modified August 15, 2013. http://www.bsminfo.com/doc/reasons-to-switch-from-analog-cameras-and-dvrs-to-ip-cameras-and-nvrs-0001.

Malatesti, C. "Physical Security in the IT Space." *ISSA Journal* (July 2008): 32–35.

Matthews, B. "Physical Security: Controlled Access and Layered Defense." In *Information Management Security Handbook* (6th ed.), ed. H. Tipton and M. Krause, 1327–1338. Boca Raton, FL: Taylor and Francis. 2007.

McCready, C. "Growing the Role of Analytics in Video Surveillance: Adding Value to Video Surveillance." *Security Today*. Last modified February 1, 2015. https://security-today.com/Articles/2015/02/01/Growing-the-Role-of-Analytics-in-Video-Surveillance.aspx?Page=1.

McKinnon, S. "Alarms: Intrusion Detection Systems." In *Effective Physical Security* (4th ed.), ed. L. Fennelly, 191–212. New York, NY: Butterworth-Heinemann. 2013.

Nelson, J. "Access Control and Badges." In *Effective Physical Security* (4th ed.), ed. L. Fennelly, 257–268. New York, NY: Butterworth-Heinemann. 2013.

Newcombe, T. "Are Smart Street Lights the Future of Security Tech?" *Emergency Management*. Last modified February 27, 2014. http://www.emergencymgmt.com/safety/Smart-Street-Lights-Security-Tech.html.

Olson, E. "Using Video Analytics with Pan-Tilt-Zoom Cameras." *Security Magazine*. Last modified February 1, 2015. http://www.securitymagazine.com /articles/86077-adding-thermal-cameras-for-better-intrusion-detection.

Prenzler, T. *Preventing Burglary in Commercial and Institutional Settings: A Place Management and Partnerships Approach*. Alexandria, VA: ASIS Foundation, Inc. 2009.

Ritchey, D. "Using Smartphone-Based Access Control to Keep Students Happy." *Security Magazine*. Last modified December 1, 2014. http://www.securitymagazine .com/articles/85957-using-smartphone-based-access-control-to-keep-students -happy.

Saenez, A. "Robots Guarding U.S. Nuclear Stockpile." Singularity HUB. Last modified October 8, 2010. http://singularityhub.com/2010/10/08/robots-guarding -us-nuclear-stockpile-video/.

Saptharishi, M. "The New Eyes of Surveillance: Artificial Intelligence and Humanizing Technology." *Wired*. Last modified August 2014. http://www.wired.com /insights/2014/08/the-new-eyes-of-surveillance-artificial-intelligence-and -humanizing-technology/.

Schaffhauser, D. "Student-Invented Mobile App Could Replace Security Access Badges." *Campus Technology*. Last modified February 13, 2012. https:// campustechnology.com/articles/2012/02/13/student-invented-mobile-app -could-replace-security-access-badges.aspx?=CTMOB.

Shallcross, J. "Your Hotel Key Is the Smartphone You Already Own." *Conde Nast Traveler*. Last modified September 9, 2015. http://www.cntraveler.com/stories /2015-09-09/your-hotel-key-is-the-smartphone-you-already-own.

Simpson, T. "Physical Safety Is Becoming Digital Security." *AVG*. Last modified September 2, 2015. http://now.avg.com/physical-safety-is-becoming-digital -security/.

Sloan Security Group. "Specialized Solutions." Sloan Security Group. Accessed in January 2016. http://www.sloancompanies.com/sloan_security_group/solutions/.

Southwest Microwave, Inc. "Buried Cable Detection Systems." Southwest Microwave, Inc. Accessed in January 2016. http://www.southwestmicrowave.com /products/buried-cable-detection-systems/.

Space and Naval Warfare Systems Center—Atlantic. *SAVER Program Highlight: Video Analytics Systems*. Charleston, SC: Space and Naval Warfare Systems Center—Atlantic. 2013.

Strohm, P. "Enterprise Level Systems Integration Delivers ROI." *Security Technology Executive* 25, no. 2 (2015): 16–19.

Tyco. "IP: Taking Video Surveillance to a New Level." *Tyco*. Last modified 2016. http://www.tyco.com/resource-library/articles/ip-taking-video-surveillance-to -a-new-level.

Tyco. "The New Age of Video Surveillance: Not Just Security Anymore." Tyco. Last modified 2016. http://www.tyco.com/resource-library/articles/the-new-age -of-video-surveillance-not-just-security-anymore.

U.S. Department of Homeland Security. "Imaging System for Immersive Surveillance: New Video Camera Sees It All." U.S. Department of Homeland Security.

Last modified August 24, 2015. http://www.dhs.gov/imaging-system-immersive-surveillance-new-video-camera-sees-it-all.

The White House. *Comprehensive Preparedness Guide (CPG) 201: Threat and Hazard Identification and Risk Assessment Guide.* Washington, DC: U.S. Department of Homeland Security. 2013.

The White House. *Imaging System for Immersive Surveillance.* Washington, DC: U.S. Department of Homeland Security, Science and Technology Directorate. 2014.

The White House. *National Infrastructure Protection Plan: Partnering for Critical Infrastructure Security and Resilience.* Washington, DC: U.S. Department of Homeland Security. 2013.

The White House. *The National Strategy for the Physical Protection of Critical Infrastructures and Key Assets.* Washington, DC: The White House. 2003.

The White House. *Presidential Policy Directive 21: Critical Infrastructure Security and Resilience.* Washington, DC: The White House. 2013.

Wilt, G. "Argus Oversees and Protects All." *Science and Technology Review* (April 1998): 13–15.

CHAPTER SEVEN

Cybersecurity Threats and Technology Applications in Homeland Security

S. Kristopher Bowerman

Learning Objectives

After reading this chapter, readers should be able to:

- Identify the challenges to combating electronic information threats.
- List and describe the threats to computers and networks.
- Explain the need for increased cybersecurity measures in an evolving era of increased cyberattacks.
- Apply information systems risk management techniques to a computer/ networking infrastructure.
- Summarize the different technologies and strategies used to combat the threats to cyber security.

Key Terms

Cyberattack
Cybersecurity
Data Breach
Denial of Service

Disaster Recovery Plan
Encryption
Firewall
Incident Response Teams
Internet Content Filtering
Malware
Malware Protection
Risk Management
Risk Mitigation
Social Engineering

Introduction

IN AN EVER-CHANGING WORLD OF information technology, a trend exists with an increased number of cyberattacks. Global threats have expanded through digital mechanisms, and overall Internet availability has drastically increased. Although organizations rely on technology, experts in the field are tasked with prevention and subsequent mitigation of cyberattacks. A myriad of threats to computers and networks are an everyday problem and include malicious attacks, specific security breaches, virus and malicious software (spyware, adware, ransomware), and social engineering. The manner in which information is obtained can occur in many different fashions, including, but not limited to, poor security, lost/stolen media, lost/stolen computers, hacking, inside jobs, and even the accidental publishing of information. Organizations are susceptible targets of cyberattacks, and necessary proactive measures must be put in place to mitigate these potential attacks.

According to the Identity Theft Resource Center's Breach Report, the United States experienced a record high number of data breaches in 2014. The report states that "the number of U.S. data breaches tracked in 2014 hit a record high of 783 [which] represents a substantial hike of 27.5 percent over the number of breaches reported in 2013 and a significant increase of 18.3 percent over the previous high of 662 breaches tracked in 2010. The number of U.S. data breach incidents tracked since 2005 also hit a milestone of 5,029 involving more than 675 million estimated records."[1] Examples include the January 29, 2015, cyberattack on Anthem's information technology (IT) system in which stolen information "included names, dates of birth, Social Security Numbers, health care identification numbers, home addresses, email addresses, and employment information, including income data."[2] Another example was the U.S. Office of Personnel Management (OPM) attack that affected over 20 million people and included information "such as Social Security Numbers; residency and educational history; employment history; information about immediate family and other personal and business acquaintances; health, criminal, and financial history;" and other sensitive information.[3] Additionally, approximately 1.1 million fingerprint records were compromised. These breaches are considered very damaging on record because of its scale and, more importantly, the sensitivity of the material taken.

Businesses of all sizes have advanced threat protection needs, and with the evolving trends of mobility, cloud computing, and the Internet of Everything, cyber criminals are continually searching and exploiting new gaps in security. Establishing a scalable, proactive threat-centric security solution to protect businesses across the entire attack continuum—before, during, and after an attack—is essential. Criminal activity in this realm will not diminish, and the objective of information security professionals will be to keep systems and networks secure to keep the undesirables out while maintaining the business functioning with the least amount of downtime.

A National Institute of Standards and Technology (NIST) special publication (800-30) defines risk as "a function of the likelihood of a given threat source exercising a particular potential vulnerability, and resulting impact of that adverse event on an organization."[4] As with all risk, the job of the information security professional is to manage and mitigate with respect to information systems by answering common risk management questions.

- What risk is there to information systems?
- Why is it important to understand risk?
- How is risk evaluated?
- How is risk managed?
- What are some common risk assessment/management methodologies and tools?

Steve Elky states in his 2006 SANS Institute publication, *An Introduction to Information System Risk Management*, "From the IT security perspective, risk management is the process of understanding and responding to factors that may lead to a failure in the confidentiality, integrity or availability of an information system."[5] With the vast number of threats to computer and networking systems compared with limited resources, risk management policies need to efficiently (and effectively) protect information in accordance to how the risk is identified and prioritized.

Common Cyber Security Threats

From an information systems risk management standpoint, information threats, attacks, and vulnerabilities are categorized as either outsider or insider threats. The hacker is considered the most significant outsider threat to the information infrastructure. A hacker is someone who uses a computer to maliciously access data without permission. Atkinson explains that "the understanding of the processes, techniques, and skills of hackers or cyber-criminals can be ascertained through the practical application of forensic psychology techniques and behavioral analysis."[6] Atkinson categorizes a hacker in Table 7.1 by stereotype.

Malware is a term for any piece of software that once installed on the computer or network performs unwanted tasks, usually without the user's knowledge and typically for the benefit of someone else. It can range from being as simple as an annoying pop-up advertisement to causing serious

Table 7.1 Categorizing Hackers by Stereotype

Black Hat Actor	Example	Motive	Actions
Script Kiddie	Newbies and tinkerers	Curiosity	Very loud, no specific target and lots of attempts
Malicious Insider	Work force or ex-employee	Revenge	Stealing information or wreaking havoc with internal systems
Activist	Snowden	Revelation	Revealing trade secrets or bringing light to a cause
Spy	Nation States	Espionage	Better understand your enemy or ally
Terrorist	Sony hack	Destruction	Infiltrate, discredit or destroy data/systems
Organized Crime	Russian Mob	Making money	Making money but maintaining the computer infrastructure

Source: Adapted from Atkinson, *Psychology and the Hacker*, p. 2.

invasion and damage such as stealing information or infecting other computers across a network with the malicious intent of compromising data. On the other hand, some malware programs are designed to transmit information on browsing habits on the Internet to advertisers or other third-party interests, all unbeknownst to the user.[7]

A virus is a piece of software that is transmitted over a network or the Internet that can replicate itself and infect a computer without the permission or knowledge of the user. The worst case scenario of some viruses and malware is that it can delete files, corrupt files, cause erratic system behavior, and even cause systems to crash, rendering the computer unusable.

Spyware is a piece of software secretly installed on a computer that monitors and interferes with control over the user's computer systems. The greatest fear about spyware infection is that it can collect a user's personal information such as usernames/passwords, Web site tracking, and banking details; change computer settings; and redirect to malicious Web sites.

Ransomware can result in rendering a computer system useless by holding a computer or files for ransom. As with the virus, malware, and spyware, there are several different types of ransomware that typically require the user to complete a task or demand financial compensation before a user can regain control of the computer system and files. At its worst, ransomware can prevent users from accessing Windows and encrypt files and software, rendering them unusable.

Additionally, a Trojan horse or Trojan is a piece of software that disguises a payload (often malicious) while appearing to perform a legitimate action. Trojan horses often install programs that allow hackers discrete access into computer systems. Its damage could be quite extensive such as erasing a computer, corrupting files, allowing remote access, and logging keystrokes. There are a myriad of different scenarios in which Trojan's can inflict havoc on a computer system.

A Denial of Service (DoS) is an attempt to render a computer/network resource unavailable. This attack is one of the most common, with a goal to flood the computer/network resource using a massive amount of external communication requests. The computer/network resource cannot determine which requests are valid, thereby making the systems slow or unavailable.

Finally, Social Engineering is a method to bypass existing security systems on electronic devices. It does not break through or exploit a vulnerability, but rather it exploits the human factor around the system. The attacker, who is the social engineer, breaks in or cracks a password and tries to convince the user to reset the password, thus giving access to it to the attacker.

Computer/Networking Technology

The firewall is the oldest of proactive network security strategies and is considered one of the most important parts of network infrastructure security. Networking infrastructure has evolved into a complex topic in computer information security. The firewall placement in a network setting is the outer edge of the network with the size and function of the organization determining what type of firewall is needed to maintain a secure network. For example, in an enterprise setting, a multifunction/multilayer firewall security appliance may be necessary; however, in a small business/home office environment, a less sophisticated technology may be an option. Firewalls can be implemented as a software or hardware solution with the purpose of deciding what Internet traffic should be allowed or denied access to a networking infrastructure. This decision is based on rules set by the administrator of the network. With network attacks increasing substantially over the last decade, hackers and their tactics have become so sophisticated that businesses must address the threat by investing in the necessary preventive equipment to protect against network downtime and potential loss of data. According to Bernstein Global Wealth Management, the firewall security appliance represented 53 percent of the overall network security market in 2009, with firewall/virtual private network (VPN) software accounting for 7 percent ($351 million) of the

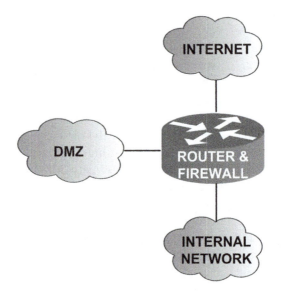

Figure 7.1   Firewall in Relation to Network Infrastructure.

market and integrated security appliances with core firewall functionality representing 46 percent ($2.3 billion) of the market.[8]

Firewalls are the fundamental building blocks of an organization's network security architecture and should be deployed at every intrusion point throughout a network. Next-generation firewalls will offer many different applications to include VPN technology, intrusion prevention, content filtering, unified communications security, and integrated threat defense.

As previously noted in this chapter, the term *computer virus* is often used interchangeably with malware, although the two do not have the same meaning. In the strictest sense, a virus "is a program that copies itself and infects a computer or device, spreading from one file to another, and then from one computer to another. Antivirus software is vital for computer systems to function properly. In 2014, more than 317 million new pieces of malware—computer viruses or other malicious software—were created with nearly one million new threats released each day."[9]

When computers operate without antivirus programs, they have an increased risk of acquiring malicious software that could render the system inoperable, compromising security or deleting important information. The purpose of virus/malware protection is to protect fully the computer system by scanning the entire operating system, files, email, and all downloaded files. Computer systems are an expensive investment and a resource relied upon by many, so system scans are important to ensure the computer's functionality. Browsing the Internet increases the risk of viruses, spyware, malware, and malicious Trojans on computer systems. The purpose of antivirus software is to detect suspicious Web sites and files that contain malicious programs before they enter the computer. Additionally, the software provides a proactive means to block malicious tracking software from being downloaded to a computer. Tracking software is used to steal personal information such as credit card numbers, banking account information, and copyrighted material; that information is then sold to organizations that run identity theft rings. Finally, antivirus programs have the ability to update their virus definitions regularly. These updates are critical because new viruses are released daily, and they can go undetected should the virus software not be up to date.

Internet content filtering software is a tool used to block Internet Web site threats. This technology-based solution can be implemented as a hardware/software solution on an existing networking infrastructure. Its purpose is to proactively protect an enterprise against the latest advanced threats, malware, and phishing techniques, thereby reducing the risk of network intrusion and data loss. Internet content filtering has a myriad of different security and filtering categories and Web application and protocol controls. It allows for monitoring in real time and provides a comprehensive view of network activity and threat levels, similar to antivirus software receiving updates near real time. Finally, its reporting feature allows the capability for customization and provides real-time administrative alerts.

Common Protection Strategies

Encryption

How is corporate data protected on portable/mobile devices and removal media? Only one-third of missing laptops have full-disk encryption for preventing data breaches. Lost laptops cost $1.8 billion per year in the United States. In a recent U.S. study, 329 organizations surveyed lost more than 86,000 laptops over the course of a year. With many users on laptops, tablets, mobile devices, and removal media, the chances of sensitive data being "mobile" is significant. Whether it is a computer with sensitive information, a thumb drive with trade secrets, or a mobile device, data must be protected in a manner that ensures no unauthorized access in case of loss or theft. Encryption technology (which typically includes disk encryption and removable media encryption) protects data on the device rendering it unreadable to an unauthorized user. At the computer level, disk encryption works in a similar manner: Once the encryption software is installed, it loads at the pre-boot requiring authentication before the execution of the operating system. For example, a computer protected with encryption software displays a modified boot sequence environment for the user to authenticate the computer. The user will be prompted by a modified pre-boot software prompting authentication of the user assigned credentials. Additionally, depending on the business environment and security policy in place for the organization, the computer or device may ask for additional credentials such as a smart card, token, or other two-factor authentication. After the user authenticates with valid credentials, the operating system continues to load as normal, and the user can access the computer. Disk encryption protects the organization in the event laptops, tablets, mobile devices, and removal media are lost or stolen. If data is encrypted, it cannot be accessed by unauthorized users. To any other computer, the device appears to be unformatted, and any data is inaccessible.

Incident Response Teams

An incident response team is a group of trained people whose purpose is to promptly and correctly handle an incident to examine and regain control of information systems infrastructure. The group is comprised of members from within the organization who are able to respond immediately and have the authority to make decisions and take actions on demand. When a risk assessment is conducted, critical information may be identified that requires the organization to implement use of the incident response team. The team will investigate and resolve computer security incidents and has the responsibility to review and respond to security incident reports and activity. This team is specifically identified within the organization (corporate, governmental, or educational), a region or country, a research network, an individual or a business. They monitor all attempts, whether failed or successful, to gain unauthorized access to a system or its data as well as unwanted disruptions or denial of service, and finally any unauthorized use of the computer networking infrastructure.

Disaster Recovery Plans

A disaster recovery plan (DRP) provides a process to ensure a business recovers from disrupted information services and helps it resume normal operations. Its purpose is to minimize any negative impacts to an organization. Bryan C. Martin of the SANS Institute states "the term 'disaster' is relative because disasters can occur in varying degrees. So, this plan has considered this issue and incorporates management procedures as well as technical procedures to ensure provable recovery capability."[10] The DRP process identifies critical IT systems and networks, prioritizes their recovery time, and describes the steps needed to recover. Included in the DRP are all important vendor contracts, hardware and software configurations, and necessary backups. Computer information systems response team members will have a system of action to take for a smooth recovery. After having completed a risk assessment and identifying potential threats to information systems infrastructure, the next step is to determine what is most critical to the performance of the organization's business. Reprinted from the NIST *Special Publication 800-34: Contingency Planning for Information Technology Systems*, the following summarizes an ideal structure for an IT disaster recovery plan:

- Develop the contingency planning policy statement. A formal policy provides the authority and guidance necessary to develop an effective contingency plan.
- Conduct the business impact analysis (BIA). The business impact analysis helps to identify and prioritize critical IT systems and components.
- Identify preventive controls. These are measures that reduce the effects of system disruptions and can increase system availability and reduce contingency life-cycle costs.

- Develop recovery strategies. Thorough recovery strategies ensure that the system can be recovered quickly and effectively following a disruption.
- Develop an IT contingency plan. The contingency plan should contain detailed guidance and procedures for restoring a damaged system.
- Plan testing, training, and exercising. Testing the plan identifies planning gaps, whereas training prepares recovery personnel for plan activation; both activities improve plan effectiveness and overall agency preparedness.
- Plan maintenance. The plan should be a living document that is regularly updated to remain current with system enhancements.[11]

Having a disaster recovery plan is crucial to an organization's risk management and mitigation plan and for business continuity.

Other Strategies

Precautionary measures mixed with technology hardware and software are essential to mitigating the myriad of potential threats that exist. Although any plan needs to be tailored to the specific entity it serves, the following are some general strategies that should be included in every plan, adapted from the 2016 FBI's Cyber Division's Private Industry Notification news letter:

- Maintain copies of sensitive data both on-site and at a secure off-site location.
- Implement a mitigation strategy for dealing with DoS attacks.
- Monitor network using firewall security appliance with logs enabled.
- Carefully review links contained in e-mail attachments for social engineering or phishing tactics.
- Set up backup imaging of data and critical system files.
- Establish a password policy that meets the needs of an organization, including changing passwords frequently and setting up limitations so as not to reuse passwords.
- Be cautious of information available from such open sources as social media and the Internet.
- Proactively review social engineering techniques used to obtain sensitive information.
- Patch software as updates become available.
- Conduct annual computer and information systems training.[12]

Every business or entity should have a disaster recovery plan in place to avoid breaches of data and information as well as interruption of operations.

Conclusion

Hackers have been around for as long as computers have existed and cybercrime is not going away. With the evolution of technology and the rise of the Internet, the legal system struggles to keep up with crime. New viruses, malware, and hacking techniques are becoming increasingly sophisticated. To combat these cybersecurity threats, having a proactive approach is essential by using all tools and educational resources available through collaboration with individuals and public/private partnerships. Additionally, it is necessary to continually conduct annual risk assessments and implement a hardware and software strategy within a computer/networking infrastructure. Finally, companies must have a well-documented cybersecurity plan that includes a disaster recovery/business continuity plan and an available incident response team. There will be challenges ahead, both expected and unexpected. The job of an information and security professional is to ensure, with these strategies, that the cybercriminal is unsuccessful by providing a secure and trustworthy environment.

Discussion Questions

1. Explain the term malware. How does this malicious code and activity affect computer systems and a networking infrastructure?
2. Explain and provide examples of how malware is a threat to a business organization.
3. List and describe five different types of malware. Which do you deem the greatest threat to an organization and why?
4. Explain how risk management and disaster recovery planning are necessary for business continuity.
5. List and explain five motivators driving the establishment of an incident response team.

Notes

1. Identify Theft Resource Center, "Identity Theft Resource Center Breach Report Hits Record High in 2014"
2. Anthem, Inc., "How to Access and Sign Up for Identity Theft Repair and Credit Monitoring Services."
3. Zengerle and Cassella, "Millions More Americans Hit by Government Personnel Data Hack."

4. National Institute of Standards and Technology, *Guide for Conducting Risk Assessments.*

5. Elky, *An Introduction to Information System Risk Management,* 4.

6. Atkinson, *Psychology and the Hacker—Psychological Incident Handling,* 5.

7. Bernstein Global Wealth Management, *Black Book,* 25.

8. Harrison and Pagliery, "Nearly 1 Million New Malware Threats Released Every Day."

9. Schwartz, "Lost Laptops Cost $1.8 Billon per Year."

10. Martin, *Disaster Recovery Plan Strategies and Processes,* 2

11. Swanson, et al., *Contingency Planning for Information Technology Systems.*

12. Adapted from Federal Bureau of Investigation, *Private Industry Notification,* 2.

Bibliography

Anthem, Inc. "How to Access and Sign Up for Identity Theft Repair and Credit Monitoring Services." Anthem, Inc. Last modified August 25, 2015. https://www.anthemfacts.com/.

Atkinson, S. *Psychology and the Hacker—Psychological Incident Handling.* Bethesda, MD: SANS Institute. 2015

Bernstein Global Wealth Management. *Black Book: The Art of Cyber War—Asymmetric Payoffs Lead to More Spending on Protection.* New York, NY: Bernstein Global Wealth Management. 2010.

Elky, S. *An Introduction to Information System Risk Management.* Bethesda, MD: SANS Institute. 2006.

Federal Bureau of Investigation. *Private Industry Notification: Alert Number 160616-001.* Washington, DC: Federal Bureau of Investigation, Cyber Division. June 16, 2016.

Harrison, V., and J. Pagliery. "Nearly 1 Million New Malware Threats Released Every Day." *CNN.* Last modified April 14, 2015. http://money.cnn.com/2015/04/14/technology/security/cyber-attack-hacks-security/.

Identity Theft Resource Center. "Identity Theft Resource Center Breach Report Hits Record High in 2014." Identity Theft Resource Center. Last modified January 12, 2015. http://www.idtheftcenter.org/ITRC-Surveys-Studies/2014databreaches.html.

Martin, B. *Disaster Recovery Plan Strategies and Processes.* Bethesda, MD: SANS Institute. 2015.

National Institute of Standards and Technology. *Guide for Conducting Risk Assessments: NIST Special Publication 800-30, Revision 1.* Gaithersburg, MD: U.S. Department of Commerce, National Institute of Standards and Technology, Computer Security Division. 2012.

Schwartz, M. "Lost Laptops Cost $1.8 Billion per Year." *Information Week.* Last modified April 21, 2011. http://www.informationweek.com/mobile/lost-laptops-cost-$18-billion-per-year/d/d-id/1097314.

Swanson, M., P. Bowen, A. Phillips, D. Gallup, and D. Lynes. *Contingency Planning for Information Technology Systems: NIST Special Publication 800-34*. Gaithersburg, MD: U.S. Department of Commerce, National Institute of Standards and Technology, Computer Security Division. 2010.

Zengerle, P., and M. Cassella. "Millions More Americans Hit by Government Personnel Data Hack." *Reuters*. Last modified July 9, 2015. http://www.reuters.com/article/us-cybersecurity-usa-idUSKCN0PJ2M420150709.

CHAPTER EIGHT

Unmanned Aircraft Systems in Homeland Security

Robert Coullahan

Learning Objectives

After reading this chapter, readers should be able to:

- Describe an Unmanned Aircraft System (UAS) and its associated elements.
- Summarize the history of unmanned aircraft and vehicles.
- Summarize current and potential UAS uses by mission area.
- Describe example sensor technologies that UAS support.
- Describe the federal laws and regulations that govern the civilian use of UAS.
- Explain privacy issues associated with UAS.
- Describe methods to comply with applicable laws and regulations.
- Recognize the issues associated with the implementation and use of UAS by homeland security partners.

Key Terms

Aircraft
Civil Rights and Civil Liberties Privacy Policy
Ground Control Station
Line of Sight
National Airspace System (NAS)

Remote-Controlled Model Aircraft (RCMA)
Remote Piloted Vehicle (RPV)
Unmanned Aerial Vehicle (UAV)
Unmanned Aircraft System (UAS)

Introduction

DUE TO ADVANCES IN TECHNOLOGY, the use of Unmanned Aircraft Systems (UAS) to perform missions related to homeland security, national security, emergency management, public safety, military operations, scientific research and applications, and commercial and industrial applications has continued to increase. Few regulations, however, exist that address modern UAS despite recent policy development and rulemaking by the Federal Aviation Administration (FAA). At the same time a robust new industry of UAS manufacturers, sensor and payload developers, and training and technical support infrastructure is developing. That industrial emergence is happening as the nascent policies, regulations, and laws guiding use of the technology are rapidly transforming.

The development of multiple U.S.-based UAS test sites and recent FAA policy guidelines[1] are among the developments, both in policy and in programs, that will have impacts on the operational deployment capabilities of UAS in the homeland security arena. As the technology is adapted and integrated for domestic security applications, homeland security partners need to comprehend the architecture, security, and opportunities for safe and effective use of these potentially lifesaving systems.

As defined by the FAA, "a UAS is an aircraft that must comply with safety requirements."[2] Given this definition in the FAA's authorizing statutes, it is therefore subject to regulation by the FAA. The U.S. Code of Federal Regulations (C.F.R.) 49 U.S.C. § 40102(a)(6) defines an aircraft as "any contrivance invented, used, or designed to navigate or fly in the air."[3] In sum, the FAA views a UAS as aircraft "because it is a contrivance/device that is invented, used, and designed to fly in the air."[4] Due to this, the FAA and others have "promulgated regulations that apply to the operation of all aircraft, whether manned or unmanned, and irrespective of the altitude at which the aircraft is operating."[5]

The purpose of this chapter is to facilitate an understanding of emerging applications and integration of UAS within homeland security partners. The chapter elevates topics for further research and analysis and organizes policy, operational, and technical information to facilitate understanding of requirements, capabilities, and acquisition challenges related to rapidly maturing UAS technologies.

Evolution of UAS Technologies

Among the first reported use of UAS for weapons delivery systems was in 1849. *The Presse*, the newspaper of Vienna, Austria, reported that there was a plan to bombard Venice, Italy, with balloons carrying bombs as a way to get around its natural protection from shipboard artillery by the geography of its lagoon. The diabolical plan was for five balloons, each 23 feet in diameter, to be directed as near to Venice as possible enabling the release of bombs by means of a long isolated copper wire with a galvanic battery placed on the shore to trigger the bombardment.[6]

The use of radio-controlled plans in warfare and training accelerated the development of UAS technologies especially during and after World War I. Examples of early UAS technologies included A. M. Low's "Aerial Target," which was developed in 1916 and is considered the earliest attempt at a powered unmanned aerial vehicle. After World War I, further UAS advances followed, which included the first scale Remote Piloted Vehicle (RPV) developed by Reginald Denny as well as the Hewitt-Sperry Automatic Airplane. During World War II, advances in technologies enabled UAS to be used in both antiaircraft training for gunners as well as to conduct attack missions. Germany also heavily utilized UAS during World War II in the form of radio-guided airborne torpedoes[7] and bombs, which were directed via wire or radio from aircraft[8] or early television cameras.[9] However, full implementation of UAS in the U.S. military did not occur until the late 1950s/early 1960s (under the code name of Red Wagon) with additional expansion during the Vietnam War all of which was classified. In fact, the U.S. Air Force did not confirm the use of UAS in offensive military actions until 1973 during congressional testimony in which it was revealed that more than 3,400 UAS missions were flown during the Vietnam War (more than 550 UAS were destroyed in these missions).

Today, the definition of a UAS is a "system whose components include the necessary equipment, network, and personnel to control an unmanned aircraft."[10] This "system" view definition includes more than just the aircraft, such as the associated "equipment, networks, and personnel."[11] Further, "UAS come in a wide range of shapes and sizes designed for diverse applications" with wingspans that range from "as large as a Boeing 737 or smaller than a radio-controlled model aircraft."[12] Table 8.1 identifies the five principal categories of UAS in production and use today. Table 8.2 provides the fundamental components supporting a UAS implementation.

Table 8.1 UAS Categories

UA Category	Maximum Gross Takeoff Weight (lbs)	Normal Operating Altitude (ft)	Speed (KIAS)	Representative UAS
Group 1	0–20	< 1,200 AGL	100	WASP III, TACMAV RO-14A/B, BATCAM, RO-11B, RO-16A, Puma AE
Group 2	21–55	< 3,500 AGL	< 250	ScanEagle, Silver Fox, Aerosonde
Group 3	< 1,320	< 18,00 MSL	< 250	RO-7B Shadow, RO-15 Neptune, XPV-2 Mako
Group 4	> 1,320	< 18,00 MSL	Any Speed	MO-5B Hunter, MO-8B Fire Scout, MO-1C Gray Eagle, MO-1A/B Predator
Group 5	> 1,320	> 18,000 MSL	Any Speed	MO-9 Reaper, RO-4 Global Hawk, MO-4C BAMS

Legend			
AGL	above ground level	lbs	pounds
ft	feet	MSL	mean sea level
KIAS	knots indicated airspeed	UA	unmanned aircraft
kts	knots	UAS	unmanned aircraft system

Table 8.2   Elements of a UAS Implementation

Air Vehicle Element	Control Element	Data and Voice Communications Element
Airframe and structure	Mission planning	Landline or communication relay services
Propulsion system	Mission control and operations	
Flight control system		
Communication suite	Conflict avoidance monitoring	Uplink/downlink spectrum (e.g., line of sight, over the horizon)
Conflict avoidance system	Maintenance and logistics	
Navigation system		
Electrical system	Supply and provisioning	
Flight recovery system	Support and training	
	Launch and recovery	
	Towing and taxiing	

These include the air vehicle with payloads, communications element, and ground control element.

Policy and Program Initiatives

The FAA Modernization and Reform Act of 2012 defines that a final rule be developed to enable small UAS, and later all civil UAS, to operate in the United State airspace. Some of the UAS provisions in the FAA bill include:

- Setting a deadline for full integration of UAS into the national airspace.
- Requiring the FAA to create a five-year UAS road map (which should be updated annually).
- Requiring small UAS (under 55 pounds) to be allowed to fly within 27 months.
- Requiring six UAS test sites within six months (similar to the language in the defense bill).
- Requiring small UAS (under 55 pounds) be allowed to fly in the U.S. Arctic, 24 hours a day, beyond line of sight, at an altitude of at least 2,000 feet, within one year.
- Requiring expedited access for homeland security partners.
- Allowing first responders to fly very small UAS (4.4 pounds or less) within 90 days if they meet certain requirements.
- Requiring the FAA to study UAS human factors and causes of accidents.[13]

Operational Scenarios

UAS provide an effective and affordable solution for specific mission support of homeland security partners. In fact, UAS can be viewed as force multipliers. However, the utilization of UAS go far beyond law enforcement activities as illustrated in Table 8.3. Beyond the public safety and security realm, UAS can be used for such applications as professional aerial photography; inspection related to farming, utility, and pipeline operations; traffic monitoring; telecommunication signal relaying; and crop dusting. Despite the advantages provided by UAS, homeland security partners must also address privacy concerns. One source of support in this arena is the International Association of Chiefs of Police (IACP) Aviation Committee. Specifically, the IACP Aviation Committee recommended the following guidelines for law enforcement agencies contemplating the use of UAS:

- Determine how they will use this technology, including the costs and benefits to be gained.
- Engage their community early in the planning process, including their governing body and civil liberties advocates.
- Assure the community that it values the protections provided citizens by the U.S. Constitution. Further, the agency will operate the aircraft in full compliance with the mandates of the Constitution and federal, state, and local laws governing search and seizure.
- Provide the community with an opportunity to review and comment on agency procedures as they are being drafted.[14]

Data Management

Given the torrent of additional sensor and video data that could be generated through UAS systems deployment, records retention and data management strategies must be reviewed and updated. It is recommended that homeland security partners review data records every five years to determine whether the data should be retained or purged. This time frame is consistent with 28 CFR Part 23.[15] Further, the five-year time frame should be applied to data that are not considered criminal intelligence.[16]

Current and Future Operational Environment

Over the next decade, the growth of the UAS market (both government and commercial) is expected to reach $90 billion.[17] Procurement of UAS is

Table 8.3 Examples of UAS Applications by Mission Area

Protection	Prevention	Response	Recovery	Mitigation
Plume Dispersion and Tracking	Surveillance	Search and Rescue	Damage Assessment	Surveying and Mapping
Shelter-in-Place and Evacuation	CIKR Monitoring	Hostage Rescue	Debris Management	Scientific Data Collection
Border Security	Evacuation and Traffic Management	Active Shooter	Site Assessment and Selection	Natural Hazards Research and Monitoring
Standoff Cargo Monitoring	Farm and Fence Inspections	Wildland Fire	Ingress and Egress Route Mapping	Risk Analysis
Monitoring Crowds/ Events	CBRNE Detection	Flood	Long Duration Monitoring	Communications
	Observation Platform	Severe Weather Events		
		Spill Monitoring		
		Criminal Activity (Alarm Response)		
		SWAT Operations		

Mission Area Definitions

Protection: The capabilities necessary to secure the homeland against acts of terrorism and man-made or natural disasters.

Prevention: The capabilities necessary to avoid, prevent, or stop a threatened or actual act of terrorism.

Response: The capabilities necessary to save lives, protect property and the environment, and meet basic human needs after an incident has occurred.

Recovery: The capabilities necessary to assist communities affected by an incident to recover effectively.

Mitigation: The capabilities necessary to reduce the loss of life and property by lessening the impact of disasters.

expected to top $60 billion with the remaining $30 billion associated with research and development.[18] However, continued worldwide growth of the UAS market will only be achieved with the development and implementation of necessary regulations that specifically focus on overall safety as well as integration into the national airspace.[19]

UAS can help in countering threats, vulnerabilities, and hazards by reducing risk to human life and increasing standoff from hazardous areas. Potential civil, scientific, and commercial applications of UAS include those indicated in Table 8.4.[20]

Understanding Airspace Integration

Recognizing that UAS pose several obstacles to operating safely and routinely in the NAS, the FAA and others are continuing their efforts to address these challenges, which include:

- Inability of UAS to detect, sense, and avoid other aircraft and airborne objects in a manner similar to "see and avoid" by a pilot in a manned aircraft.
- Vulnerabilities in the command and control of UAS operations.
- Limited human factors engineering incorporated into UAS technologies.
- Unreliable UAS performance.
- Lack of technological and operational standards needed to guide the safe and consistent performance of UAS.
- Lack of final regulations to guide the safe integration of UAS into the NAS.
- Transition to NextGen.[21]

Initially, FAA UAS COA regulations required that the operator must have passed pilot training ground school to operate within line of sight and must have a full pilot's certificate if piloted beyond line of sight or in instrument flight rules conditions. This quickly becomes complicated since possession of a flight medical certificate dramatically affects life insurance rates, and it presents a cascading set of administrative actions and costs that are inherent in assuring compliance and safety. In 2015, the FAA issued a Notice of Proposed Rulemaking that recommended creation of a new "UAS Operator" certification that along with other conditions, would permit small UAS operations under 500-feet altitude, with less than 55 pounds of total vehicle weight, for daytime, line-of-sight operations less than 100 miles per hour.[22] The rules and regulations concerning UAS operations within the NAS continue to evolve and these developments cannot be adequately treated within this chapter. The reader should visit the FAA UAS Web site for current and timely resources (http://www.faa.gov/). The professional membership organization, Association of Unmanned

Table 8.4 Examples of UAS Civil, Scientific, and Commercial Applications

Civil Applications	Scientific Applications	Commercial Applications
Avalanche/rockslide/landslide monitoring	Aerosol source determinations	Utility inspection
Border patrol	Atmospheric monitoring	News and media support
Chemical and petroleum spill monitoring	Environmental monitoring and mapping	Crop monitoring
Communications relay	Hyperspectral imaging	Communications relay
Damage assessment, post-incident recovery planning	Natural hazards research and monitoring	Fish spotting
Drug surveillance and interdiction	Sea ice flow observations	Surveying and mapping
Emergency response	Soil moisture imaging	Commercial imaging
Flood inundation mapping		Cargo
Forest fire monitoring		Commercial security
High altitude imaging		
Humanitarian aid planning and logistics support		
Land use mapping (right-of-way mapping for utilities, transportation easements)		
Law enforcement surveillance		
Monitoring of sensitive sites (critical infrastructure, special events, mass gatherings)		
Nuclear, biological, chemical (NBC) sensing/tracking		
Pipeline or transmission power line patrol		
Plume dispersion and tracking		
Port security		
Radiological plume monitoring		
Search and rescue		
Traffic surveillance and traffic accident reporting		

Vehicle Systems International, offers an extensive library of technical and policy related references (http://www.auvsi.org/).

The Integration Challenge

Due to the increasing popularity of UAS, it is expected that small UAS will make up the majority of UAS in use throughout the NAS. The challenge of this is that small UAS can be operated outside of line of sight and for long durations. Large UAS also pose integration challenges due to their ability to operate at high altitudes (some above 60,000 feet) and remain in flight for several days in order to support surveillance, data gathering, communications, and other missions. Figure 8.1 provides a representation, although illustrative and not comprehensive, of UAS and the altitudes at which they operate.

Sensor Solutions

Along with the various UAS operational scenarios, agencies must identify and implement sensors that make those scenarios possible. Many sensor possibilities include, but are not limited to, remote sensing to gamma

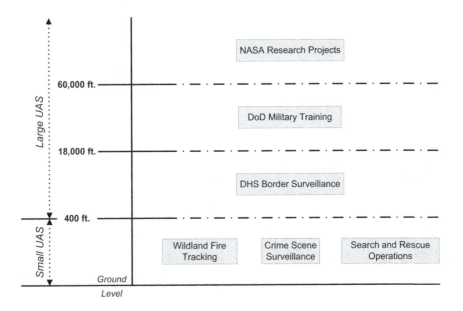

Figure 8.1 Typical UAS Operating Altitudes.

ray, electromagnetic spectrum, biological, and chemical. Electro optical (EO) sensors include visual spectrum and a variety of infrared sensors. The following sections will identify and briefly explain several varieties of sensors and detectors. While the listing is not exhaustive, it will help the reader further understand the capabilities of UAS.

Observation and Sensing

Since earliest times, vision from above has been the primary driving goal of observation at altitude. If balloons (tethered or self-contained aerostats) are to be included in the mix of tools grouped as UAS, observation is where it all started and is still the most common use of UAS. Though the perceived view has broadened dramatically and advances in computational analysis have transformed raw images into actionable intelligence through instantaneous post-processing, the idea remains to get above the area or object in question and gather data not possible through terrestrial means.

This "remote-controlled helicopter with a camera" concept remains one of the most affordable, practical, and effective tools for homeland security partners today. The advances that occur almost weekly in microelectronics for consumer use in cell phones, tablet computers, and digital cameras (still and video) include precise three-axis-locating (generally Global Positioning System [GPS] signals augmented by terrestrial information and accelerometers [inertial navigation]) and very responsive flux-gate directional compasses that are all highly suited for UAS adaptation due to their low weight and mass and tiny electrical current demands.

Optics, Chips and Post-Processing

Modern digital cameras are computer chips that respond to light. These advanced electronics produce high-quality images inexpensively while only requiring a tiny amount of power. Closed-circuit television has long defined basic standards for low-light, high-definition (resolution) image capture devices, universal optical lens mounting, and signal encoding-decoding. Due to enormous competition in video security systems, the choices are virtually limitless and generally based on mission and budget. They give the responder a critical view not otherwise available by going above the trees, down the ditch, around the corner, and up the stairs into a dangerous building.

The nature of these devices is that a current flows through them and an image is created by the embedded microcircuitry then wirelessly, but securely, transmitted to the need-to-know pilot or command team. Since the current creating the image data is both small and constant, still or moving (video) images make little difference other than the amount of data that is transmitted or captured to a removable memory chip. Thus most systems use live video to help a human operator (pilot) guide the UAS on its mission as well as capturing the data, which is the purpose of the mission. Post-processing of the UAS captured imagery is readily available through security technology that can enhance photographs to clarify identifying marks such as license plate numbers, process facial recognition, and even "stitch" together multiple live video feeds from both UAS and stationary camera systems to produce a seamless image that tracks marked targets such as a specific person for long distances including travel inside buildings.

Human eyes respond to a narrow sliver of the electromagnetic spectrum. Imaging chips and sensors do not have this same limitation, so they can see things that a person cannot, then represent it as an image easily recognized by the untrained human eye. The most commonly known version and perhaps the most useful is thermal temperature differential. Many names for this are well-known, including thermal imaging, forward-looking infrared, and near infrared.

These expanded-range systems are roughly divided into cameras that image in the infrared portion of the electromagnetic spectrum that humans cannot see or cameras that actually are activated to create images by very minute changes of temperature of the objects they are viewing. Second only to visual imaging, these are the most affordable and useful tools in the UAS payload arsenal. By imaging objects by their temperature, the outline of the human form or other visually recognizable object is readily seen through the use of a change in the image (bright area versus dark) or commonly seen as a more quickly discernible false color image where red is hot, blue is cold, and green is foliage. Infrared, being a type of "light" in another part of the spectrum, has the added advantage of artificial illumination, which turns nighttime into daytime without the use of physical lighting. Infrared cameras, however, are highly dependent on the stability of the camera itself when the image is being captured. Camera technological advances that have enhanced UAS operations include:

- Use of nearly silent, vibration-free electric motors for rotors and propellers in the UAS itself
- Development of carbon-fiber-based micro-gyroscope-driven camera mounts
- Optical image stabilization of digital video and still camera technology (moving prisms in lenses)
- Digital image stabilization of digital systems (dot alignment)

- Advanced post-processing systems
- Miniaturization

By using highly advanced sensors that collect information in many sections of the spectrum, a high-probability conclusion of a specific item can be discerned. Ten years ago this was highly specialized equipment owned only by the military with payload weights starting at over 300 pounds. Today, through mass production and microminiaturization, hyperspectral devices can be as small as a human hand and weigh as little as a pound, inclusive of optics and electronics.

Other Sensing Technologies

Standoff sensing of chemical warfare agents has an ancient history, though it usually involved some sacrifice of life. Affordable UAS are capable of carrying chemical agent sensing devices that sense, analyze, and relay their findings in real time while in flight. Or, they can carry aloft tiny tubes that "inhale" the air being traveled through for later bio-survey analysis when back on the ground where the contents of the tubes may be safely analyzed by highly accurate portable pathogen detection systems.

As microminiaturization continues at a rapid pace, it is envisioned that homeland security UAS systems could remain equipped at all times with chemical, biological, and radiological sensing systems linked to a regional or national network to provide umbrella-like sensing protection from deadly airborne threats. Very small ionizing radiation detectors have been available (radiation pagers as they are frequently called due to their size and shape), and adaptation to UAS is in early stages after recent incidents at nuclear power facilities.

Locating, Identifying, and Communicating

An emerging highly useful variation of multispectral is combining visual imaging with highly sensitive directional radio frequency receivers. This combination of video with superimposed radio signature detection is capable of discovering the exact location of a cell phone or other radio device and showing it on a live video image (visible or thermal) or aerial or road/terrain/sea map or chart.

This "augmented reality" is considered by many to be the next frontier of surveillance imaging. The ability to pick up electronic signatures or radio transmissions from watches to cell phones to electronic vehicle, vessel, and aviation ignition systems and primary drive motors and to display them in real time on a visual-like image has possibilities not yet envisioned but of immense value to homeland security partners.

Since more and more electronics either communicate their information via cellular, wireless fidelity (Wi-Fi), Bluetooth, and public/private radio frequencies, this is an increasing valuable way of looking at the world for homeland security partners. Even nontransmitting devices such as GPS receivers frequently include "superheterodyne" antennas that "charge" the antenna with a sending radio frequency to provoke a more sensitive reception of the GPS satellite signal. Therefore, a person lost with no communication device or an intruder or smuggler finding his or her way with nothing more than a GPS can be detected and shown in real time on the UAS surveillance video stream.

The near-silent operation of modern UAS platforms provides not only "eyes in the sky" but also ears. From listening to rubble piles for signs of life to gunshot identification and locating, both directional and omnidirectional microphones on UAS are inexpensive, lightweight, low-power providers of valuable actionable information. By using near-infrared frequency imaging cameras, vehicle, vessel, and aircraft identification names and numbers can be read from great distances. Quickly searching all pertinent databases instantaneously identifies or catalogues identifying marks for further action or simply recording the movement for later discovery of patterns of movement, such as a drug runner making the same long trip on the same day over a period of time.

Wide Area Augmentation System (WAAS), first used by the FAA, was soon matched by a host of related navigation and location GPS enhancing systems such as Differential GPS (DGPS—popular for maritime applications), Global Navigation Satellite System, and Multifunctional Satellite Augmentation Systems or simply Satellite-Based Augmented Systems. Sometimes the earth-based signal makes the satellite signal more accurate; sometimes the satellite signal makes the earth-based signal better. Either way, it works very well, and precise three-dimensional (3-D) locating has become commonplace. An important recent addition to this development is discerning the location of a distant "target" object from an object of a known altitude and location, such as a UAS. By combing optical laser range finding and/or Doppler radar range finding, highly precise locations of the actual objects being observed at great distances can be determined, greatly advancing the utility and practicality of the UAS itself.

Originally, the government-initiated way to make GPS locating more predictable was superseded by patented commercial solutions to the extent that the common smartphone uses many different inputs to create a highly precise location based on:

- GPS data from 12 or more satellites
- Microscopic fluxgate technology magnetic compass
- Microscopic gyroscope or multidimensional "accelerometer"
- Known Wi-Fi hot spot locations
- Cellular tower location (signal-based triangulation)
- WAAS
- DGPS

Now combined into a single commodity chip, frequently further integrated into the signal amplifier chip of the cell phone or UAS navigational guidance system, modern UAS and their pilots know precisely where they are and their exact direction of travel or surveillance with great accuracy. This exact 3-D location knowledge thus greatly enhances the precision of the UAS payload.

Mechanical Payloads—Dropping Off, Picking Up, and Corrective Actions

Although observation, investigation, sampling, and tracking have been the primary payloads, UAS are expanding their roles in the functional domain of their terrestrially bound robotic counterparts. Due to the issue of payload weight restrictions on smaller UASs, development of grabbing or object capture devices has been limited; however, the speed at which a UAS can be deployed and guided to an object, can secure the object, and can move it out of harm's way creates a logical market for robotics developers, especially with small UAS power and propulsion system advances.

While most any UAS can be rigged to release a package, commercial systems have concentrated on the larger UAS devices that can deploy supplies, weapons, or destructive devices as needed. As the homeland security technology market evolves, this technology, which has been available for decades in traditional aviation, should quickly be adapted for UAS use allowing rapid delivery of supplies, tools, food, or protective gear. True to the mission of homeland security, such delivery systems hold the promise of protecting not only the innocent bystander victims from mob or gang-related actions, but also the rioters themselves from escalation into very regrettable situations where lives are lost. UAS deployment with counter-insurgency measures could be quick and effective solutions to senseless outbreaks of mob violence, gang or prisoner fights, or destructive rioting.

Training and Exercises

The UAS applications impact a broad training audience from the aviation division that may be responsible for the flight operations and ground control stations to the collaborating disciplines that have a stake in forensic data collection requirements, data management, and information sharing. Not unlike the challenges experienced in managing communications interoperability, rational UAS asset management must involve a wide range of regional partners often with competing and divergent priorities for system capabilities and operational access.

Several varieties of training courses must be made available for the UAS user community that focus on topics such as pilot/flight officer, ground control stations, sensors, and payloads as well as overall program management. Early planning efforts should be undertaken to establish how training can be more widely accessible to homeland security partners. In order to meet training objectives to a geographically dispersed audience in not only an effective but efficient manner, multiple modalities of training must be implemented. These modalities could include a mixture of Web-based, hands-on, and traditional classroom-based opportunities.

Additionally, in the category of hands-on training, exercises must be planned and conducted in an effort to simulate real-world events. Homeland security practitioners should ensure utilization of the Homeland Security Exercise and Evaluation Program and the doctrine within that program. The doctrine will outline essential exercise components such as design, coordination, preparation of injects, implementation, and evaluation/ assessment.

State Statutes and Local Ordinances

The variance across state and local jurisdictions and the rapidly changing legal aspects of UAS operations preclude a careful treatment of this topic in this chapter. Simply put, the laws, statutes, and ordinances are undergoing enormous evolutionary changes and many have yet to be tested in the courts. It is incumbent upon the UAS user to understand the ramifications of their operations on public and private lands, including FAA rules and regulations as well as the state and local constraints placed upon use. They operate at the risk of civil and criminal penalties for unauthorized use.

Technologies and Tactics for Protective Measures

Adversary low, slow, and small UASs can operate in all environments, from attacks on the NAS to precision attacks on key public figures, mass gatherings, or critical infrastructure. Current air and missile defense programs focus on large, fast, and lethal platforms relying on radar as the primary means of detection. The introduction of low, slow, and small UASs flying at low altitude in high-clutter areas is often difficult for fielded systems to detect. This has created new challenges for domestic air defense and homeland security.

The increased use of Remote-Controlled Model Aircraft (RCMA)/UAS incidents prompted the U.S. Government to develop and disseminate recommended protective measures and response procedures for stadium and other mass gathering venues. Unfortunately, the recreational misuse of UAS from RCMA hobbyists (such as flying in restricted airspace, disrupting first responders, and so on) has further complicated the delineation of malicious from nonmalicious activity. The potential mission set of adversary UAS ranges from airborne improvised explosive devices (IEDs) to information gathering around critical infrastructure or military facilities and to propaganda efforts demonstrating unchallenged unauthorized access to the NAS.

The downside of UAS operations is that the same tool that can save lives and prevent widespread damage and injuries in the service of the public good can be used for nefarious and criminal activities by those of ill will. The dangers and threats posed by UAS may include their use to deliver or conduct the following activities:

- Convey explosives.
- Deliver dangerous chemicals.
- Deliver biological agents.
- Project weapons (machine guns have been mounted on commercial UASs).
- Drop in surveillance payloads.
- Conduct kamikaze missions (the platform as the weapon).
- Engage in critical infrastructure surveillance (probing of defenses and observation of defensive measures).
- Monitor security staffing, equipment, and preventive measures (casing for future attack).
- Monitor law enforcement activities (e.g., to protect a meth lab, drug operations).
- Conduct Very Important Person (VIP) executive protection surveillance.
- Smuggle contraband into prisons (e.g., illicit cell phones, weapons).
- Engage in illegal recordings and harassment (civil).
- Engage in corporate espionage.

Significant work has been accomplished in programs across the U.S. government to meet the threat of adversary UAS operations; however, much of the technology and concepts of operations associated with that capability are not yet fully transitioned to homeland security partners.

Assumptions in Adoption of UAS Technologies

Assumptions useful for homeland security partners to adopt as part of deploying UAS assets include the following, reprinted from Legislative Task Force on Unmanned Aircraft Systems, *Final Report to the Legislature*:

- **Public Navigable Airspace:** The question of what constitutes "public navigable airspace" for UAS operated by the government is central to privacy policy. The most likely scenario is already protected by existing law.
- **Role of Imaging Technology:** Rules and case law exist that protect citizens from inappropriate use of capturing data that is more than the human eye could ever see.
- **Extended Surveillance:** It is unlikely that law enforcement would use UAS for standard patrol activities due to cost considerations. Limiting flight hours is not an acceptable control because long duration flights may be necessary to support search and rescue or disaster recovery operations.
- **Obtaining a Warrant:** It is widely agreed that use of a UAS to gather data would require a warrant in situations similar to using any other data gathering device (such as voice recording, photography, and thermal imaging with manual technology). No additional laws are required to obtain a warrant for UAS data gathering. Law enforcement agencies must first obtain a court order to use UAS over private property for criminal investigation against any person.
- **Weaponized Aircraft:** FAA guidelines do not allow anything to be dropped from an unmanned aircraft.
- **Visibility:** Use of high-visibility marking on any UAS is likely to become standard practice. Application of navigational lighting and/or high-visibility paint is used by several jurisdictions.
- **Public Education:** The demand for public education regarding those agencies using UAS will continue to be high; however, the sensitivity is heightened for homeland security partner uses, and appropriate public outreach and community engagement will be beneficial.[23]

Impacts, Benefits and Consequences of UAS Implementation

Given the acceleration of activities in development of UAS and supporting applications, it is imperative that homeland security partners get in front of a new technology with the proper technical and policy guidance. With every new capability comes new responsibility. There is little doubt that airborne robotic sensing and surveillance capabilities will protect many lives and property as well as guard homeland security partner personnel entrusted with their proper and effective use, ensuring their safety. UAS solutions also hold the promise of operational budget savings through more effective and expeditious performance at a lower overall cost.

New advances in technology have made cameras and other sensors dramatically lighter with higher resolution and broader spectrum while lowering power consumption. Advances in cell phone technology have created such new secure radio waveforms as long-term evolution capable of carrying significant amounts of high-speed encrypted data for very low cost and their universal presence, especially in urban environments across the country. The once intractable legal issues regarding privacy and due process have been framed into policy guidelines.

Privacy

As introduced in chapter 2 of this textbook, ethics and privacy in technological applications must remain a prevalent consideration for the homeland security practitioner. Case in point, privacy in UAS applications continues to be a frequently debatable issue in the media, academia, and other circles. Please note that this chapter will not provide a comprehensive review of privacy issues associated with UAS surveillance and monitoring. However, several primary points will be addressed that allow the reader to further investigate the topic based on need and interest. Two key actions related to privacy considerations include the American Civil Liberties Union (ACLU)'s recommendations regarding the use of "drones."[24] Further, in 2012, the Electronic Privacy Information Center submitted a petition to the FAA requesting a public rulemaking on the privacy impact of drone use in U.S. airspace.[25]

The following list, reprinted from American Civil Liberties Union, *Protecting Privacy from Aerial Surveillance*, provides a set of recommendations from the ACLU regarding use of drones:

- Drones should be prohibited for mass surveillance or spying on activities protected by the First Amendment. Unmanned Aerial Vehicles (UAVs) should only be used for collecting evidence allowed under a search warrant and for emergencies such as a fire, hostage crisis, or search-and-rescue operation.
- Images captured by UAVs should not be retained or shared unless there is reasonable suspicion they contain evidence of criminal activity, or pertain to an ongoing investigation or pending criminal trial.
- Policies for using UAVs should be explicit, written, and available to the public.
- UAV deployments and policy decisions should be democratically decided based on public information.
- Independent audits should be used to track UAV deployments so that citizens can assess how and how often drones are used, and if they are being used, whether it is a worthwhile public expense.

- Drones for domestic use should not be equipped with lethal or nonlethal weapons.[26]

In further defining statutes designed to protect the collection of Personally Identifiable Information (PII), two laws should be highlighted: the Privacy Act of 1974 and the privacy provisions of the E-Government Act of 2002. In its simplest form, the Privacy Act limits an agencies' "collection, disclosure, and use of personal information maintained in systems of records."[27] Next, the E-Government Act of 2002 was designed to protect PII in government information systems or information collections through the use of Privacy Impact Assessments (PIA).[28] PIAs were discussed in chapter 2 of the textbook.

In addition to laws, many federal agencies are required to employ a privacy officer and/or chief privacy officers to ensure privacy rules are enforced on various programs, projects, technologies, and systems. It is interesting to note that the Department of Homeland Security was the first federal agency to be statutorily required to establish a privacy officer and has subsequently demonstrated leadership in policy development and implementation for privacy protection of civil rights and civil liberties.

Privacy and the Importance of a Civil Rights and Civil Liberties Privacy Policy

The subject of privacy and data security associated with UAS surveillance and monitoring data products cannot be adequately treated in a single chapter. Therefore, the reader is encouraged to review Chapter 2: Ethical and Privacy Implications of Technology, which provides information that can be generally applied to all homeland security technologies, including UAS. However, this chapter would be remiss if a discussion of a Civil Rights and Civil Liberties Privacy Policy was not addressed. The purpose of the Civil Rights and Civil Liberties Privacy Policy is to promote and ensure the collection and storage of information complies with applicable federal, state, local, and tribal laws, regulations, and policies and assists participants in:

- ensuring individual privacy, civil rights, civil liberties, and other protected interests;
- increasing and improving national security;
- protecting the integrity of systems for the observation and reporting of terrorism-related criminal activity and information;
- encouraging individuals or community groups to trust and cooperate with the justice system;
- promoting governmental legitimacy and accountability;

- making the most effective use of public resources allocated to homeland security agencies;
- minimizing the threat and risk of injury to specific individuals;
- minimizing the threat and risk of physical or financial injury to law enforcement and others responsible for public protection, safety, or health;
- minimizing the threat and risk of damage to real or personal property; and
- protecting individual privacy, civil rights, civil liberties, and other protected interests.[29]

Eight Privacy Design Principles, designed to guide policy, are incorporated into the Privacy policy. The principles, as developed by the Organization of Economic Cooperation and Development's Fair Information Practices, reprinted here from Southern Nevada Counter-Terrorism Center, *Privacy, Civil Liberties, and Civil Rights Protection Policy*, include:

1. **Purpose Specification:** Define agency purposes for information to help ensure agency uses of information are appropriate.
2. **Collection Limitation:** Limit the collection of personal information to that required for the purposes intended.
3. **Data Quality:** Ensure data accuracy.
4. **Use Limitation:** Ensure appropriate limits on agency use of personal information.
5. **Security Safeguards:** Maintain effective security over personal information.
6. **Openness:** Promote a general policy of openness about agency practices and policies regarding personal information.
7. **Individual Participation:** Allow individuals reasonable access and opportunity to correct errors in their personal information held by the agency.
8. **Accountability:** Identify, train, and hold agency personnel accountable for adhering to agency information quality and privacy policies.[30]

Conclusion

In this chapter, several items have been considered, including the UAS utility, critical steps in defining UAS requirements, acquisition strategy, and operational planning, training, exercise, and system life-cycle issues that accompany the adoption of the technology. The story of how UAS will fully serve homeland security partners remains to be written as organizations lurch forward through the uncharted territories of evolving laws, statutes, policies, and concepts of operation. There is little doubt that UAS can be put into service to save lives, protect communities, and safeguard critical infrastructure. Cost-effective, safe, and effective insertion of UAS into the domestic NAS and into the inventories of homeland security partners requires discipline, definition of best practices, formal testing, and a robust technical assistance framework to assure this airborne capability joins other systems and technologies that safely serve the public good.

Discussion Questions

1. Explain the elements of a UAS beyond the aircraft.
2. You are a captain of a city police department who is responsible for technology implementation across the department. The police chief has asked you to implement the use of UAS within the department. Knowing that you cannot simply purchase a UAS and start using it, explain the initial activities you would complete to ensure your department follows all federal, state, and local laws and regulations and addresses privacy and other concerns that may arise from citizens.
3. Select and research a U.S. incident or natural disaster that occurred prior to 2010 while paying close attention to the jurisdiction's preparedness, response, and recovery efforts. Analyze the selected incident/natural disaster and explain if and how the use of UAS could have assisted with preparedness, response, and recovery efforts, thereby creating different outcomes.

Notes

1. Federal Aviation Administration, *Fact Sheet—Unmanned Aircraft Systems (UAS)*.
2. Ibid., para. 1.
3. *Transportation, U.S. Code 49*, § 40102(a)(6).
4. Greco, *Press Release*, para. 1.
5. Ibid., para. 9.
6. Scientific American, "More about Balloons."
7. Nowarra, *German Guided Missiles*, 30–37.
8. Ibid., 21.
9. Ibid.
10. Coullahan and Desourdis, "Planning Considerations for Unmanned Aircraft Systems Deployment in the Public Safety Mission," 4.
11. Ibid.
12. Ibid.
13. Reprinted from *FAA Modernization and Reform Act of 2012*, Public Law 112–095 (2012).
14. Reprinted from International Association of Chiefs of Police, *Recommended Guidelines for the Use of Unmanned Aircraft*, 2.

15. Executive Order 12291 of February 17, 1981, Criminal Intelligence Systems Operating Policies, *Code of Federal Regulations.*

16. Ibid.

17. Ibid.

18. Teal Group Corporation, *World Unmanned Aerial Vehicle Systems.*

19. Ibid.

20. DeGarmo, *Issues Concerning Integration of Unmanned Aerial Vehicles in Civil Airspace.*

21. Reprinted from U.S. Government Accountability Office, *Unmanned Aircraft Systems.*

22. Federal Aviation Administration, *Operation and Certification of Small Unmanned Aircraft Systems.*

23. Reprinted from Legislative Task Force on Unmanned Aircraft Systems, *Final Report to the Legislature.*

24. American Civil Liberties Union, *Protecting Privacy from Aerial Surveillance.*

25. Electronic Privacy Information Center, *Petition to the FAA.*

26. Reprinted from American Civil Liberties Union, *Protecting Privacy from Aerial Surveillance.*

27. *The Privacy Act of 1974* (Public Law 93–579).

28. *The E-Government Act of 2002* (Public Law 107–347).

29. Reprinted from Southern Nevada Counter-Terrorism Center, *Privacy, Civil Liberties, and Civil Rights Protection Policy.*

30. Ibid.

Bibliography

Adelman, T. "Under New Leadership, FAA's Unmanned Aircraft Systems Integration Office Meets Its Deadline." *UAS News.* Last modified May 14, 2012. https://www.suasnews.com/.

American Civil Liberties Union. *Protecting Privacy from Aerial Surveillance: Recommendations for Government Use of Drone Aircraft.* New York, NY: American Civil Liberties Union. 2011.

Bennett, W. *Issues in Governance Studies (Number 55)—Unmanned at Any Speed: Bringing Drones into Our National Airspace.* Washington, DC: The Brookings Institution. 2012.

Concannon, R. *COA How to Book.* Grand Forks, ND: Department of Aviation, University of North Dakota. 2008.

Congressional Research Service. *Intelligence, Surveillance, and Reconnaissance (ISR) Acquisition: Issues for Congress (CRS Report R41284).* Washington, DC: Congressional Research Service. 2011.

Congressional Research Service. *Unmanned Aerial Systems (CRS Report R42136).* Washington, DC: Congressional Research Service. 2012.

Coullahan, R., and R. Desourdis Jr. "Planning Considerations for Unmanned Aircraft Systems Deployment in the Public Safety Mission." *The CIP Report* 11, no. 7 (2013): 4–5, 14–16.

Criminal Intelligence Systems Operating Policies. *Code of Federal Regulations,* Title 28, Chapter 1, Part 23.

Criminal Justice Information Systems. *Code of Federal Regulations,* Title 28, Chapter 1, Part 20.

DeGarmo, M. *Issues Concerning Integration of Unmanned Aerial Vehicles in Civil Airspace.* McLean, VA: Center for Advanced Aviation System Development, MITRE Corporation. 2004.

Deltek, Inc. *Unmanned Aerial Systems Market Overview.* Reston, VA: Deltek, Inc. 2012.

The E-Government Act of 2002 (Public Law 107–347). *Electronic Communications Privacy Act of 1986,* Public Law 99–508 (1986): 2510–2522, 2701–2709.

Electronic Privacy Information Center. *Petition to the FAA: Drones and Privacy.* Washington, DC: Electronic Privacy Information Center. 2012.

Elias, B. *Pilotless Drones: Background and Considerations for Congress Regarding Unmanned Aircraft Operations in the National Airspace System (CRS Report 42718).* Washington, DC: Congressional Research Service. 2012.

Executive Order 12291 of February 17, 1981, "Criminal Intelligence Systems Operating Policies." *Code of Federal Regulations,* Title 28 (1998): 127.

FAA Modernization and Reform Act of 2012, Public Law 112–095 (2012).

Federal Aviation Administration. *AFS-407: Evaluation of Candidate Functions for Traffic Alert and Collision Avoidance System II (TCAS II) on Unmanned Aircraft System (UAS).* Washington, DC: Federal Aviation Administration. 2011.

Federal Aviation Administration. *Fact Sheet—Unmanned Aircraft Systems (UAS).* Washington, DC: Federal Aviation Administration. 2015.

Federal Aviation Administration. *Law Enforcement Guidance for Suspected Unauthorized UAS Operations.* Washington, DC: Federal Aviation Administration. 2015.

Federal Aviation Administration. *NextGen Implementation Plan.* Washington, DC: Federal Aviation Administration. 2012.

Federal Aviation Administration. *Notice of Proposed Rulemaking Regulatory Evaluation, Small Unmanned Aircraft Systems, 14 CFR Part 107.* Washington, DC: Federal Aviation Administration. 2015.

Federal Aviation Administration. *Operation and Certification of Small Unmanned Aircraft Systems, Notice of Proposed Rulemaking, RIN 2120-AJ60, Docket No. FAA-2015-0150, Notice No. 15-01.* Washington, DC: Federal Aviation Administration. 2015.

Federal Aviation Administration. *Overview of Small UAS Notice of Proposed Rulemaking.* Washington, DC: Federal Aviation Administration. 2015.

Federal Records Act, U.S. Code 44 (1976), Chapter 33, § 3301.

FLIR Corporation. http://www.flir.com/US/.

Greco, K. *Press Release—FAA Statement on Texas Equusearch UAS Search Decision.* Washington, DC: Federal Aviation Administration. July 18, 2015.

Integration Innovation, Incorporated. *Technical Exchange Meetings with Mr. Jon Daniels.* Las Vegas, NV: Integration Innovation, Incorporated. 2012.

International Association of Chiefs of Police. *Recommended Guidelines for the Use of Unmanned Aircraft.* Alexandria, VA: International Association of Chiefs of Police. 2012.

International Association of Chiefs of Police. *Recommended Guidelines for the Use of Unmanned Aircraft.* Washington, DC: International Association of Chiefs of Police. 2012.

Johnson, E., E. Koski, W. Furman, M. Jorgenson, and J. Nieto. *Third-Generation and Wideband HF Radio Communications.* Norwood, MA: Artech House. 2012.

Legislative Task Force on Unmanned Aircraft Systems. *Final Report to the Legislature.* Juneau, AL: Legislative Task Force on Unmanned Aircraft Systems. 2014.

National Aeronautics and Space Administration. *Topic 2: A2 Air Traffic Management Research and Development / A2.01 Unmanned Aircraft Systems Integration into the National Airspace System Research.* Washington, DC: National Aeronautics and Space Administration. 2012.

Nowarra, H. *German Guided Missiles.* Atglen, PA: Schiffer. 1993.

Privacy Act, U.S. Code 5 (1974), Part I, Chapter 5, Subchapter II, § 552a.

The Privacy Act of 1974 (Public Law 93–579).

Readiness Resource Group Incorporated. *Roadmap for a Public Safety Unmanned Aircraft Systems Technical Assistance Program.* Las Vegas, NV: Readiness Resource Group Incorporated. 2013.

Scientific American. "More about Balloons." *Scientific American* 4, no. 26 (March 17, 1849): 205.

Southern Nevada Counter-Terrorism Center. *Privacy, Civil Liberties, and Civil Rights Protection Policy.* Las Vegas, NV: Southern Nevada Counter-Terrorism Center. n.d.

Teal Group Corporation. World Unmanned Aerial Vehicle Systems. Fairfax, VA: Teal Group Corporation. 2012.

Transportation, U.S. Code 49 (2010).

United States Code, Title 42, Chapter 140, Subchapter II, § 14611.

U.S. Department of Defense. *Unmanned Systems Integrated Roadmap: FY2011–2036 (Reference Number: 11-S-3613).* Washington, DC: U.S. Department of Defense. 2011.

U.S. Department of Homeland Security. *National Preparedness Goal* (2nd ed.). Washington, DC: U.S. Department of Homeland Security. 2015.

U.S. Department of Homeland Security. *Recommended Protective Measures and Response Procedures for Remote-Controlled Model Aircraft / Unmanned Aircraft System at Stadiums and Mass Gatherings.* Washington, DC: U.S. Department of Homeland Security. 2014.

U.S. Department of Homeland Security. *Request for Information (RFI) Number DHS 13-01: Robotic Aircraft for Public Safety (RAPS).* Washington, DC: U.S. Department of Homeland Security. 2012.

U.S. Federal Aviation Administration. http://www.faa.gov/.

U.S. Government Accountability Office. *Unmanned Aircraft Systems: Use in the National Airspace System and the Role of the Department of Homeland Security (GAO-12-889T).* Washington, DC: U.S. Government Accountability Office. 2012.

U.S. Government Accountability Office. *Unmanned Aircraft Systems: Measuring Progress and Addressing Potential Privacy Concerns Would Facilitate Integration into the National Airspace System (GAO-12-981)*. Washington, DC: 2012.

USA PATRIOT Act. Public Law 107– 156 (2001).

Wire and Electronic Communications Interception and Interception of Oral Communications, U.S. Code 18 (1994), Part I, Chapter 119, §§ 2510–2522, 2701–2709, and 3121–3125.

CHAPTER NINE

Chemical, Biological, Radiological, Nuclear, and Explosive (CBRNE) Detection Systems and Data Interoperability

David Lamensdorf and Chad S. Foster

Learning Objectives

After reading this chapter, readers should be able to:

- Assess the problems that Chemical, Biological, Radiological, Nuclear, and Explosive (CBRNE) detection systems aim to address, overcome, or mitigate.
- Explain the purpose of and benefits provided by CBRNE detection systems.
- Distinguish between CBRNE tactical and strategic alerts.
- Identify and explain types of CBRNE threats and instrumentation available to detect those threats.
- Assess the importance of sensor data interoperability and standards such as the Common Alerting Protocol (CAP) in the context of CBRNE threat detection and response.
- Identify and explain CBRNE system detection components, as well as supporting tools and services.

- Apply the CBRNE detection system design to a planned event or disaster scenario.

Key Terms

CBRNE Detection Systems and Technologies
Common Alerting Protocol (CAP)
Detection Instrumentation
Map Integration
Sensor Data Interoperability
Strategic Alerts
Tactical Alerts

Introduction

AT FIRE STATION 4, THE LOS ANGELES Fire Department (LAFD) receives a data message alert from sensors in a chemical storage warehouse indicating abnormal heat levels and possible agent release. A hazardous materials (HAZMAT) response team is dispatched to the warehouse. While en route, onboard data receivers are continuously updated with readings from the building sensors, allowing the responders to plan their approach for building entry and hazard containment. Once on scene, HAZMAT technicians wearing full protective gear and equipped with individual environmental monitoring sensors/meters enter the building hot zone. The technicians have limited visibility in the toxic haze and cannot see their instrument's portable sensor readings. Fortunately, wireless local area network (WLAN) data messaging is being used to relay their sensor readings through a cellular gateway back to receivers on a fire apparatus in the cold zone. Subject matter experts (SMEs) monitor the sensor readings and alert the technicians when conditions exceed safe levels, prompting technicians to exit the "hot" zone. Readings can be pushed as needed to other locations so authorized personnel can monitor conditions for plume prediction, initiating area evacuations, prestaging arriving units, and taking other measures as warranted.[1]

Thanks to many factors such as support and commitment across the Los Angeles region, programming, and the adoption of standards, the vision above is within reach. First responder agencies in the Los Angeles area have a history of working together to respond to large emergencies that exceed the capabilities of a single jurisdiction, most notably in the response to large wildfires. However, these multiagency, multijurisdictional response efforts have not been without complications. With agencies and jurisdictions relying on disparate equipment and communication platforms, responders have had difficulty integrating various public safety agencies for a combined response. Drawing on these experiences, HAZMAT response agencies in the area began a grassroots effort to foster more effective multiagency response by overcoming interoperability issues.

The experiences and the problems encountered by response agencies in the greater Los Angeles region exemplify challenges encountered by many agencies nationwide. At first glance, a discussion of Chemical, Biological, Radiological, Nuclear, and Explosive (CBRNE) detection technologies may seem to be specifically focused on the instrumentation used to sense specific environmental hazards, but as this chapter will reinforce, there are significantly more elements needed to make the information collected from these devices actionable.

This chapter will discuss the family of different environmental detection and monitoring devices, and the manner in which their data is collected, shared, visualized, analyzed, and utilized to support either a tactical response or a preventive–strategic component of an environmental event.

CBRNE Detection Systems and Threats at a Glance

Several years ago, a radiological sensor was triggered in a cargo storage facility at the Los Angeles World Airport. After donning the appropriate multilayered, Level A HAZMAT suits, responders entered the facility to measure the amount of radiation present. While looking through multiple foggy face shields in a poorly lit area, a responder misread his meter's reading by a decimal point. He saw a false positive for a radiological event that resulted in a response of significant stress, risk, time, money, and operational impact to one of the world's busiest airports.

That same scenario would likely not occur today. Interagency emergency responders, managers, and leaders in the Los Angeles region have created a culture and policy to employ CBRNE detection systems to share CBRNE alarm data with each other. Now, a wide range of legacy sensors are connected by a wireless network, sharing real-time information with responders and operations centers at every level of government to enhance decision making and response capabilities. In addition, CBRNE detection systems aim to:

- Save money
- Improve situational awareness among operational decision makers and responders
- Decrease risk to responders

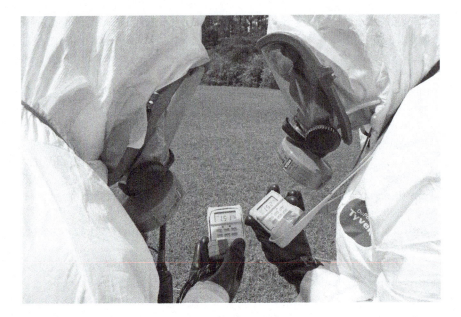

Figure 9.1 Monitoring of Detector Readings

As implied in the name, this chapter views the problems—the lack of situational awareness, heightened risks to responders, and so on—from a systems perspective. For example, situational awareness is achieved through the effective operation of many components, which includes the CBRNE detection technologies and the interoperability of their readings with other user interfaces. This concept requires that various types of technologies be implemented that overcome locational differences, data language disparities, lack of standardization, and viewer types.

Even more fundamentally, these systems aim to protect the public and responders from a range of hazards and threats, which may be a result of an accidental release of a substance in a community (e.g., train derailment, chemical plant incident), or the intentional release of a substance or use of a weapon of mass destruction (WMD) by terrorists. Table 9.1 provides a brief description of CBRNE threats as provided by the U.S. Department of Homeland Security (DHS).

CBRNE Detection Concept of Operations

The CBRNE detection concept of operations is based on widespread, accessible, and standardized sensor readings and alerts. There are two categories

Table 9.1   CBRNE Threats

Chemical Threats: Chemical agents are poisonous vapors, aerosols, liquids, and solids that have toxic effects on people, animals, or plants. They can be released by bombs or sprayed from aircraft, boats, and vehicles. They can be used as a liquid to create a hazard to people and the environment. Some chemical agents may be odorless and tasteless. They can have an immediate effect (a few seconds to a few minutes) or a delayed effect (2 to 48 hours). While potentially lethal, chemical agents are difficult to deliver in lethal concentrations. Outdoors, the agents often dissipate rapidly. Chemical agents also are difficult to produce.

A chemical attack could come without warning. Signs of a chemical release include people having difficulty breathing; experiencing eye irritation; losing coordination; becoming nauseated; or having a burning sensation in the nose, throat, and lungs. Also, the presence of many dead insects or birds may indicate a chemical agent release.

Biological Threats: Biological agents are organisms or toxins that can kill or incapacitate people, livestock, and crops. A biological attack is the deliberate release of germs or other biological substances that can make you sick. The three basic groups of biological agents that would likely be used as weapons are bacteria, viruses and toxins. Most biological agents are difficult to grow and maintain. Many break down quickly when exposed to sunlight and other environmental factors, while others, such as anthrax spores, are very long lived. Biological agents can be dispersed by spraying them into the air, by infecting animals that carry the disease to humans and by contaminating food and water.

Radiological Threats: Terrorist use of a Radiological Dispersion Device (RDD)—often called "dirty nuke" or "dirty bomb"—is considered far more likely than use of a nuclear explosive device. An RDD combines a conventional explosive device—such as a bomb—with radioactive material. It is designed to scatter dangerous and sublethal amounts of radioactive material over a general area. Such RDDs appeal to terrorists because they require limited technical knowledge to build and deploy compared to a nuclear device. Also, the radioactive materials in RDDs are widely used in medicine, agriculture, industry and research, and are easier to obtain than weapons grade uranium or plutonium.

The primary purpose of terrorist use of an RDD is to cause psychological fear and economic disruption. Some devices could cause fatalities from exposure to radioactive materials. Depending on the speed at which the area of the RDD detonation was evacuated or how successful people were at sheltering-in-place, the number of deaths and injuries from an RDD might not be substantially greater than from a conventional bomb explosion.

The size of the affected area and the level of destruction caused by an RDD would depend on the sophistication and size of the conventional bomb, the type of radioactive material used, the quality and quantity of the radioactive material, and the local meteorological conditions—primarily wind and precipitation. The area affected could be placed off-limits to the public for several months during cleanup efforts.

Nuclear Blast: A nuclear blast is an explosion with intense light and heat, a damaging pressure wave, and widespread radioactive material that can contaminate the air, water, and ground surfaces for miles around. A nuclear device can range from a weapon carried by an intercontinental missile launched by a hostile nation or terrorist organization, to a small portable nuclear devise transported by an individual. All nuclear devices cause deadly effects when exploded, including blinding light, intense heat (thermal radiation), initial nuclear radiation, blast, fires started by the heat pulse, and secondary fires caused by the destruction.

The nuclear threat present during the Cold War has diminished; however, the possibility remains that a terrorist could obtain access to a nuclear weapon. Called improvised nuclear devices (INDs), these are generally smaller, less powerful weapons than we traditionally envision.

Explosives: Terrorists have frequently used explosive devices as one of their most common weapons. Terrorists do not have to look far to find out how to make explosive devices; the information is readily available in books and other information sources. Explosive devices can be highly portable, using vehicles and humans as a means of transport. They are easily detonated from remote locations or by suicide bombers.

Conventional bombs have been used to damage and destroy financial, political, social, and religious institutions. Attacks have occurred in public places and on city streets with thousands of people around the world injured and killed.

Source: U.S. Department of Homeland Security, "Terrorist Hazards."

of alerts that emergency responders deal with: tactical and strategic. A tactical alert is by far more common, and refers to alerts that pertain to information used to expediently resolve a situation or to temporarily gain an advantage while additional resources are brought to muster.

Numerous methods to deliver sensor data and alarm notifications are in place. These include Transmission Control Protocol (TCP) / Internet Protocol (IP), Web services, e-mail, and pushed Hypertext Markup Language (HTML). All data, messages, and notifications are delivered typically in DHS's Common Alerting Protocol (CAP) format, although conversion into other standard formats is enabled as needed for interoperability with

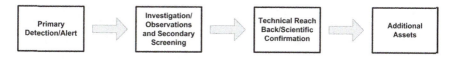

Figure 9.2   Strategic Alerts Process Illustration.

diverse systems. Message/alert brokering is performed through a variety of commercial companies and federal services.

On the other hand, strategic alerts are issued only in connection with planning and directing coordinated responses in larger operations. There is no formal playbook for strategic alerts; strategies differ depending on the nature of an incident.[2] However, chemical, radiological, or biological events for the most part follow National Incident Management System (NIMS) protocols. The best documented series of alerts are in radiation/nuclear detection. A simple concept of operations would involve four steps: (1) initial detection and alerting, (2) investigation and secondary screening, (3) technical reach-back and ancillary confirmation, and (4) deployment of additional assets. See Figure 9.2 for a process illustration.

Although the arrows in Figure 9.2 point to the right, it's important to note that shared information for this concept of operations must flow in both directions. The key is to utilize shared information across the organizations and federated levels in both directions and to reach out to extended resources, expertise, and decision contributors, and then to funnel the resulting assessments, resources, and advice back down to the incident managers and decision makers.

Detection Instrumentation Overview

Detection instrumentation is used to detect the various environmental hazards categorized in the CBRNE family. This instrumentation is very diverse in its use and sophistication and can span the gamut from small, handheld personal detectors to instruments capable of detecting specific gases from a mile away.

Table 9.2 provides a high-level overview of CBRNE detection technologies identified in the Federal Emergency Management Agency (FEMA)'s Authorized Equipment List (AEL) under category 07—Detection. Homeland security partners are permitted to use federal grants to purchase detection technologies that fit within these categories.

Table 9.2   CBRNE Detection Technologies

Title	Description
	Biological Detection
Kit, Field Assay	Field assay kit.
Detector, Optical	Handheld detector utilizing optical technology to discriminate between bacterial spores and benign material.
Kit, Protein Test	Protein test kit.
Analysis, DNA/RNA Detection	DNA/RNA detection analysis (example: PCR, ECL).
Kit, Biological Batch Sampling / Evidence Recovery	Biological batch sampling and evidence recovery kit. Collects samples for later analysis.
Sampler, Biological, Portable Air	Portable air sampler for biological sampling/ evidence.
Kit, Biological Sampling/ Evidence; Automated Perimeter Sampling Systems	Biological sampling/evidence kit; automated perimeter sampling systems.
	Chemical Detection
Strips, Classifier (pH, Waste Water, Chemical)	Waste water classifier strips, pH and chemical.
Detector, Flame Ionization (FID), Point, VOC	Flame ionization detector (FID) for point detection of volatile organic compounds (VOC).
Detector, Flame Photometry, Point, Chemical Agent	Flame photometry detector for point chemical agent detection.
Detector, Infrared Spectroscopy, Point, Chemical Agent	Point chemical agent detector utilizing infrared spectroscopy. These detectors may also have explosive detection capability when equipped with appropriate spectra libraries.
Detector, Multisensor Meter, Point, Chemical	Multisensor meter with minimum of O2 and LEL for point chemical detection.
Detector, Photo-Ionization (PID), Point, Volatile Organic Chemical (VOC)	Photo-ionization detector (PID) for point detection of volatile organic chemicals (VOC).
Detector, Raman Spectroscopy, Point, Chemical Agent	Point chemical agent detector utilizing Raman spectroscopy. These detectors may also have explosive detection capability when equipped with appropriate spectra libraries.

Detector, Ion Mobility Spectrometry, Point, Chemical Agent	Ion mobility spectrometry (IMS) or Differential Ion Mobility Spectrometry (DMS) detector for point chemical agent detection.
Detector, Surface Acoustic Wave (SAW), Point, Chemical Agent	Surface acoustic wave detector for point chemical agent detection.
Detector, Fourier Transform Infrared, Point, Chemical Agent	Point chemical agent detector utilizing infrared spectroscopy with Fourier Transform capability. These detectors may also have explosive detection capability when equipped with appropriate spectra libraries.
Paper, Indicating, (M-8)	Indicating paper, chemical warfare agent.
Tape, Indicating (M-9)	Indicating tape, chemical warfare agent.
Kit, Colorimetric Tape/Tube/Chip	Colorimetric tape/tube/chip kit specific for TICs and WMD applications.
Kit, Chemical Classifying	Chemical classifying kit for unknown liquids, solids, and vapors.
Kit, PCB Test	PCB test kit.
Kit, Mercury Test / Mercury Vapor Test	Mercury and mercury vapor test kit.
Kit, Chemical Agent Water Test	Chemical agent water test kit.
Kit, M-256(A1)	M-256(A1) detection kit for chemical agent (military grade; blister: HD/L; blood: AC/CK; and nerve: GB/VX) detection.
Detector, Single Chemical Sensor	Single gas meter with point chemical detection.
Detector, Reactive Polymer	Reactive polymer point chemical agent detector.
Detector, Spectroscopic, Laboratory, Chemical Agent	Laboratory-grade chemical detector using Raman spectroscopy, Fourier Transform Infrared (FTIR) spectroscopy, Laser-Induced Breakdown Spectroscopy (LIBS), or a combination of multiple types in a single device chassis.
Detector, Gas Chromatograph / Mass Spectrometer, Chemical Agent	Gas chromatograph and/or mass spectrometer detector for chemical agent detection (GC and/or MS).

Detector, Fixed Site, Chemical	Chemical detection devices designed to be mounted in buildings or on fixed exterior mounts that utilize infrared/vibrational detection technologies such as Fourier Transform Infrared (FT-IR) Raman, FT-IR/Raman, or photoacoustic infrared (PIR) for chemical detection.
Detector, Standoff, Chemical	Standoff chemical detector. FTIR system.
Kit, Air/Vapor Chemical Sampling	Air/vapor chemical sampling/evidence kit.
Kit, Liquid Chemical Sampling	Liquid chemical sampling/evidence kit.
Kit, Solid Chemical Sampling	Solid chemical sampling/evidence kit.

Explosive Detection

Canines, Explosive Detecting	Explosive detecting canines, related CBRNE training, protective equipment/garments, handling and training accessories. Includes transport accessories such as vehicle heat alarms.
Trace Detector, Explosive, Handheld	Handheld trace explosive detectors using air-sampling, particulate sampling, or dual mode operation. Underlying technology is Ion Mobility Spectrometry (IMS), Differential Ion Mobility Spectrometry (DMS) or equivalent.
Detector, Explosive, Infrared Spectroscopy	A transportable or handheld detector that utilizes infrared spectroscopy to detect explosive material. Examples include infrared (IR) and Fourier Transform Infrared (FTIR) devices.
Detector, Explosive, Laser-Based	A transportable or handheld detector that utilizes laser technology and spectral analysis to detect explosive material. Raman Spectroscopy and Laser Induced Breakdown Spectroscopy (LIBS) are examples of current technologies.
Portal, Explosive Detecting	Walk-through/drive-through explosives screening equipment. Sampling technologies include, but are not limited to Ion mobility spectrometry (IMS) and Mass Spectrometry (MS) for explosives detection, as well as X-ray/backscatter and millimeter wave for anomaly detection.

Swipe System, Trace Explosive Detection	An explosive detection system that utilizes cloths, papers, strips, or other media to wipe or otherwise contact a surface to collect a sample. The sampling medium is then placed in or near a device that detects/ identifies an explosive based upon its unique signature.
Detector, Explosive, Laser-Based, Standoff	A standoff explosive detector based upon active laser-based interrogation of targets from a distance using an unconfined laser beam. The laser-target interaction produces a spectral signature denoting the chemical composition of the target. Explosive materials exhibit unique spectral signatures.
Detector, Explosive, Passive, Standoff	An explosive detector that uses sensor-based passive interrogation of area targets from a distance to create a target image. Analyzing the spectral signature indicates the chemical nature of the unknown material.

Radiological Detection

Dosimeter, Personal	Personal dosimeter, including film, Thermoluminescence Dosimetry (TLD), and Optical Stimulated Luminescence (OSL).
Dosimeter, Self-Reading	Self-reading dosimeter (SRD) or pocket ionization chambers (PIC).
Dosimeter, Personal, Electronic	Electronic personal dosimeter (EPD).
Meter, Survey, Handheld	Handheld survey meter such as Geiger-Mueller (GM) meter or ionization chamber. Various probes allow detection of alpha, beta, beta/gamma, and neutron.
Detector, Radiation, Alarming, Personal (Gamma and Neutron)	Personal radiation (gamma and neutron) detection device which provides an alarm based on detection, but may not quantify dose-rate.
Identifier, Isotope, Radionuclide	Handheld spectrometer for nuclide identification using crystals such as NaI, CZT, LaBr, Boron Triflouride, and Germanium.
Detector, Radionuclide, High-Sensitivity	Radionuclide detector utilizing high-purity crystal such as germanium.

Detector, Elemental, Laser-Based, Standoff	A laser-based detector capable of detecting specific radioactive elements (uranium, plutonium, cesium, etc.) without immediate proximity to the target. Laser-Induced Breakdown Spectroscopy (LIBS) is the best example of current line-of-sight technology.
Detector, Gamma/Neutron, Standoff	A detector that can detect gamma/neutron radiation at a standoff distance of at least 50 feet and specify the type and location of radiation sources, while maintaining sufficient energy resolution and sensitivity to discriminate between normally-occurring radioactive materials, background, and potential threats.
Equipment, Air Sampling	Air flow calibrators for samplers. Personal air sampler. Area air sampler (high volume).

Source: U.S. Department of Homeland Security, *Authorized Equipment List (CSV File)*.

Incident Sensor Data Interoperability

In many circumstances, the data acquired from public safety sensors is vetted by either on-scene HAZMAT specialists or directly sent to remote SMEs. At this stage of the process, the data is in its raw format—appearing the same as the readings on the faceplate of the meter—because it is being viewed by specialists familiar with the instrument. If a condition warrants that an alert be disseminated for any reason, including the need for involvement of other experts, the local specialist has the option of either forwarding the raw reading with other alert information to others or just sending alarm and alert conditions.

Sensor analysis is performed using several methods and factors, such as the following:

- Remote display of raw sensor readings
- Filtering of raw data to only show alarm conditions
- Trend analysis showing sensor values over time (Note: Depending on the sensor, this can also be a trigger for alarm conditions when weighted averages need to be considered such as Short-Term Exposure Limits [STEL] or Time Weighed Averages [TWA].)
- Sensor readings integrated as part of a Geographic Information System (GIS)

Conducting this analysis requires interoperable sensor data or sensor data interoperability—sensor-to-sensor, sensor-to-user interface, and so on. Without wireless telemetric data transmission, sensor users face numerous challenges. One of the foremost problems is reading sensor values from an instrument's faceplate though several layers of fogged-up face masks. Another is the distraction of trying to read the instrument data while mitigating the hazard. Voice transmission of sensor values can also cause problems. Users may hold the transmit key down, inadvertently blocking instructions, and may misspeak vital data readings. There is also a risk of interception of sensitive information by an eavesdropper.

Further challenging the need for remote sensor data acquisition is the limited use of a standard data format, protocol, or connector associated with the instrument. In general, no two manufacturers handle data acquisition the same way. This problem can even be found across similar models of the same manufacturer.

Utilization of the Common Alerting Protocol

To overcome this problem, many systems convert the unformatted, nonstandard data into a structured standard format called the Common Alert Protocol (CAP), which enables reliable sensor information sharing. Through the use of a standard, systems designed to this specification will work together.

Developed by the Organization for the Advancement of Structured Information Standards, CAP is one of the most useful, familiar, and supported emergency management standards; it is the principal standard used for CBRNE systems communications. CAP has a large international presence and is used as a notification method by organizations such as the National Oceanic and Atmospheric Association for weather alerts; the U.S. Geological Service for seismic (earthquake) alerts; the Federal Communications Commission for emergencies; and a large variety of commercial, federal, and defense systems.

This federally approved standard gave the public safety community confidence that the information flowing from sensors and to sensor utilization applications was in a nonpropriety format. Utilizing CAP and other Emergency Data Exchange Language (EDXL) standards, such as the Distribution Element (EDXL-DE), the sensor data can be packaged with other information representing the associated hazards of the incident and routed to the appropriate users based on policies and geospatial coordinates.

CAP was carefully studied to determine what was minimally needed to maintain the standard knowing that bandwidth would be a consideration in any wireless deployment. Initially the "Headline" was picked as the most data-efficient element within CAP to transport sensor information. As working knowledge of CAP matured, so has the utilization of sensor data in CAP, which now utilizes the "Parameter" fields.

Alert messaging standards for the public safety sector are rapidly converging around the CAP standard. The judicious use of this CAP message can provide a convenient alert and messaging mechanism for sensor data.

The CAP used for CBRNE detection is an extended message that contains the actual summary data and alert status of the sensor(s). The data is contained in the <Parameter> tag in a comma delimited text string. The sensor data is therefore not readable by users unacquainted with the data string. However, for the community of users that require the data, it is easily read by specific applications attached to their situational awareness tools. The message is relatively short and fits easily into small, dedicated applications on handheld devices.

Revisiting the Los Angeles Case Study

HAZMAT responders in Los Angeles County have historically used hand-carried sensors or meters with visual displays when probing HAZMAT environments. Typically, they read the integrated display meters' readings over voice radio links to their deployed mobile communication centers. The difficulty of this operation is that they have to manually initiate voice calls to SMEs at the communications center and relay sensor meter readings via voice radio. The HAZMAT SME interprets these readings to detect the agent(s) present and to determine if the environment is dangerous for the sensor-equipped personnel or any human, plant, or animal potentially threatened by the incident.

Los Angeles HAZMAT responders desired the capability to automatically transmit sensor data from responders operating in a "hot" zone to an apparatus located in a "cold" zone. In researching potential sensors, the region discovered that each sensor was putting out data in a different format, complicating efforts to attain a common operating picture among various response organizations. Rather than requiring each response organization to purchase new software from a single vendor, Los Angeles HAZMAT responders identified the use of common communications and information standards, CAP and EDXL-DE, as the solution to ensure common data was produced from all monitoring devices.

Los Angeles County HAZMAT officials added an 802.11 WLAN and cellular capability to their sensors and sensor networks. By formatting with CAP in the EDXL-DE framework, a continuous standardized data feed has been provided from the sensor to the nearby mobile command center. The HAZMAT SME aboard the vehicle is then able to monitor the sensor output without relying on the engaged responder and can warn them via voice radio. This data can also be distributed over wireless networks to provide wide-area situational awareness, enabling greater responder safety awareness, better-informed command decisions, and timelier public alerting.

These anticipated benefits of CAP are being realized within the scope of the Los Angeles County HAZMAT data networking implementation. Responders have reported a substantial increase in their operational capability as a result of this effort.

CBRNE detection systems have been utilized in support of many large-scale disasters and planned events, including those listed below:

* American Music Awards, Los Angeles, California (2011–2012)
* Arizona Wildfires (2012)
* Boston, Massachusetts, Marathon (2011–2013)
* Democratic National Convention, Charlotte, North Carolina (2012)
* Emmy Awards, Los Angeles, California (2008–2012)
* Fukushima (Japan) Nuclear Disaster (2011)
* Joplin, Missouri, Tornado (2011)
* National Football League (NFL) Pro Bowl, Honolulu, Hawaii (2012)
* New Jersey Train Derailment (2012)
* Olympic Pre-Trials (2012)
* Republication National Convention, Baltimore, Maryland (2012)
* Rose Bowl Parade, Pasadena, California (2010–2013)
* Special Olympics, Los Angeles, California (2015)
* Super Bowl XLVII, New Orleans, Louisiana (2013)
* Superstorm Sandy, 2012
* U.S. Presidential Inauguration, Washington, DC (2013)
* West Texas Fertilizer Explosion (2013)

The New Year's Day Rose Bowl game was attended by more than 96,000 fans and provided an opportunity to deploy a full complement of radiation and chemical detection systems. Radiation portals were set up in a side scan configuration at each ticket entrance. Wireless MESH/wireless fidelity (Wi-Fi) portable repeaters were set on top of roofs at various support buildings surrounding the bowl forming a daisy chain path for data to travel back to the command vehicle. Mobile point source and standoff chemical detection systems were mounted to two six-wheel gators that drove the bowl perimeter relaying data back to the command area. Data was also exchanged between the Integrated Chemical, Biological, Radiological,

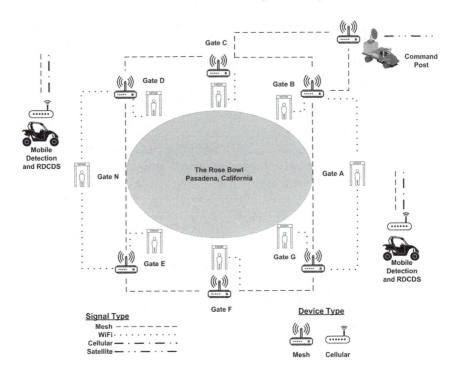

Figure 9.3   New Year's Day Rose Bowl Game Deployment Conceptualization.

Nuclear, and Explosives (ICBRNE) program and the DHS/Sandia Rapid Deployable Chemical Detection System (RDCDS) that had 12 chemical warfare agent detection systems located both inside and outside the Rose Bowl. See Figure 9.3 for a conceptualization of the game day configuration.

Sensor-Map Integration

As the CBRNE interoperability grows, the evolution of contextual information becomes more important. Today, users want the ability of knowing where their sensor information is coming from so they can start correlating data about the incident.

To accomplish the location component, global positioning system (GPS) receivers have been added to the wireless telemetry feeds coming from most of the instrumentation. This GPS feed is specific for the instrument that has matured from a grouped-based GPS location, which was originally provided the same GPS feed for the instrumentation at a specific location. With independent GPS feeds, specific users and/or specific instruments can be tracked as independent sources.

With the use of map-based data, consideration of the origin of the maps is a very important component. Currently, there are two map sources. The first map source is a live Internet-based map such as Google or Bing. The second source is a more permanent or reliable software platform installed on the personal computer used to view the data such as an ESRI product or MapPoint.

The availability of an Internet connection may determine the map source. Users who could potentially go off-line or want to use the system in a completely local network should consider local permanent maps. Users who have the ability of going to the Internet to acquire data and feel that this connection will be appropriately robust should consider live map feeds. For the map component, data is available in a variety of protocols, including a direct Keyhold Markup Language (KML) or Geographically Encoded Objects for Really Simple Syndication (GeoRSS) feed.

Two types of maps are typically used for CBRNE interoperability—an instrument-specific map and a regional map. The instrument-specific map provides a view of the exact instrument location. Often it is particularly useful to identify the location of the instrument as opposed to viewing the complete group of all instruments. In the regional or group view, all instruments can be viewed concurrently on one map; however, since sensor instruments can be located all over a city, region, state, or nation, the zoom-level and perspective of the map must be considered in relation to where the sensors are located.

Alerting and Notification

A component of several CBRNE detection systems is the ability to alert and notify in relation to CBRNE events. This process utilizes developed policies to filter automated messages generated from detection instrumentation. Once filtered, these messages are broadcasted to a subscription list of emergency responders. Manual operation of this system is also provided. Delivery options include short message service (SMS), e-mail, text-to-speech, and fax. Most data exchanged with the CBRNE detection systems follow strict adherence to federally endorsed open standards. Alert messaging specifically utilizes the CAP standard, which defines the minimal necessary data elements to clearly define an alert. For CBRNE-based alerts, it is necessary that the message also contains information about the substance detected. In addition to required minimal fields, the following four items were added to the alert message:

- **Detection Type:** This field designates the substance being detected, such as radiation, ammonia, or nerve/blister agent.
- **Reading:** This field includes the alphanumeric amount of the substance being monitored.
- **Units:** This field represents the quantity of the substance being measured.
- **Alert Color:** This field indicates the severity of the combination of the substance monitored and its readings and units. Typically, Red indicates an alarm condition, Yellow indicates a warning for radiation only, and Green indicates a safe condition. These trigger points are typically provided by SMEs for radiation values and industry exposure limits as established by the National Institute for Occupational Safety and Health (NIOSH) for chemicals. These threshold values exist within an administrative password-protected window and are typically configured at the time a new instrument is brought online.

Policies may be created to determine who gets what alert and notification, and under what circumstances. Alerts and notifications are generated by creating a policy for one or more of the rules listed below:

1. **No Filter:** All data is available. All information received from the server will be pushed out to subscribers of this group. No special filtering will be applied. This is a pass through service.
2. **Pre-Filter:** This filter provides for the creation of subgroups based on the CAP "incident" field.
3. **In-Test Filter:** The CAP field "Status" is monitored, and data with this field set to "test" is disregarded.
4. **Extreme Alert Filter:** All data is disregarded unless the CAP field of "Severity" is set to Extreme.
5. **Geographical Alert Filter:** Associated with the Test filter, all registered users in a geographical area defined by a polygon wherein an alert is occurring receive the notification.
6. **Agent Alert Filter:** Specific sensor types will trigger an alert grouping as defined in number four.
7. **Multiple Detection Filter:** Multiple instrument alarms coming from the same location will trigger an alert grouping as defined in number four.

Tools and Services

This section provides an overview of common tools and services that support operation of CBRNE detection systems.

Wireless Communications

There are two common ways of sending wireless sensor data from point A to point B: One way is telemetry and the other is through a network. The telemetry typically involves a process wherein each point sequentially interrogates each other point for the exchange of data. A network connection can almost be considered a continuous exchange of data between all devices on the network. Also note that a network connection can be routed across other network devices to extend the range, which includes utilization of tools such as the Internet.

Network Devices

A network device arbitrates data as it passes through it. These devices are routers, switches, cellular modems, access points, gateways, serial servers, and satellite terminals. The data-sharing requirements of several CBRNE detection systems require data to be routed through the Internet. To accomplish this requirement, most end points utilize a cellular connection. Cellular has the benefit of being the most pervasive and cost-effective network available, but it does not offer the same level of a guarantee of service as a private, proprietary wireless network.

Sensor Views[3]

Two primary views of the sensor data worked best for the majority of users in the ICBRNE program: the Subject Matter Expert (SME) View and the Emergency Manager (EM) View. The SME View recreated an exact replica of the meter displays on the computer screen. This design has many benefits. SMEs are trained with their meters, so there is no extra training required to understand the computer displays. The sensor manufacturers' meter displays become de facto standards of their own, and the reuse of the designs leverages their lessons learned. SMEs require that meter views display specific sensor data for specific sensors. The meter displays can be viewed individually or multiple meters may be displayed on one screen, if necessary.

The second primary view is the Emergency Manager (EM) View. Emergency managers have a more holistic and broader perspective than the SMEs, so they need a map of the region with highlighted areas and points that describe the sensor readings from a region-wide perspective. The goal is situational awareness derived from multiple sensor detections to guide management of the entire region.

Both views, SME and EM, can be delivered to any location in near real time, whether in the back of a fire truck, on a mobile device, or on a desktop anywhere in the region or around the world. The views are accessible through a variety of installed commercial software viewers as well as through a user's browser without any additional installation of software. Although technical details are not addressed in this chapter, it's important to understand the flexibility of these visualizations and the implied inter-operability with a variety of commercial tools that are enabled by utilizing open standards and open architectures; these allow for conversion of sensor information into a variety of standard formats. The following sections go into some depth on both kinds of views to help the reader better understand the ICBRNE program.

SME Views

The basic SME View is the actual meter readings that are shown on the remote computer display. Note that both the actual meter and SME View displays are formatted in the same manner with three columns, the first being the chemical label, the second being the values, and the third column being the units. A Multi-Meter SME View is available for SMEs who want to view numerous instruments that are operational at any one time. This Multi-Meter SME View is automated and dynamic. In this view, meters appear and disappear as they go on- and off-line, and the meters shrink in size as needed to fit the overall display size. Filters can be selected to view meters by incident, user, or instrument type. The Basic SME Web View is another form of viewing the meter emulations on a desktop display or on a cell phone or tablet.

EM Views

The Basic EM View is the regional map display. The characteristics of these views include a regional map, sensor-derived situational awareness, sensor readings in context, and "at a glance" situational awareness. As with the SME Views, these EM Views are available via installable commercial software as well as Web browser-based displays. The same flexibility and interoperability are enabled through the use of open standards and open architectures.

First Responder Safety

The ability to move and share information through the use of CBRNE detection systems offers several significant safety enhancements. CBRNE responders have considerable challenges trying to see instrumentation readings through layers of face masks. High humidity levels typically fog up the lenses, making the small readings from the faceplates even more difficult to read. The CBRNE detection systems can capture the instrument's readings in real time and display them remotely as a replica of the instrument's display. This data is monitored by trained CBRNE technical representatives assisting during the response.

CBRNE instrumentation users can also have difficulty accurately reporting the correct data wherein it is easy to misreport units or decimal points. Care should also be taken when verbally reporting incident sensor data over potentially open or easily monitored radio communications. The CBRNE detection system's architecture transmits live digital data eliminating the potential of changing a unit or decimal place such as 0.10 parts per million (ppm) as 0.01 ppm.

Integration with Plumes

Often the CBRNE instrumentation is used as part of a plume tool. These tools are used to model the direction and magnitude of the agent. Several CBRNE detection systems have interfaced with different plume tools, including one that is created as a result of a detection, one that uses the sensor readings as part of its plume algorithm, and another that integrates sensor detections into its model.

Conclusion

The partnerships borne of necessity in fighting wildfires created the demand for standards-based information sharing and communications capabilities in the Los Angeles region. CBRNE detection systems implemented for planned events, for responding to large-scale disasters, and for other purposes demonstrates the expanded capability to share information among homeland security partners in the region. Both on-scene responders and remote management facilities can receive the same HAZMAT sensor readings and alerts, and distribute situational awareness as appropriate.

The concept of CBRNE detection technology exemplifies effective interoperability wherein decisions and subsequent actions are a result of systems working together. Regardless of the sophistication of the sensor itself, the utilization of the sensor's readings are based on the effective workings of a system and cumulative sequence of events that permits the recipient to act with confidence on the data they are receiving. This chapter introduced the threats associated with CBRNE, the instrumentation used to sense environmental hazards, the policies associated with hazard information dissemination, the methods for collecting and distributing

CBRNE information, and how these systems are implemented in the field. In total, these systems provide enhanced safety solutions both for public safety and the people they protect.

Discussion Questions

1. Responding to HAZMAT incidents requires donning of personal protective equipment (PPE) that often limits the visibility of the responder and hinders the usability of equipment. How do emerging CBRNE detection systems help to maintain capabilities despite the challenges associated with operating in a "hot" zone?

2. Plans and procedures for responding to a HAZMAT incident requires the involvement of specialized teams and technical specialists operating within the Operations Section, technical specialists operating in support of the incident command, and emergency managers and other key decision makers providing coordination support. What design features of a CBRNE detection system may be modified to support various functions performed at the incident scene and within the incident command and coordination structure?

3. You have been tasked to oversee the development of a grant proposal for the city to support future year homeland security priorities. After working through the Threat and Hazard Identification and Risk Assessment (THIRA) process, the accidental or intentional release of hazardous substances surfaced as a high priority hazard/threat for the city. Specifically, the many large-scale planned events each year was cited as concern in the THIRA context. What requirements for a CBRNE detection system would you cite both in the grant proposal and then in a formal solicitation or Request for Proposal (RFP) for commercial vendors?

Notes

1. The authors investigated and arrived at many findings presented in this chapter relating to the Los Angeles case study in a previous project sponsored by the Federal Emergency Management Agency, U.S. Department of Homeland Security. (Source: Federal Emergency Management Agency. *NIMS Standards Case Study: Los Angeles Regional Interoperability.* Washington, DC: Federal Emergency Management Agency. 2008. https://www.fema.gov/txt/emergency/nims/Los_Angeles _CAP%20EDXL.txt.)

2. The U.S. Department of Homeland Security's Domestic Nuclear Detection Office in conjunction with the Los Angeles Secure the Cities program is completing a formal radiological/nuclear operational plan (July 2015).

3. This section references the U.S. Department of Homeland Security Science and Technology Integrated Chemical, Biological, Radiological, Nuclear, and Explosives (ICBRNE) Program's utilization of the Safe Environment Engineering's CBRNE detection system.

Bibliography

Federal Emergency Management Agency. *Authorized Equipment List (CSV File).* Washington, DC: U.S. Department of Homeland Security. https://www.fema.gov/authorized-equipment-list.

Federal Emergency Management Agency. *NIMS Standards Case Study: Los Angeles Regional Interoperability.* Washington, DC: Federal Emergency Management Agency. 2008. https://www.fema.gov/txt/emergency/nims/Los_Angeles_CAP%20EDXL.txt.

U.S. Department of Homeland Security. "Prepare for Emergencies." *Ready.gov.* Accessed February 2016. https://www.ready.gov/prepare-for-emergencies.

CHAPTER TEN

Public Safety Communications

The Technology behind the Call

Jay English

Learning Objectives

After reading this chapter, readers should be able to:

- Explain the basic functions of the 9-1-1 system in the United States and types of 9-1-1 calls.
- Explain the purpose of and functions performed by Public Safety Answering Points (PSAPs).
- Identify and explain positions within a PSAP.
- Explain requirements for locating an emergency caller.
- Distinguish the routing of traditional wireline and wireless 9-1-1 calls.
- Distinguish between Phase I and Phase II wireless calls to 9-1-1.
- Assess challenges associated with implementing Internet Protocol (IP)-based emergency communications systems such as Voice over Internet Protocol (VoIP).
- Identify and explain emergency notification systems (ENS) and additional systems used by PSAPs.
- Summarize processes and radio systems used by PSAPs to communicate with responders.
- Compare and contrast emerging technologies such as Next Generation (NG) 9-1-1 to more traditional emergency communications systems.

Key Terms

Computer Aided Dispatch (CAD)
Emergency Communications
Emergency Communications Enterprise
Emergency Notification Systems (ENS)
Enhanced 9-1-1 (E9-1-1)
Next Generation (NG) 9-1-1
9-1-1 Network
9-1-1 System
Public Safety Answer Point (PSAP)
Telecommunicators
Voice over Internet Protocol (VoIP)
Wireless Service Provider (WSP)

Introduction

"9-1-1, WHERE IS YOUR EMERGENCY?" This is a phrase repeated by public safety telecommunicators more than 240 million times a year in the United States.[1] The first 9-1-1 emergency phone call was reported to have occurred in 1968 between two elected officials from Alabama; U.S. Rep. Tom Bevill supposedly answered the call with "Hello."[2] From this point forward, 9-1-1 began the journey to a nationwide, ubiquitous number for all emergency assistance.

America's 9-1-1 and emergency communications centers are a key element in the overall security of the Nation. Combined, they enable a bidirectional flow of information among homeland security partners and they enable response in times of crisis while contributing to continuity of communications and operations.

Each time a call is made to 9-1-1, a complex system of communications devices, networks, and protocols is invoked to transport the call to the appropriate Public Safety Answering Point (PSAP) within seconds of dialing these three well-known digits. The end result of this capability is that lifesaving resources in the form of law enforcement, fire, and/or emergency medical services (EMS) can be dispatched to the caller to assist with whatever emergency he or she is experiencing. In other words, 9-1-1 saves lives. This chapter examines the progress 9-1-1 systems have made and their impact on homeland security partners. The basic construct of a 9-1-1 network is discussed and how it works to include both wired and wireless systems as well as systems internal to PSAPs. Once a basic understanding of 9-1-1 and PSAP operations is established, the transition to Internet protocol (IP)-based, multimedia capable systems is explored along with the new capabilities, and challenges, they bring to public safety. Finally, the interfaces between the citizens, PSAPs, and homeland security partners are discussed that illustrate the influence that emerging technologies will have on the emergency communications enterprise as a whole.

What Is a PSAP?

A PSAP is an agency that receives 9-1-1 emergency calls for a predefined geographic area and disseminates those calls according to the policy of the governing 9-1-1 authority (e.g., local, state, or other). PSAP operations differ between agencies and regions to the point that a common saying in the industry is "if you've seen one PSAP, you've seen one PSAP." PSAPs are divided into two basic categories, primary and secondary. Primary PSAPs receive 9-1-1 calls directly from the local telephone switch. These facilities are the first to speak directly to a 9-1-1 caller and generally gather the information required to determine the location and nature of the emergency. After a 9-1-1 call is received at a primary PSAP, it may be transferred to another agency for further processing. The agency to which the 9-1-1 call is transferred is a secondary PSAP. How and when a call is transferred to a secondary PSAP depends on local policies. Whether primary or secondary, all PSAPs answer 9-1-1 calls, determine the location and nature of the incident, and prepare an initial incident record to determine what kind of help will be needed and where to send it. It is important to note that not all PSAPs fulfill the complete roles of call taking and dispatch; in the majority of smaller and medium-sized PSAPs, the PSAP serves as both the call answering and the dispatch agency.

Whether serving only the call answering function, or acting as both call takers and dispatchers, PSAPs receive calls and create incident records that usually require response by emergency services. The primary disciplines for emergency response are law enforcement, fire, and EMS. In addition to gathering information for, and providing information to, primary responders, PSAPs and dispatch centers also provide communications support to a number of secondary responders. Secondary responders that routinely interface with PSAPs include, but are not limited to, transportation departments, tow companies, emergency management agencies, emergency operations centers, hospitals, poison control centers, disaster relief organizations (e.g., American Red Cross), and other private sector and government agencies in accordance with local policies.

Personnel operating at PSAPs require specific skill sets that must be developed to support homeland security partners. For this reason, and because the telecommunicator is the first voice a caller hears when in need, today's public safety telecommunicators are truly America's first, first responders. As technologies evolve, this role will become even more connected to homeland security partners in the future.

PSAP Roles and Responsibilities

Call Takers/Telecommunicators

Personnel who receive and process incoming emergency calls are the front line of emergency communications. The professional designation of this position varies, but they are generally referred to as call takers or public safety telecommunicators. These individuals not only handle the incoming 9-1-1 calls, but also routinely handle nonemergency or administrative calls sometimes for multiple agencies. As a first step in any 9-1-1 call, it is crucial that the telecommunicator gather some basic information to locate the caller and assess and classify the situation in order to determine what resources to dispatch. The information gathered by the initial call taker generally includes location, contact information and callback number, the nature of the emergency (i.e., police, fire, or EMS), the caller's name, and any critical details (e.g., suspect descriptions, medical status, weapons, hazards to responders). Once enough information is gathered to determine what the nature of the emergency is, who to send, and where to send them, the call will generally progress to a dispatcher.

Note that there is an emerging, and important, discipline within the call-taking realm known as Emergency Medical Dispatch (EMD). This discipline consists of a combination of questions to determine the nature of the medical emergency, the status of the patient, and medically approved and predefined prearrival instructions. The development of a standardized EMD program was undertaken by the U.S. Department of Transportation under the National Highway Traffic Safety Administration (NHTSA). The following description is extracted from the NHTSA EMD Manager's Guide:

> The goal of emergency medical dispatch is to make sure that the right kind of care is given to the right patient at the right time. Today's emergency medical dispatchers are trained to interrogate callers in order to identify the nature and severity of the emergency; allocate the EMS system's resources, and give post-dispatch prearrival emergency care instructions to callers. Methods of EMD vary dramatically from place to place, depending on the

EMS assets available and the level of training and expertise of the EMD. Tomorrow's emergency medical dispatchers will be taking on expanded roles as the field of emergency medical dispatch matures. As 9-1-1 and 9-1-1 Enhanced telephone systems reach into more and more communities, the emergency medical dispatch industry will identify new and valuable roles that it can fill to meet the growing needs of the communities it serves.[3]

Dispatchers

Once the call taker has enough information to classify the call and determine the appropriate response, he or she will notify the dispatcher of the call usually via Computer Aided Dispatch (CAD) systems. The dispatcher is responsible for disseminating emergency calls to police, fire, or EMS responders. This is typically done via radio system in combination with mobile data terminals. In many small PSAPs, the responsibility for call taking and dispatch are assigned to a single individual.

Supervisors

Supervisors at agencies large enough to have a distributed management structure are the personnel who oversee and manage the daily operations at a PSAP. Medium and large PSAPs often have supervisors assigned to each duty shift. Larger PSAPs may have multiple supervisors assigned to other duties such as training and technology. Smaller PSAPs often function with only one manager who acts as the supervisor of the overall operation, and they generally rely on individual telecommunicators and dispatchers to manage daily operations during their shifts. It is often the supervisor who is responsible for training new recruits, for quality control functions in both call taking and dispatching disciplines, for handling basic public complaints, and for interfacing with field supervisors from the various agencies served by the PSAP. This model varies widely from PSAP to PSAP.

Ancillary Positions

Usually the medium- to larger-sized PSAPs have personnel assigned to positions to manage tactical channels, major incidents, motor vehicle data, or other duties such as tow requests and warrant checks. In smaller agencies, all of these duties are still required, but they are carried out by on-duty personnel who are responsible for many, if not all, PSAP functions required during their respective shifts.

As the reader may conclude from the various duties performed in PSAPs, they are busy places, regardless of size or staffing. PSAPs are generally classified by their size (i.e., number of seats or positions within the PSAP). The sizing schema is organized as follows:

- Small PSAP: 5 or fewer seats
- Medium PSAP: 6 to 49 seats
- Large PSAP: 50 or more seats

It is estimated that 80 percent of PSAPs in the United States are considered "small" and contain five positions or less. In these PSAPs, a single individual may answer phone calls, dispatch emergency units, and perform all of the administrative and ancillary tasks discussed previously in this chapter. In many cases, even small PSAPs are responsible for taking 9-1-1 calls and dispatching resources for multiple homeland security partners. Medium and large PSAPs are often responsible for dispatch of multiple homeland security partners and have annual call volumes that may number into the millions of calls per center per year. For example, the City of New York PSAP averages 11 million calls per year.[4]

Given the amount of work that must be done by any PSAP, regardless of size, some PSAPs and jurisdictions have begun to move toward one of several types of consolidations. Co-location consolidation is accomplished when multiple homeland security partners share common facility but maintain separate call-taking and dispatch capabilities and functions. Virtual consolidation occurs when multiple PSAPs and/or agencies are connected via secure networks and share certain services. Full consolidation occurs when multiple homeland security partners from different disciplines share a common facility and share all call-taking and dispatch functions. Multipurpose consolidation, which is less common though becoming more popular, occurs when public safety and nonpublic safety agencies share a common facility, networks, systems, and technologies. Now that the basic function and construct of a PSAP along with some of the particular duties involved to support daily operations have been established, it is time to discuss the technologies behind 9-1-1 calls and emergency communications.

How Calls Get to PSAPs

Landline calls are the first mechanism for which 9-1-1 systems were designed. Many people think that as soon as they dial 9-1-1 the call proceeds directly to the local PSAP. This is far from the reality of how a basic landline call makes its way from a caller to a 9-1-1 call taker.

A landline or wireline connection is a method of transporting either an electrical or light signal via copper wire or optical fiber, respectively, over the Public Switched Telephone Network (PSTN) and terminates at a specific customer location assigned a unique telephone number. When a customer dials 9-1-1 from the landline phone, the phone company recognizes 9-1-1 as the number dialed. It then inspects the caller identification (Caller ID) known as the Automatic Number Identifier (ANI) assigned to the phone placing the 9-1-1 call, and routes the call to the dedicated 9-1-1 Tandem—the selective router serving the local network. The selective router uses the ANI to determine which PSAP should receive the call. The mapping of the caller's ANI to the serving PSAP is determined in advance of the call typically during service provisioning.

There are two "types" of landline 9-1-1 calls. Basic 9-1-1 connects the caller to the appropriate PSAP, but provides only audio data (voice) to the PSAP. No additional caller information is sent with a basic 9-1-1 call. Enhanced 9-1-1 (E9-1-1) includes both the audio portion of the call as well as the calling party's telephone number and their physical location, expressed as a civic address. The E9-1-1 location is validated against a Master Street Address Guide (MSAG). The MSAG is a database that describes the exact spelling of streets, street number ranges, and other address elements. All addresses entered into Automatic Location Identification (ALI) databases must be validated against the MSAG for the region in which the address is located. MSAG addresses are in civic address format. The community name associated with an address is assigned by the 9-1-1 addressing authority and may not be the same as the community name assigned by the U.S. Postal Service. Addresses in the MSAG are also associated with a field called the Emergency Service Number (ESN). Each ESN is assigned to a specific geographic area—sometimes referred to as an emergency service zone—within a PSAP's jurisdiction. The telephone switching equipment uses the ESN to identify the correct PSAP for routing a 9-1-1 call.

Once the call has been properly identified and located, it is routed to the PSAP via the selective router based on the flow previously detailed. The selective router, which is typically provided by the local incumbent carrier (LEC), serves as a tandem switch in the 9-1-1 network. At a basic level, the selective router uses logic and data from other network elements to route a 9-1-1 call to the appropriate PSAP.

During a 9-1-1 call, the caller's phone number, also referred to as the ANI, is passed to the PSAP. The PSAP equipment automatically uses the ANI to look up the associated address in an ALI database. PSAP equipment, in conjunction with the services just described, will look up the location information in conjunction with the initial delivery of the 9-1-1 call. This lookup function is commonly referred to as an "ALI dip." The ANI and ALI are then displayed on a computer screen at the PSAP. A common display includes the caller's phone number, address, and Class of Service (COS), which is the type of phone service being used to call 9-1-1. Some common COS values are Residential (RESD), Business (BUSN), Multiline (e.g., MLTS, CNTX, OPX, PBX), Wireless Phase 1 or 2 (WPH1 or WPH2), and Voice over Internet Protocol (VoIP).

A landline call to 9-1-1 is known as fixed/static access, which refers to a geographic location or civic address that is mapped to a specific access point. For this reason, a landline call is the easiest to process and to obtain a dispatchable location. Conversely, wireless calls are not made from fixed locations; the geographic locations from cell phones and smartphones, for example, change even during the 9-1-1 call itself in some circumstances. Wireless services offered to the public are classified by the Federal Communications Commission (FCC) as Commercial Mobile Radio Service (CMRS), "a designation for any wireless carrier or license owner whose wireless service is connected to the PSTN and/or is operated for profit, and is available to the public."[5] Voice calls are routed over cellular radio networks—Code Division Multiple Access (CDMA), Global System for Mobile Communications (GSM), and Universal Mobile Telecommunications System (UMTS)—via a mobile switching center (MSC) and based on the location of the caller.

Long-Term Evolution (LTE) is also becoming widely deployed; however, at the time of this writing LTE is limited to data transport only. Specifications are currently in development by the 3rd Generation Partnership Project (3GPP), an international standards body, to facilitate Voice over LTE (VoLTE); however, the service has not yet deployed. Wireless 9-1-1 call routing is based on the location of the cell tower that transmits the call to the PSAP; cell towers can be omnidirectional or may be divided into sectors.

The destination PSAP for each tower or cell sector is predefined by the PSAP in conjunction with the wireless service provider (WSP). WSPs are commonly referred to as cell phone companies or cell service providers. Examples in the United States include AT&T, Verizon, T-Mobile, and Sprint. The WSP works with the mobile positioning center (MPC) vendor who updates this routing information in the appropriate ALI database. As illustrated in Figure 10.1, wireless calls are a great deal more complex than wireline calls. An originating cell site/sector has a static address assigned to it, which is MSAG valid and verified/registered by the governing authority. The system utilizes a number of interfaces and technologies to determine the appropriate destination PSAP. These functions are all part of the

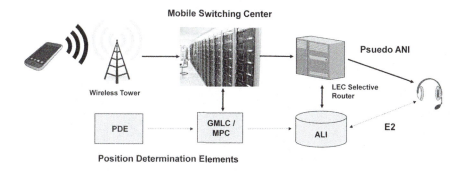

Figure 10.1   Wireless 9-1-1 Call.

intricate communication that takes place internal to the MSC, MPC, the selective router, and the PSAP.

It is important to note that there are two types of wireless calls to 9-1-1: Phase I and Phase II. Phase I (COS WPH1) calls deliver locations as a cell site sector. The latitude and longitude of the tower or cell sector centroid may also be provided.

Phase II (COS WPH2) calls display the MSAG valid address of the cell tower that delivered the 9-1-1 voice call. The latitude and longitude of the caller is also provided using a combination of technologies, including global positioning system (GPS) hardware and software, assisted GPS, Time Delay of Arrival (TDOA), and other triangulation methods; see Figure 10.2. Basically, either a signal is acquired from a number of satellites in geosynchronous orbit, with triangulation calculated based on the combined returned data (i.e., GPS), or active radio signals are measured for the time it takes them to arrive at, and return from, multiple tower locations (i.e., TDOA). Regardless of the method used, outdoor location is more easily obtained, and generally more accurate, than indoor location for wireless calls. According to the National Emergency Number Association (NENA), 99 percent of PSAPs have at least some Phase I capabilities, 98.1 percent of PSAPs have some Phase II, 96.9 percent of counties in the United States have some Phase I, and 95.7 percent of counties have some Phase II capabilities.[6]

The voice portion of the call may arrive at the PSAP before a Phase II location is provided and callers are often mobile during the 9-1-1 call. Wireless calls are routed based on Phase I data to ensure speedy delivery of the call to the PSAP. Upon initial receipt of a wireless call, the PSAP has the capability to perform a "rebid" to obtain Phase II location information. APCO and NENA have both published documents encouraging PSAPs to

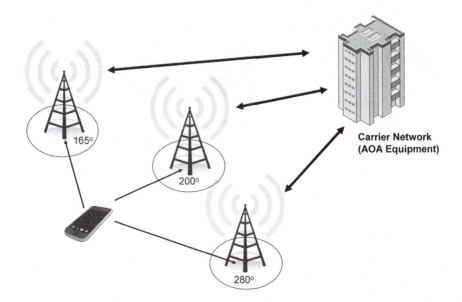

Figure 10.2   Example of Time Delay of Arrival.

rebid early and rebid often to ensure accurate initial and updated location for wireless callers. When used properly, Phase II wireless provides a much better location estimate to the PSAP.

VoIP is a newer technology utilizing IP transport in lieu of traditional circuit switched systems. Interconnected VoIP service is defined by the FCC as "bearing the following characteristics: the service enables real-time, two-way voice communications; the service requires a broadband connection from the user's location; the service requires IP-compatible customer premise equipment (CPE); and the service permits users to generally receive calls that originate on the PSTN and to terminate calls to the PSTN."[7] Basically, a VoIP call is a communication service that originates or terminates via IP networks rather than the circuit switched PSTN.

For a VoIP call to reach 9-1-1, a VoIP Position Center (VPC) determines which selective router and PSAP will receive a VoIP call. The VPC maintains the call information, caller location information, ESN, and dynamic ALI records. The destination PSAP for VoIP 9-1-1 calls is predetermined by the PSAP in conjunction with the VSP. The VPC uses an emergency service query key (ESQK) to route calls to the correct PSAP. One of the major challenges in implementing VoIP service for 9-1-1 is the nomadic nature of VoIP telephones and devices. According to the Communications Security,

Reliability, and Interoperability Council, "Nomadic access refers to multiple locations for connection points / calling devices. A common example is a VoIP service that can be registered at a primary residence and updated when the caller is staying at their vacation home. Nomadic devices are not mobile and thus cannot update their registered location during a 9-1-1 call."[8]

There are additional VoIP services that cannot "call" or reach 9-1-1. Over-the-top (OTT) voice services—Yahoo Instant Messenger (IM), Skype, Google Voice, Gizmo, Oovoo, and others—may be implemented as software applications that are not capable of connecting the user directly with 9-1-1. As discussed previously, the 9-1-1 architecture is generally a "closed loop" and requires access permission as well as conformance to accepted standards for 9-1-1 voice and location data. The OTT applications do not provide a voice path, data path, or caller location. As a result, the OTT application providers are required to inform the public that they may not use the application to contact 9-1-1.

As should be obvious to the reader by now, it is important to have standards by which this type of information flow can be guided. There are a number of standards development organizations in the United States that are engaged in such work specifically as it relates to public safety and emergency communications. APCO, NENA, the Alliance for Telecommunications Industry Solutions, and other organizations such as the National Fire Protection Association are all actively involved in writing standards related to data controls, network flow, network elements, and data transfer in the emergency communications realm. Creation of and adherence to standards helps to ensure interoperability as technology progresses. It is also important to note that all standards in the United States are voluntary. Therefore, while standards may exist, not all vendors and service providers will comply with them. This is an important consideration for public safety agencies when creating Requests for Proposal to solicit bids from potential suppliers. In the event a vendor chooses not to comply with established standards, the agency should be prepared to ask some detailed questions as to why, and how that particular vendor intends to meet the intent, if not the letter, of the standards in question. In some cases, such as the Project 25 (P25) radio interoperability standard, compliance may be tied to grant monies. However, even in these situations compliance is still voluntary rather than statutory.

Indoor Location

There is currently work under way by various industry organizations as well as APCO and NENA to improve location accuracy for wireless calls, both indoor and outdoor. There are a number of challenges associated with determining location indoors, not the least of which is the lack of a usable signal from typical outdoor location services such as GPS. On November 14, 2015, APCO, NENA, and the four major wireless carriers reached a voluntary agreement on indoor location referred to as the road map.[9] Subsequent to this agreement, the FCC issued an order (PS Docket No. 07-114) setting the course for indoor location determination in the United States.[10]

As a result of this order, a number of organizations are engaged in standards development and technology proof and testing activities. There are numerous options when considering indoor location technologies. Wireless fidelity (Wi-Fi) access points providing floor-level details into the public safety data flow, Bluetooth beacons that triangulate using an active signal and may provide x–y coordinates and compensated barometric pressure, and variants of assisted GPS for indoor use are all in play at the time of this writing.

Key to utilizing commercially available technologies is the ability to integrate those technologies into a very well-defined, controlled, and critical 9-1-1 location infrastructure. While it may seem "simple" to locate a caller using commercial technologies, there is nothing simple about putting such information into a usable format for public safety entities, translating that data into a defined data flow and infrastructure, then porting it to multiple types of PSAPs, using multiple types of equipment and ensuring that the call is properly routed, transferrable, and contains all of the required data every time. If commercial entities "miss" on a location, you may not find your favorite restaurant or you may have to wait another five minutes for a cab ride. If that same "miss" occurs in 9-1-1, people's lives are put at risk. For this reason alone, it is critical that the standards and technologies deriving and delivering a 9-1-1 caller's location result in a truly "dispatchable location" as envisioned in the road map and encouraged by the FCC.

As the reader has probably already determined, the increasingly mobile society and the advancement of technologies has had a major impact on homeland security partners. Not only is the PSAP affected, but so is every support element involved with locating, delivering, and sustaining a 9-1-1 call. In addition, as technology evolves, so must the personnel who are tasked with using that technology. Training in the form of both initial and continuing education for 9-1-1 telecommunicators, dispatchers, supervisors, technologists, and managers has never been more important. Not only are these personnel tasked with the responsibility of handling multiple types and varying volumes of calls every second of every day, but also they are tasked with learning multiple roles, using ever-changing technologies, understanding those technologies, and incorporating constantly changing methods and systems into their everyday tasks.

Other Equipment and Services

In order to support the ability of wireline, wireless, and VoIP calls to get to the PSAP, a great deal of hardware and software is required within the PSAP. CPE is the terminal or system that typically controls the PSAP's E9-1-1 call-handling functions. It is connected to the local exchange carrier's network at a demarcation point. It may consist of computer telephony, mapping, and ANI/ALI controllers. 9-1-1 call takers answer and interact with callers via the CPE equipment. The CAD system at a PSAP is typically used by call takers to create a computerized record of emergency and nonemergency incidents. Once created, these incident records are then displayed at a dispatch terminal for dissemination to the appropriate responding agencies. CAD systems typically contain additional components for call taking and dispatch such as map display, geographic information system (GIS) databases, training modules, and mobile data management information.

PSAPs may be required by local or state law to record all telephone and radio transmissions that originate from or terminate at their facility. There are a variety of systems available to perform these functions from within a PSAP or remotely. There are numerous support systems that interface with 9-1-1 CPE and CAD systems, such as the following information technology systems: camera feeds, shots fired listening systems, EMS information systems, external alarm interface exchanges, the National Crime Information Center, and state law enforcement and intelligence databases. In addition to the equipment located either in the PSAP or in the PSAP's network, there are additional systems and support tools used by PSAPs and emergency communications centers, including:

• Mobile Data Systems
• Automatic Vehicle Locators
• Management Information Systems
• Records Management Systems
• Jail Management Systems
• Emergency Notification Systems

Given their importance in communicating with the public, it's worth noting and briefly explaining the purpose of emergency notification systems (ENS), a subset of emergency communications, which may also be identified as public alert and warning systems, or mass notification systems. ENS includes systems that provide both one-way and two-way communication between emergency communications staff and impacted individuals; two-way communication requires an acknowledgement of receipt of a message. Mass text messaging services offered by many vendors, as well as social media services such as Twitter, are increasingly being used as ENS systems both formally and informally. Mass automated dialing services, commonly referred to as Reverse 9-1-1, are examples of formal systems used for alerting and warning the public. These systems evolved from the town siren, an early warning system that is still in use today for tornadoes, floods, and other hazards and threats.

PSAPs are becoming ever more connected to outside resources, allowing the PSAP to serve as a focal point for information exchange. PSAPs can offer the ability to deploy a single ENS solution, and interconnect multiple agencies and jurisdictions. This approach reduces costs, enables multiple agencies to benefit from a single solution, and helps to ensure better coordination and control. The opportunity exists and will expand for PSAPs to provide integrated ENS capabilities and services to the fire service, EMS, and law enforcement. With the interconnected disciplines, networks, and systems of Next Generation 9-1-1 (NG9-1-1), and other emerging technologies, ENS becomes an even more valuable tool for both emergency communications and emergency response.

Radio

No discussion of emergency communications would be complete without mention of the "lifeline" for field responders, which is the radio. Although homeland security technologies are discussed in more detail elsewhere in this book, a brief description of radio as it applies to the dispatcher and communications center follows since the radio is one of the most important tools used by PSAPs and dispatch centers. From the emergency communications center perspective, radios are critical tools with which to relay information about calls, update responders, and maintain a "lifeline" with personnel in the field. This is typically done by way of a radio console. Consoles connect directly to radio and/or IP networks using combinations of interface boxes, digital voice gateways, or backroom electronics. Consoles allow dispatch and centralized management of communications for both trunked and conventional audio, auxiliary inputs/outputs, and configuration/fault management. The use of consoles in a centralized-system configuration provides for uniformity in the deployment and use of equipment and can foster more effective fault management allowing changes to be centrally controlled and distributed throughout the system. Additionally, the use of consoles fully integrated into the RF communications network allows for scalability, fault tolerance, failover capabilities, and redundant operations. All of these capabilities are critical to both the PSAP and the responders.

FirstNet

The next generation of "over the air" communications for PSAPs and responders is the National Public Safety Broadband Network (NPSBN) administered by the First Responder Network Authority or FirstNet. As part of Middle Class Tax Relief and Job Act of 2012, the National Telecommunications and Information Administration (NTIA) established FirstNet as an independent entity within NTIA. FirstNet is intended "to take all actions necessary to ensure the design, construction, and operation of a nationwide public safety broadband network (NPSBN), based on a single, national network architecture."[11]

As part of the overall approach to next generation broadband data services for public safety, FirstNet includes provisions for the use of mobile applications to share data in near real time between PSAPs and responders, and between the responders themselves. Mobile applications can be powerful tools for public safety communications. Serving both citizens and homeland security partners, FirstNet and the mobile applications are driven by new features and innovations, faster networks, and better devices. The FirstNet NPSBN will bring advanced communications technology to homeland security partners and enable new lifesaving technologies and practices to develop and unfold. The transition to advanced, IP-based platforms, including FirstNet and NG9-1-1 systems, will enable the use of new applications that will become essential components of emergency response.

Next Generation 9-1-1 (NG9-1-1)

NG9-1-1 systems will be a network of networks providing connectivity between PSAPs within a specified geographic area to other networks both regionally and nationally. NG9-1-1 systems will also provide a mechanism for the transport of multimedia information (e.g., voice, text, video, and photos) from the public to the PSAP. With this advancement in technology comes an increased opportunity to gather actionable data at the PSAP level and to facilitate improved situational awareness for responders before they arrive at the scene.

The intent of NG9-1-1 is to provide solutions intelligent enough to listen in whatever language the customers' devices speak. NG9-1-1 is predicated on the fact that in the very near future, callers may utilize third-generation (3G) / fourth-generation (4G) LTE, Wi-Fi, digital subscriber lines (DSL), cable, or fiber optics as a method of contacting PSAPs. NG9-1-1 systems are designed to translate whatever form of communication the caller chooses into IP protocol, and then translate it back again ensuring a uniform flow of both data and voice, providing a content-rich environment for both the callers and emergency services.

On one side of this equation is the commercial IP network, which is content rich and increasingly pervasive. It offers a variety of location-based services for those who can "speak its language." This enterprise, accessible by the public and used daily, includes a myriad of devices connecting to the Internet using a variety of access technologies; many applications include valuable location information. In order to take advantage of these technologies, NG9-1-1 must also be IP based and capable of speaking the language of the many commercial technologies available to the public today. Accomplishing this goal is no small task.

Fundamental to the formation of NG systems is the creation and deployment of Emergency Services IP Networks (ESINets). The ESINet is a network of networks designed to achieve specific Quality of Service (QoS), security, and reliability levels while facilitating enhanced call routing and delivery. The ability to reroute calls to and share data with any PSAP served by the ESINet is a benefit of the transition. NG9-1-1 systems are made up of functional elements that will provide multiple features and capabilities. A functional element does not have to correspond to a specific product or position in a PSAP. Some of the most common and critical functional elements are discussed in the following paragraphs.

As with wireless Phase II and VoIP calls, there is a complex system of location determination tools used to locate the caller, route the call, and pass location information to the PSAP. Unlike these legacy technologies, NG9-1-1 location services offer a great deal of additional information to the PSAP. The location server (LS) stores location information for subscribers and/or access points. It may support telephone numbers, subscriber uniform resource identifier (URI), or any unique identifier for a subscriber, device, or network entry point. This system is also being designed to provide geo-based routing. When realized, this will allow for the location and routing of a caller based on his or her actual location on the planet in the form of x–y coordinates, and also includes provisions for z-axis or vertical/elevation location. While not yet operational, the basic protocols and tenets of this technology have been tested. Once fully realized, geo-spatial routing will be another revolutionary step in the evolution of 9-1-1.

The DNA of the 9-1-1 call is the Emergency Services Routing Proxy (ESRP). The ESRP queries the LS for location information, obtains routing instructions for the call, and utilizes a number of protocols and proxies to determine where the call goes, and what data goes with it. Incident and call identifiers are assigned when a request first hits the ESINet and are delivered with the call.

There are also a number of gateways involved in both the fully implemented NG9-1-1 system and in transitional networks. The legacy network gateway is a media gateway solution with additional 9-1-1 features that allows legacy, TDM-based carrier networks to access the emergency services.

At a high level, NG9-1-1 can be summed up as the evolution of older, analog-based calling systems to scalable, cost-effective, and agile IP-based solutions providing public safety with the much-needed ability to interface with multiple sources of data and receive critical, real-time information from callers in need.

In spite of the measurable benefit to making the transition, many PSAPs are finding that they are limited by equipment and networks that are incapable of providing a realistic evolution to NG9-1-1. This is a challenge that must be addressed from both the political and financial perspectives. The operational reality is that NG9-1-1 is critical to improved response, and it will save lives. At present, there are no fully implemented NG9-1-1 networks or systems. However, a number of jurisdictions have made or are making substantial progress toward implementation. Many states have already begun implementation of NG9-1-1 networks and systems. According to NENA, at least six states have implemented NG9-1-1 at the state or substate level, and another 11 states are in the process of implementing NG9-1-1 at the state or substate level.[12]

NG9-1-1 Cybersecurity

As NG9-1-1 networks are ever more reliant on data rather than voice, there is tremendous potential for achieving a new level of interoperability. With this potential, of course, comes an increased risk of cyberattack. The increased ability to share data via IP-based networks and systems also opens up paths to emergency communications networks that are not currently accessible and, as a result, the threat of infiltration and exploitation of the system will likely increase. Legacy 9-1-1 systems are relatively secure, and while threats exist, they are somewhat limited to events such as telephony denial of service (TDoS), carrier outages, and capacity issues. Secure, legacy systems are extremely dated and may have location limitations, limited media capabilities, and reliance on aging centralized automatic message accounting trunks and circuit switched technology. With advancement of technology comes an increased threat of infiltration and exploitation of the system.

NG9-1-1 systems and ESINets will be vulnerable to the same threats as existing IP networks and systems. Training and awareness are important considerations. People, not just the equipment, are key to success on the cyber battlefield. There are a number of resources available to assist in the protection, mitigation, and investigation of cyberattacks involving public safety. The FCC Task Force on Optimal PSAP Architecture has a working group specifically tasked with making cybersecurity recommendations for PSAPs and public safety. The National Institute of Standards and Technology (NIST) has created the *Framework for Improving Critical Infrastructure Cybersecurity*.[13] In addition, the U.S. Department of Homeland Security (DHS) and the U.S. Computer Emergency Readiness Team (US-CERT) have numerous resources dedicated to cybersecurity.[14]

Conclusion

Regardless of the type, location, or extent of an emergency, there is one common denominator: all emergencies are local. From the perspective of either the emergency communications centers that initially process the call, or the law enforcement, fire, or EMS personnel who initially respond, all emergencies begin at the local level and as a local event. This holds true for a structure fire, shoplifting case, difficulty breathing incident, or major terrorist attack. As any emergency unfolds it can become more far-reaching, more complex, and more difficult to manage, but it is still the first call to 9-1-1 and the first local dispatch of resources that will begin the life cycle of every incident. Whether the incident remains local, becomes regional, or develops into a national crisis, communications are at the center of any emergency response.

From the call taker, to the dispatcher, to the responders on scene, the flow of information and maintenance of situational awareness will determine the ultimate success or failure of the response. As experienced on September 11, 2001, and seen many times since, interoperability of both voice and data services is critical as incidents unfold and expand. NG9-1-1, FirstNet, and the other emerging technologies that are already being tested and deployed in the public safety space can facilitate this interoperability at levels never before obtained.

As homeland security partners around the nation go about their day-to-day business, respond to calls, and save lives, never before has it been more important that the communications infrastructure that supports this mission be resilient, redundant, and continuously improved. The mission of homeland security partners worldwide is one that is clear and unified. Whether at the local, state, or federal level, the mission is to save lives and protect property. One must never forget that without communications, without the telecommunicator and dispatcher, and without the networks and systems in place to provide up-to-the-minute information to, from, and between the public and responders in the field, this important mission cannot and will not be accomplished.

As was said previously, in the 9-1-1 profession, there is a well-known saying that sums up just how diverse the emergency communications landscape can be: "If you've seen one PSAP, you've seen one PSAP." As our society becomes more reliant on technology, and PSAP personnel receive increasing numbers of calls, including many from mobile callers and indoor locations, it is important to remember that at each end of every call, behind all of this technology, and with every emergency, there is a human being.

Discussion Questions

1. Recent local elections resulted in significant turnover among the city's councilmembers. Given that budget deliberations for the following year will begin soon, the director of emergency communications tasks you with developing a short brief to inform new councilmembers on the importance of 9-1-1 systems and the operation of the PSAP. Develop a short brief that explains the purpose of the system and PSAP, generally, as well as critical system components or subsystems.
2. Today's newspaper cited a recent incident in which a distressed resident called 9-1-1 from her cellular phone, but the communications center didn't have the capability to trace her location. The city mayor called the director of the emergency communications asking how this might be possible when she can track her own location using an application on his smartphone. Prepare a response for the mayor in the form of bullet points that describe the problem.
3. Recent survey data on your community indicates that 30 percent of residents no longer maintain traditional landline phone service, but rather exclusively use a mobile cellular or smartphone as their sole form of communications. However, 100 percent of residents expect a response to 9-1-1 emergency calls regardless of type of phone service. Analyze the problem(s) associated with this scenario, as well as alternative(s) available to the local PSAP.

Notes

1. National Emergency Number Association, "9-1-1 Statistics."
2. Association of Public-Safety Communications Officials International, "About APCO."
3. U.S. Department of Transportation, National Highway Traffic Safety Administration, *Emergency Medical Dispatch: EMD Program Implementation and Administration—Manager's Guide*, vi–vii.
4. City of New York, "911 Performance Reporting."
5. Cellular Telecommunications Industry Association, *Wireless Glossary of Terms*, 3.
6. National Emergency Number Association, "9-1-1 Statistics."
7. Federal Communications Commission, *E911 Requirements for IP-Enabled Service Providers*, 13–14.
8. Communications Security, Reliability, and Interoperability Council, *Technical Options for E9-1-1 Location Accuracy: Final Report*, 12.
9. Association of Public-Safety Communications Officials International, "APCO and NENA Reach Consensus Plan with Major Wireless Carriers on Improvements to Locating 9-1-1 Callers."
10. Federal Communications Commission, *Wireless E911 Locations Accuracy Requirements*.
11. First Responder Network Authority, "Project Overview."
12. National Emergency Number Association, "Status of NG9-1-1 State Activity."
13. National Institute of Standards and Technology, "Cybersecurity Framework."
14. U.S. Computer Emergency Readiness Team, "Home Page."

Bibliography

Association of Public-Safety Communications Officials International. "APCO and NENA Reach Consensus Plan with Major Wireless Carriers on Improvements to Locating 9-1-1 Callers." *APCO International*. Last modified November 15, 2014. http://psc.apcointl.org/2014/11/15/apco-and-nena-reach-consensus-plan-with-major-wireless-carriers-on-improvements-to-locating-9-1-1-callers/.

Association of Public-Safety Communications Officials International. "Comm Center and 9-1-1." *APCO International*. Accessed January 2016. https://www.apcointl.org/resources/9-1-1.html.

Cellular Telecommunications Industry Association. *Wireless Glossary of Terms*. Washington, DC: Cellular Telecommunications Industry Association. Accessed November 2016. http://files.ctia.org/pdf/Telecom_Glossary_of_Terms.pdf.

City of New York. "911 Performance Reporting." City of New York. Accessed January 2016. http://www.nyc.gov/html/911reporting/html/home/home.shtml.

Communications Security, Reliability, and Interoperability Council. *Technical Options for E9-1-1 Location Accuracy: Final Report*. Washington, DC: Federal Communications Commission. 2011.

Federal Communications Commission. *E911 Requirements for IP-Enabled Service Providers (FCC 05-116; WC Docket No. 04-26 and 05-196).* Washington, DC: Federal Communications Commission. 2005.

Federal Communications Commission. *Wireless E911 Locations Accuracy Requirements (FCC 15-9; OS Docket No. 07-114).* Washington, DC: Federal Communications Commission. 2015.

First Responder Network Authority. "Project Overview." FirstNet. Accessed January 2016. http://www.firstnet.gov/content/project-overview.

National Emergency Number Association. "9-1-1 Statistics." National Emergency Number Association. Last modified December 2015. https://www.nena.org/?page=911Statistics.

National Emergency Number Association. "Status of NG9-1-1 State Activity." National Emergency Number Association. Last modified May 18, 2015. http://www.nena.org/?NG911_StateActivity.

National Institute of Standards and Technology. "Cybersecurity Framework." National Institute of Standards and Technology. Last modified February 9, 2016. http://www.nist.gov/cyberframework/.

U.S. Computer Emergency Readiness Team. "Home Page." U.S. Computer Emergency Readiness Team. Accessed January 2016. https://www.us-cert.gov/.

U.S. Department of Transportation, National Highway Traffic Safety Administration. *Emergency Medical Dispatch: EMD Program Implementation and Administration—Manager's Guide.* Washington, DC: U.S. United States Government Printing Office. 1995.

CHAPTER ELEVEN

Mobile Communications and Decision Support Applications

Chad S. Foster

Learning Objectives

After reading this chapter, readers should be able to:

- Assess challenges associated with emergency communications that have surfaced during the past century.
- Explain the components of the interoperability continuum and apply the components to a scenario or problem.
- Identify and distinguish among types of redundant communications systems.
- Explain the concept of cloud computing and the impacts of cloud computing on emergency communications.
- Assess the opportunities and challenges associated with the FirstNet initiative.
- Explain the value of standards to emergency communications and decision support applications, and identify and explain example applications of standards.
- Given a problem, select and apply the appropriate decision support software applications.
- Assess contemporary challenges associated with mobile computing and decision support applications, and create alternatives for overcoming those challenges.

Key Terms

Cloud Computing
Decision Support Software
Emergency Alert System (EAS)
Emergency Communications
First Responder Network Authority (FirstNet)
Geographic Information Systems (GIS)
Interoperability
Interoperability Continuum
Land Mobile Radios (LMR)
Project 25 (P25)
Voice over Internet Protocol (VoIP)
Wireless Emergency Alerts (WEA)
Wireless Networks

Introduction

HURRICANE KATRINA MAKES LANDFALL on August 20, 2005, near New Orleans, Louisiana, and results in the costliest natural disaster in U.S. history. The storm results in the destruction or degradation of 3 million landlines, 2,000 cell towers, more than 30 Public Service Answering Points (PSAPs), 37 of 41 broadcast radio stations, and first responder land mobile radio service across the region. Satellite phones are in short supply and unable to be charged due to lack of electrical power and fuel to run emergency generators. The New Orleans Police Department and the Mississippi National Guard are unable to establish effective communications for several days. In addition to operable communication, situational awareness is nonexistent due to a lack of interoperability between federal, state, and local communications systems.[1]

Similar results and case studies are documented across a range of incidents and disasters during recent history. In response to the September 11, 2001, terrorist attacks, for example, the National Commission on Terrorist Attacks Upon the United States ("9/11 Commission") found the following:

> The inability to communicate was a critical element at the World Trade Center, Pentagon, and Somerset County, Pennsylvania, crash sites, where multiple agencies and multiple jurisdictions responded. The occurrence of the problem at three very different sites is strong evidence that compatible

and adequate communications among public safety organizations at the local, state, and federal levels remains an important problem.[2]

The use of wireline and wireless communications has become a fundamental requirement for homeland security partners to effectively manage both routine duties in the field and disasters that might require large-scale response and multiagency coordination. On one hand, advances in communications and information technologies since the turn of the last century have offered partners with tremendous capabilities. Beyond voice communications, for example, new networks and mobile broadband connections offer responders in the field with access to vast amounts of information in the form of documents, procedures, and maps, among others. Mobile devices are now designed for deployability (e.g., lightweight, rugged, and small in size) since computing is handled by external servers accessed via the cloud.

On the other hand, competition for limited spectrum, the need for redundant systems, including traditional radio-to-radio communications, information security, and simply keeping abreast of advancements and managing change in the form of governance, policies, and procedures present a sample of daunting challenges. The aforementioned cases— Hurricane Katrina and the 9/11 terrorist attacks—only scratch the surface of problems encountered by partners operating in today's environment.

The importance of communications and information technologies is recognized at all levels and scales of response. At the national level, communications and information management occupies one of six key components of the National Incident Management System (NIMS).[3] Operational communications is listed as a core capability under the most recent version of the National Preparedness Goal (see Table 11.1 for a description of this core capability and preliminary targets).[4]

At the state and local levels, operational communications remains a priority for funding and training. A national needs assessment conducted in 2014 and 2015 by the Rural Domestic Preparedness Consortium found that operational communications topped the list of capabilities most in need of training among responders from small and rural communities. As displayed in Figure 11.1, approximately two-thirds of respondents or 1,766 agencies identified training was needed within this core capability.[5] Furthermore, a nationwide survey conducted by Motorola in 2015 found that 70 percent of agencies surveyed say it is "critical" or "very important" for first responders to access real-time data in the field, 73 percent need to connect different devices and networks together, and 78 percent want to easily interoperate with neighboring agencies.[6]

Table 11.1   Operational Communications and the National Preparedness Goal

Background	The National Preparedness Goal is used by partners nationwide to help assess needs and justify funding proposals for annual federal grant programs. The following provides a description of this capability as identified in the 2015 version of the doctrine.
Description	Ensure the capacity for timely communications in support of security, situational awareness, and operations by any and all means available, among and between affected communities in the impact area and all response forces.
Capability Targets	1. Ensure the capacity to communicate with both the emergency response community and the affected populations and establish interoperable voice and data communications between Federal, tribal, state, and local first responders.
	2. Reestablish sufficient communications infrastructure within the affected areas to support ongoing life-sustaining activities, provide basic human needs, and transition to recovery.
	3. Reestablish critical information networks, including cybersecurity information sharing networks, in order to inform situational awareness, enable incident response, and support the resiliency of key systems.

Source: U.S. Department of Homeland Security, *National Preparedness Goal,* 2nd ed., p. 16.

The convergence of voice and data communications—not long ago considered separate sectors—offers users in the field working in many different capacities with significant capabilities. This chapter describes communications and information technologies, and provides a summary of hardware used to support mobile applications and software systems that aim to enhance situational awareness and decision making. It begins with an overview of trends in voice communications and then presents infrastructure that has enabled the convergence between voice and data applications. The final section is dedicated to software decision support applications commonly used in the field.

Voice Communications and Interoperability

According to the 2014 National Emergency Communications Plan, *emergency communications* is defined as "the means and methods for exchanging

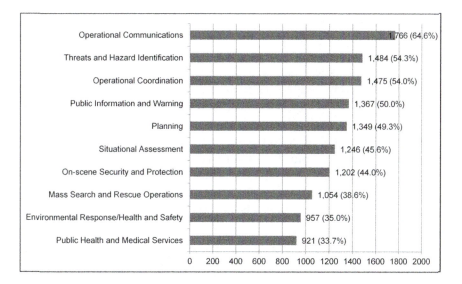

Figure 11.1 Highest Priority Training Needs among Responders from Small and Rural Communities.

communications and information necessary for successful incident management."[7] Before the widespread use of two-way wireless voice communications in the mid-20th Century, the use of rudimentary landline police call boxes was the primary means of emergency communications.[8] During World War II in the 1940s, the military invested in wireless radios nicknamed "walkie-talkies" that, on average, weighed approximately 35 pounds and could reach up to 20 miles.[9] Popularized during the war, civilian applications became apparent, though public safety encountered challenges with analog radios that were only capable of transmitting shared messages on a finite number of frequencies.[10]

The advent of digital communications during 1980s and the trunked radio system helped to address this problem. Radio systems and handsets became programmable; the embedded computers could now distinguish multiple channels that relied on the same frequency or authorized frequency spectrum.[11] In other words, more users could benefit from use of the same frequencies than before through the use of programmable channels. Simultaneously, manufacturers of radios developed proprietary systems that were often incapable of interoperability. From a historical perspective, the response to the September 11, 2001, terrorist attacks placed a national spotlight on this problem.

This lack of interoperability among disparate products is a common phenomenon today given the nation's market economy, which promotes competitiveness and innovation over standardization and uniformity. However, public safety and national security are commonly viewed as public goods and within the realm of government responsibility. Though a movement was afloat well before 2001 to establish standards for communications interoperability—including the release of select standards in 1995 as part of the Project 25 (P25) initiative[12] (see information below)— the outcry resulting from the terrorist attacks added a sense of urgency among policy makers and senior officials to incentivize adoption of interoperability standards.

According to NIMS, *interoperability* is the:

> Ability of systems, personnel, and equipment to provide and receive functionality, data, information and/or services to and from other systems, personnel, and equipment, between both public and private agencies, departments, and other organizations, in a manner enabling them to operate effectively together. Allows emergency management/response personnel and their affiliated organizations to communicate within and across agencies and jurisdictions via voice, data, or video on demand, in real time, when needed, and when authorized.[13]

The technical aspects of interoperability comprise only a portion of what is considered the *interoperability continuum*.[14] This concept aims to capture a more holistic and multidimensional perspective of the interoperability problem. To have a successful interoperability "solution," a community must adequately plan for governance, standard operating procedures, technology, training and exercises, and usage of interoperable communications.

Note that technology is now segmented into voice and data elements. Conceptually, communities are encouraged to make interoperability progress by moving from left to right on the continuum. In support of technology dimension of the interoperability continuum, the P25 initiative is aimed at developing voluntary, consensus standards for digital radio equipment and systems.[15] The development of P25 standards is organized by the Telecommunications Industry Association, an accredited standards organization, and the testing of equipment is conducted by recognized laboratories. Purchasing P25-compliant equipment provides users confidence their systems will be interoperable with others.

Two-way, point-to-point or radio-to-radio communications devices are commonly referred to as land mobile radios (LMRs) among practitioners and manufacturers. Most LMRs operate in the radio frequency (RF) range of 25 Kilohertz (KHz) to 300 Gigahertz (GHz) or gateways to patch LMRs that operate on different frequencies. RF communications include the very high frequency (VHF) (30 Megahertz [MHz] to 300 MHz) and the ultra high frequency (UHF) (300 MHz to 3 GHz) bands. Historically, LMRs are the most common type of communication used by emergency responders.

For responding to common incidents, the existing wireless communications infrastructure in a community may provide an appropriate level of communications coverage and reliability. Many emergency responders, however, operate in rural or vast wilderness areas where wireless communications coverage is weak, thereby resulting in the need to deploy a temporary communications network. Likewise, responders deployed through mutual aid agreements may need to establish wireless networks in areas with unfamiliar terrain and infrastructure. Urban areas also present unique challenges to communications officials due to their complex array of structures with interior spaces and a landscape that continually evolves due to development. According to Pine, *wireless networks* are "communication networks that connect users by radio or wireless means . . . provide a stable and flexible means to communicate."[16] Having wireless networks available to response agencies is critical to avoid the loss of communications that may result when existing systems are degraded or the lines of communications are disrupted.

To overcome problems associated with distance or obstacles hindering radio propagation, many communities rely on fixed or mobile *repeater systems.*[17] Repeaters are often deployed to circumvent natural or man-made features, and for communicating indoors or in subterranean locations. Sophisticated propagation modeling software is available to responders to aid in the placement of repeaters.

While efforts were under way to improve LMR interoperability during the past three decades, significant changes were taking place involving cellular and satellite communications, and other platforms that support the sharing of data. Baggett's overview of trends relating to social media generally reflects much broader changes that have taken place with regard to communications infrastructure.

As some are commercially available to the public today, a wide range of redundant communications systems can now be accessed by homeland security partners, such as the following:

- The 802.11 a/b/g/n standard set (also known as wireless fidelity, or Wi-Fi) was developed by the Institute of Electrical and Electronics Engineers for the purpose of enabling wireless computer communications in the 2.4, 3.6, and 5 GHz frequency bands.

- Worldwide Interoperability for Microwave Access (WiMAX), also known as 802.16, combines the benefits of broadband and wireless. WiMAX is designed to provide high-speed wireless Internet over very long distances and Internet access to large areas, such as cities.
- A cellular network, often called a "cell," is a communications network that is served by fixed-location base stations. When joined together via base stations, these cells provide communications coverage that enables a large number of portable (e.g., mobile phones, pagers) and fixed (e.g., land-based telephones) receivers to communicate with each other. The most common example of a cell is found in a mobile phone network.
- Satellite provides telephony and data services to users worldwide via special surface-based terminals (e.g., satellite phone, Broadband Global Area Network [BGAN] terminals), which communicate to ground stations through a constellation of telecommunications satellites.

The use of cellular services has become one of the most common forms of communications today in all facets of society. In addition to phones, laptops and tablets now often come equipped with cellular capabilities made possible through advancements in Long Term Evolution (LTE) broadband technology. The expanded infrastructure and enhanced broadband connectivity now supports the use of both Voice over Internet Protocol (VoIP) and data sharing in devices that were once relegated to either voice or data. VoIP involves sending voice information in digital form over the Internet rather than by using landline phones or LMRs. Being connected to the Internet also supports the capability to send and receive data, including live audio and video feeds for video teleconferencing and other purposes.

The proliferation of mobile broadband Internet access and new mechanisms to pool computing resources remotely ("cloud computing") has enabled agencies to deploy small devices in the field capable of accessing sophisticated applications and vast amounts of data. It has also offered incident personnel with a common operating picture as situation updates are made in real time and network-wide.

The National Institute of Standards and Technology (NIST) defines *cloud computing* as "on-demand network access to a shared pool of configurable computing resources."[18] Cloud computing centralizes the management of large-scale computing capabilities that may consist of hardware (e.g., servers, storage) and software applications (e.g., operating systems, security), providing operational and information technology (IT) management benefits. For example, mobile device requirements are minimal in a cloud computing configuration, often only needing access to a Web browser.

Until recently, response agencies have operated in the field using a thick client configuration, which confines field users to the computing resources available on the device itself. Made available through the expansion of wireless local and wide area networks, thin client configurations are gaining popularity among response agencies. In this type of configuration, the services and applications are "served" to end users over a network rather than stored on responders' mobile devices. Complex processing applications may be interfaced and used from basic computing hardware, such as a smartphone or other mobile computing platform. Cloud computing is comparable to variations of thin client configurations.

While agencies commonly must seek third-party vendors to provide the entire cloud computing infrastructure, many today have acquired their own infrastructure and are capable of serving applications and data themselves. Relying on a third-party vendor to provide only the hardware necessary for serving applications is one common cloud computing model. Regardless of hardware ownership, agencies may prefer to deploy response applications via the cloud, such as decision support software (e.g., geospatial information, resource management). Agencies also have the option of serving and synchronizing back-end operating systems, databases, and middleware across their entire networks.

Opportunities and Risks

Mobile devices for interfacing with the cloud may be designed for deployability (i.e., lightweight, rugged, and small in size) since computing is handled by external resources. Through a mobile broadband connection, responders in the field could access vast amounts of information in the form of documents, procedures, and maps. Since databases are managed centrally, near real-time updates to maps and status boards provide all users on the network with a common operating picture, including personnel at command centers.

Variations of cloud computing may also make it easier for IT personnel to manage, maintain, and secure applications for the benefit of all agency personnel. Rather than having to manually update potentially hundreds of separate computers, IT personnel may update the operating system and software on one or more central servers for the benefit of all users on the network, a significant savings in personnel time. Agencies without servers and network equipment, or the funds to purchase that equipment, may rely on third-party vendors to host applications at a price they may find affordable.

Agencies may have security concerns when it comes to reliance on the cloud, especially in procuring services from a third-party vendor. Before procuring a cloud computing service from a private sector company, partners should closely consider the measures in place to isolate and safeguard agency information from public data and other private data that may be handled by the company. The need for cybersecurity and the sensitivity of data may lead an agency to host applications on their own IT equipment to closely monitor access.

The movement toward cloud-based applications for accessing critical information has called into question the reliability of commercial networks that have supported safety and security partners to date. The commercial networks supporting these applications have limitations such as inconsistent coverage nationally, but most notably in rural, remote, and vast wilderness areas. There are also lingering concerns with the interoperability of traditional LMRs[19] and the resilience of private telecommunications infrastructure to support critical operations such as those required to save lives and protect property following a disaster.[20]

In response to these and additional challenges, the U.S. Congress established the First Responder Network Authority (FirstNet) in 2012 to oversee the development of a broadband network in the 700 MHz band to support public safety.[21] As of March 2016, FirstNet was developing requirements and standards for the network, which is anticipated to include high-speed data services to support, at least initially, data, video, images, and text. Additional phases of the effort may include support for location information, streaming video, Voice over Long Term Evolution (VoLTE), and even connection to LMR networks.[22] From the perspective of the field user, this network holds the potential to reduce the number of and complexity associated with the use of mobile devices (e.g., radio, smartphone, tablet).

An evaluation of opportunities and risks may lead agencies to consider hybrid configurations that involve one or more applications managed through the cloud, while other applications critical to mission success and life safety are installed on responders' devices.

For example, urban search and rescue personnel operating in an area impacted by an earthquake may need area maps pre-installed on ruggedized computers for quick access during the initial phases of the response. After communications have been reestablished in the impacted area, these teams may gain access through the cloud to decision support software that includes status boards and incident maps monitored by the incident commander. Less mission-critical applications, such as an exercise simulation tool that provides notional scenarios, maps, and situation updates to exercise participants, may be entirely provided via the cloud.

Decision Support Applications[23]

According to NIMS, "Effective emergency management and incident response activities rely on flexible communications and information systems that provide a common operating picture to emergency management/ response personnel and their affiliated organizations."[24] To help them address these needs at the scene of an incident or within a supporting operations center, emergency response agencies are increasingly turning to software solutions.

There is a wide range of software products currently available for purchase that offer both common and unique features aimed at improving the awareness of key decision makers. The purpose of this section is to provide a summary of the features, configurations, and use of decision support software to assist partners in selecting, integrating, and leveraging these tools as part of preparedness, command, and coordination activities.

Decision support software provides Incident Commanders, emergency managers, and responders with tools to help them manage small- and large-scale incidents and events, coordinate with agencies and responders from other jurisdictions, and communicate critical information. Software supports these outcomes by reducing response times, increasing operational efficiency, and improving the overall management of resources through improved situational awareness.

Some products perform single functions such as resource management, while others are more comprehensive allowing users to employ one computer application to help them perform multiple functions. Emergency management and response agencies in small and rural communities may not have the resources available to purchase multiple software products, or the capability to integrate and manage those products simultaneously during an incident. As a result, these and other types of emergency response agencies may prefer to use comprehensive software applications in their Emergency Operations Centers to conduct multiagency coordination, make resource allocation decisions, and collect and analyze information from many different sources. These sources may range from responders at the scene of an incident to other impacted areas, neighboring jurisdictions, and other operations centers at higher levels of government.

Common software applications offer an array of analytical tools to enhance the decision making of emergency responders as it relates to command and control, implementation of plans and procedures, and the allocation of critical resources and tasking for both personnel and equipment. It also provides a means of reporting and maintaining records management and document control for archival purposes. The following decision support capabilities are offered in various combinations by manufacturers:

- **Alert and Warning Notification:** This feature allows users to receive and disseminate various types of alerts and warnings. Users may receive and monitor alerts and notifications from different sources to include the National Oceanic and Atmospheric Administration and the U.S. Geological Survey. As an example, this feature allows for the processing of weather warnings, watches, and forecasts directly to targeted personnel, such as emergency managers, who can then assess the threat and activate an emergency alert to a broader group of affected personnel. The proliferation of Internet Protocol (IP)-enabled software and other devices that leverage the Common Alerting Protocol (CAP) has made the dissemination of alerts and warnings nearly automatic and in real time.

- **Geospatial Information (Maps, Imagery, Geographic Information System [GIS] Tracking):** This function provides visual information about the location of an incident and resources. Many software applications contain mapping programs that display multilayered imagery. They may also provide the real-time geospatial tracking of resources and the capability to integrate and display blueprints and floor plans for buildings. Typically, these applications allow users to capture, store, analyze, manage, and present data that is linked to location. Commonly used GIS applications include Environmental Systems Research Institute (ESRI) ArcView™ and other ESRI products, Google Earth™, and Microsoft Bing™ maps.

- **Incident Notification and Messaging:** This feature supports incident notification and situation reporting. This may be accomplished through interfaces with other systems or integration with public and private databases to provide real-time situational awareness. An example of this capability includes receiving, completing, and processing Incident Command System (ICS) forms, such as the ICS 209 (Incident Status Summary). Many comprehensive software packages include a Records Management System to assist users in archiving incident reports. They may also provide automatic reporting capabilities such as Enhanced 9-1-1 (E9-1-1), which automatically associates a physical address with the calling party's telephone number to assist the agency in identifying the appropriate response assets.

- **Resource Management:** Resource management provides the capability to inventory and quickly identify Federal Emergency Management Agency (FEMA) typed and other resources, order and acquire resources, and track and report on the status of resources. Resource management applications may provide or be linked to Computer-Aided Dispatch (CAD) systems used at 9-1-1/dispatch centers or other resource ordering systems. They may also be shared with or connected to other agency's or jurisdiction's information management systems to support mutual aid operations. During the recovery phase, resource management features allow users to recover/demobilize assets and support reimbursement.

- **Modeling and Simulation (Plume, Weather, Forecasting):** This feature provides emergency responders with information on natural and infrastructure risks, forecasts incident consequences, and analyzes the impact of hazards based on demographic data and human needs. Modeling and simulation capabilities may assist emergency responders in assigning rescue personnel and equipment; organizing medical support; and monitoring weather conditions, environmental problems (e.g., toxic plumes), and evacuation routes. During the preparedness phase, this feature may be used to support simulated training to improve operational readiness and response to catastrophic events. Figure 11.2 shows an example modeling software application provided by FEMA called Hazus®-MH, which allows users to develop and analyze the impacts and estimated losses associated with earthquakes, flooding, and hurricanes. This image shows the reaches associated with rivers and streams within a county boundary.

- **Surveillance and Analysis (Damage Information, Responder Authentication, Intelligence):** Capabilities in this category may include video analytics, streaming video and audio coding, and data and processing/storage capabilities, which are integrated into a single interface that can be operated by multiple users. Examples of surveillance and analysis software include applications that support the sharing of camera feeds from remote locations back to the operations center or command post for displaying and storing information. The use of cameras and other sensors may be used in support of physical security, access control, and surveillance. Site security applications may be integrated with software that provides a database and runs checks of identification cards for personnel authentication and accountability purposes. Also, software in this category may support multisource collection and the production and dissemination of intelligence to incident response organizations so they can monitor threats, detect and prevent attacks, and alert authorities.

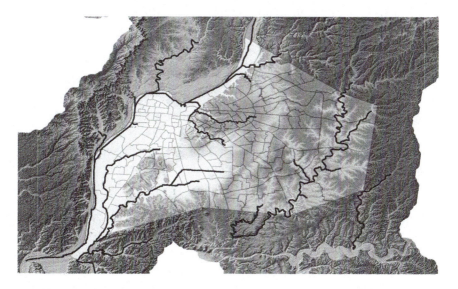

Figure 11.2   Example Hazard Modeling Application.

There are also software products that provide middleware such as data mining and gateways for supporting communications and networks that may be invisible to the end user, but they fulfill important backbone and infrastructure requirements.

Applications that rely on one or more servers allow users to post information for others to view or retrieve for their awareness; these servers may also be used as hubs for sharing data across many users of a proprietary system. Data interoperability with disparate commercial and government products and different types of equipment (e.g., smartphones, tablets) is often achieved through the use of commonly accepted data messaging standards such as the Emergency Data Exchange Language (EDXL) suite of standards.

The EDXL CAP standard, for example, has gained popularity as a means of exchanging all-hazard alerts and warnings over the Internet, including Emergency Alert System (EAS) messages. The EAS and its predecessor, the Emergency Broadcast System, have been in existence since the 1960s to "provide a method for the President to address the nation during dire national crises."[25] However, when not used by the president, state and local alerting authorities may use the system to warn the public of hazards and threats through broadcast stations and cable systems. Today, a majority of EAS messages are weather-related and originate by the National Weather Service (NWS).[26] The system may also be used for nonweather related warnings such as America's Missing: Broadcast Emergency Response (AMBER) alerts. Presently, all radio and television stations and cable systems are required by Federal Communications Commission rules and regulations to install, maintain, and test EAS equipment so that they can receive and transmit national, presidential EAS messages.

The CAP standard has afforded users of decision support software to increase the range of platforms that can receive alert and warning messages, such as EAS. It also supports the integration of other forms of multimedia. Moving Picture Experts Group (MPEG) Audio Layer 3 (MP3) files with audio messages can be transferred through CAP. Weather alerts and watches can also be more compatible for short message service (SMS)/text messaging. More and more subscription services are being offered in a variety of counties across the country.

Subscribers who register for weather alerts can also receive NWS bulletins because CAP provides a conduit for messages to be entered and packaged for text messages. A recent national initiative titled Wireless Emergency Alerts (WEA) does not require subscriptions in order to receive geographically targeted messages. Through a partnership between the federal government and commercial mobile service providers, alerting authorities are able to send WEAs to mobile devices. Most of the common service providers such as ATT, Verizon, and Sprint now offer WEA-capable phones that are designed to receive alerts even when cellular networks become overloaded and incapable of supporting voice calls, texting, and the like.

Additional EDXL standards allow for messaging among users of different software systems for other purposes, such as to request resources and to share information about hospital capacity and bed space. The National Information Exchange Model supports the exchange of EDXL-based and other types of standards by providing common semantics and packets for exchanging information across agencies for specific operational purposes (e.g., AMBER alerts).

Inherent with the use of software are information security concerns. According to NIMS, "Procedures and protocols must be established to ensure information security."[27] Response agencies should determine if the security features offered with the decision support software supports their agency's information security policies and protocols. Most commercial software products provide a login feature and individual accounts set up by an authorized person that require usernames and passwords for accessing information. This layer of security ensures that only authorized individuals are allowed to access the software and insert and retrieve data. Software products that also provide a log of activity help agencies with identifying and investigating potential security issues.

Agencies must also ensure that software applications come with mechanisms to back up and retrieve incident data, which may be an additional cost for agencies. Certain products come with automatic database backup features. Agencies should also consider archiving databases and files regularly on a separate computer system for records management and operational redundancy purposes.

Additional Challenges

Though not intended to be an exhaustive list, previous sections highlighted a sample of challenges associated with planning for communications and information technologies in the 21st century. A few additional challenges, as described below, are worth noting and addressing in the planning for future systems.

- **Security and Redundancy:** Inherent with any information management system is the security of the data, which presents new risks and costs to emergency responders. These risks include the accidental or criminal release of sensitive information, and the loss of operational data due to a system failure or loss of power. Redundant communications are backup systems that allow first responders to communicate when their primary system of communication is inoperable or disrupted. Like communications systems, the Internet is susceptible to failures during disasters due to power failures and/or severed wire connections.

- **Deployability and Usability Features:** Increased reliance on mobile devices places a higher premium on the deployability and usability of the devices themselves. For mission-critical applications, consider the power duration of and ability to recharge batteries; screen resolution, size, and brightness; the placement of keyboards and buttons, and handles and straps; and the ruggedness of the casings. In support of ruggedness, consider the ingress protection (IP) rating of the device, which generally measures protection from the ingress of foreign objects, dust, and liquids. The following military standard provides other measurements for ruggedness: Military Standard 810G (MIL-STD-810G): Environmental Engineering Considerations and Laboratory Tests.[28]

- **Managing Change and New Releases:** Software technology tends to evolve very quickly as compared to hardware; new versions of software with new capabilities are generally released more often than their hardware counterparts. An additional burden for emergency responders that regularly train on and use software is the need to manage new releases and updates from infrastructure configuration, training, and operational perspectives. Also, many commercial products are developed using proprietary applications and software rather than based on open standards for supporting interoperability and the exchange of data with other systems. Require that vendors conform to standards up front in the request for proposal or bidding process.

- **Level of Expertise:** Use of communications and software often requires some level of specialized knowledge. For example, GIS specialists may be required to configure the community's mapping applications to support homeland security functions. Personnel with a radio communications and a technical or engineering background will have the appropriate knowledge and expertise needed to program radios, install repeaters, and manage the supporting software. Keep these technical specialists in mind when planning future systems.

- **Not a "Silver Bullet":** Software applications are not a solution for reducing all of the complexities and challenges associated with the management of incidents, or a replacement for planning, training, and exercises, as well as other preparedness activities required for effective response and recovery. Likewise, training on the use of software should be part of an organization's training program.

Conclusion

This chapter briefly traced the evolution of communications from the past to the present while emphasizing key challenges, described the recent convergence between voice and data applications and the concept of cloud computing, and provided an overview of decision support software applications commonly used by partners in today's operating environment. The focus of this chapter is on mobile communications and applications used by responders themselves to communicate with each other and to improve decision making.

Keeping up with the fast pace of innovation and change in this domain is a challenge; change is commonly accompanied by increased complexities. Take, for example, the convergence of voice and data communications that will occur as FirstNet matures as an initiative and brings the LMR and LTE concepts together. It will be interesting to observe how partners manage these changes, considering all aspects of the interoperability continuum. Circling back to topics presented in the book introduction, the concepts of leadership, strategic planning, and organization culture resonate well with these trends and may be strong predictors of future institutional progress and success.

Discussion Questions

1. Why is operational communications consistently noted as a high priority for training and funding among partners?
2. Find a recent news story or report highlighting a field communications problem. Assess the problem and relate it to one or more of the components of the interoperability continuum. What problems are presented in the story or report as they relate to the continuum, and what alternatives might you consider for addressing the problems?
3. Over the past weekend, two campers went missing in the Red River Gorge area of the Daniel Boone National Forest, an expansive and heavily wooded national park. As a member of the U.S. Forest Service assigned to the Red River Gorge district, you are accustomed to working in close coordination with state and local agencies on response operations in the park. After hearing news of the missing campers, you assemble with other members of the incident management team responsible for wilderness search and rescue operations. While completing the ICS 205 form, Incident Radio Communications Plan, the need for redundant communications comes to mind. Explain multiple types of communications systems that may apply to this scenario.
4. The after action review conducted following the search for the missing campers noted the following areas for improvement: (1) lack of voice communications between ground teams and air/aviation assets used

during the search; (2) constant and disorganized traffic over shared LMR channels; (3) loss of wireless data connectively in the park that prevented teams from accessing topographic maps, tracking their positions, and providing situation updates; and (4) select mobile communications devices proved difficult to use in the rugged terrain. Relating to the fourth area identified above, condensation formed on many screens, screens were difficult to see in the sunlight, simply carrying the devices in hand or in packs proved challenging, and one responder dropped his device, shattering the screen. Within groups, explore alternatives to these problems using critical thinking and information from the chapter.

Notes

1. Select Bipartisan Committee to Investigate the Preparation for and Response to Hurricane Katrina, *A Failure of Initiative*; Miller, "Hurricane Katrina: Communications and Infrastructure Impacts."

2. National Commission on Terrorist Attacks upon the United States, *9/11 Commission Report,* 397.

3. U.S. Department of Homeland Security, *National Incident Management System.*

4. U.S. Department of Homeland Security, *National Preparedness Goal,* 2nd ed.

5. Simpkins, *2014–2015 National Rural Training Needs Assessment.*

6. Motorola Solutions, Inc. *White Paper: 5 Trends Transforming Public Safety Communications,* 3–5.

7. U.S. Department of Homeland Security, *National Emergency Communications Plan,* A–37.

8. Brown, "Police Radio History and Innovation: What Have We Learned?"

9. Montana Public Safety Communications Bureau, "Public Safety Communications."

10. Brown, "Police Radio History and Innovation: What Have We Learned?"

11. Ibid.

12. Association of Public-Safety Communications Officials (APCO) International, "Project 25."

13. U.S. Department of Homeland Security, *National Incident Management System,* 141.

14. U.S. Department of Homeland Security, *National Emergency Communications Plan,* A–20.

15. Association of Public-Safety Communications Officials (APCO) International, "Project 25."

16. Pine, *Technology in Emergency Management,* 40.

17. Portions of this section were previously developed by the authors; see Eastern Kentucky University Justice and Safety Center, *SAVER Program Report: Mobile Computing Through the Cloud;* Eastern Kentucky University Justice and Safety Center, *SAVER Program Report: Mobile Command Systems Application Note;* and Eastern Kentucky University Justice and Safety Center, *SAVER Program Report: Propagation Modeling Software Application Note.*

18. Mell and Grance, *The NIST Definition of Cloud Computing (Special Publication 800–145),* 2.

19. Schaffer, "The National Broadband (Communications) Plan: Issues for Public Safety" [National Institute of Justice conference transcript].

20. Heaton, "Making the Connection: The National Public Safety Broadband Network Moves Forward—But Hurdles Remain."

21. First Responder Network Authority, "About FirstNet."

22. First Responder Network Authority, *How Will the FirstNet Network Work with Today's Land Mobile Radio Networks?*

23. Portions of this section were previously developed by the authors; see Eastern Kentucky University Justice and Safety Center, *SAVER Program Report: Incident Decision Support Software Application Note.*

24. U.S. Department of Homeland Security, *National Incident Management System,* 7.

25. Partnership for Public Warning, *The Emergency Alert System: An Assessment (PPW Report 400–1),* 3.

26. Ibid.

27. U.S. Department of Homeland Security, *National Incident Management System,* 30.

28. U.S. Department of Defense, *Military Standard 810G (MIL-STD-810G): Environmental Engineering Considerations and Laboratory Tests.*

Bibliography

Association of Public-Safety Communications Officials (APCO) International. "Project 25." Last modified 2016. https://www.apcointl.org/spectrum-management/resources/interoperability/p25.html.

Brown, T. J. "Police Radio History and Innovation: What Have We Learned?" *Journal of Law Enforcement* 3, no. 6 (2014).

Eastern Kentucky University Justice and Safety Center. *SAVER Program Report: Incident Decision Support Software Application Note (Cooperative Agreement #EMW-2005-CA-0378 awarded by DHS).* Richmond, KY: Eastern Kentucky University. 2010.

Eastern Kentucky University Justice and Safety Center. *SAVER Program Report: Mobile Command Systems Application Note (Cooperative Agreement #EMW-2005-CA-0378 awarded by DHS).* Richmond, KY: Eastern Kentucky University. 2010.

Eastern Kentucky University Justice and Safety Center. *SAVER Program Report: Mobile Computing through the Cloud (Cooperative Agreement #EMW-2005-CA-0378 awarded by DHS)*. Richmond, KY: Eastern Kentucky University. 2012.

Eastern Kentucky University Justice and Safety Center. *SAVER Program Report: Propagation Modeling Software Application Note (Cooperative Agreement #EMW-2005-CA-0378 awarded by DHS)*. Richmond, KY: Eastern Kentucky University. 2010.

First Responder Network Authority. "About FirstNet." Reston, VA: First Responder Network Authority. http://www.firstnet.gov/about.

First Responder Network Authority. *How Will the FirstNet Network Work with To-day's Land Mobile Radio Networks?* Reston, VA: First Responder Network Authority.

Heaton, B. "Making the Connection: The National Public Safety Broadband Network Moves Forward—But Hurdles Remain." *Government Technology* 26, no. 4 (2013): 18–22.

Mell, P., and T. Grance. *The NIST Definition of Cloud Computing (Special Publication 800-145)*. Gaithersburg, MD: National Institute of Standards and Technology.

Miller, R. "Hurricane Katrina: Communications and Infrastructure Impacts." In *Threats at Our Homeland: Homeland Defense and Homeland Security in the New Century—A Compilation of the Proceedings of the First Annual Homeland Defense and Homeland Security Conference*, ed. B. Tussing, 191–204. Carlisle Barracks, PA: U.S. Army War College. 2006.

Montana Public Safety Communications Bureau. "Public Safety Communications" [online slide show]. Helena, MT: Montana Public Safety Communications Bureau. http://www.broadband.mt.gov/js_objs/fg_slideshow/pub_safety/index.html.

Motorola Solutions, Inc. *White Paper: 5 Trends Transforming Public Safety Communications*. Schaumburg, IL: Motorola Solutions, Inc. 2015.

National Commission on Terrorist Attacks upon the United States. *The 9/11 Commission Report*. Washington, DC: National Commission on Terrorist Attacks upon the United States. 2004.

Partnership for Public Warning. *The Emergency Alert System: An Assessment (PPW Report 400–1)*. McLean, VA: Partnership for Public Warning. 2004.

Pine, J. C. *Technology in Emergency Management*. Hoboken, NJ: John Wiley and Sons, Inc. 2007.

Schaffer, G. (panelist). "The National Broadband (Communications) Plan: Issues for Public Safety" [National Institute of Justice conference transcript]. Washington, DC: National Institute of Justice. 2011. http://nij.ncjrs.gov/multimedia/audio-nijconf2011-national-broadband-plan.htm#tab2.

Select Bipartisan Committee to Investigate the Preparation for and Response to Hurricane Katrina, *A Failure of Initiative, 109th Congress*, R. REP. NO. 109–377. 2006.

Simpkins, B. *2014–2015 National Rural Training Needs Assessment—Volume II: Assessing Capability and Training Needs within Rural Communities*. Richmond, KY: Eastern Kentucky University. 2015.

U.S. Department of Defense. *Military Standard 810G (MIL-STD-810G): Environmental Engineering Considerations and Laboratory Tests.* Washington, DC: U.S. Department of Defense. 2008.

U.S. Department of Homeland Security. *National Emergency Communications Plan.* Washington, DC: U.S. Department of Homeland Security. 2014.

U.S. Department of Homeland Security. *National Incident Management System.* Washington, DC: U.S. Department of Homeland Security. 2008.

U.S. Department of Homeland Security. *National Preparedness Goal* (2nd ed.). Washington, DC: U.S. Department of Homeland Security. 2015.

CHAPTER TWELVE

Fire Protection Systems for Infrastructure Protection

Scott Rockwell

Learning Objectives

After reading this chapter, readers should be able to:

- Explain the usefulness of fire protection technology.
- Describe different kinds of fire protection systems.
- Summarize what standards control the use of fire protection systems.
- Understand the use of notification systems.
- Identify many of the various uses of fire alarm systems in buildings.

Key Terms

Alarms
Emergency Notification
Fire Protection Systems

Introduction

FIRES CAUSE SIGNIFICANT DAMAGE TO property and industrial facilities in the United States and around the world every year. For instance, in 2014 approximately 1.3 million fires were reported in the United States. These fires caused $11.6 billion in direct property damage.[1] In addition to the cost of direct property damage, additional costs of fires include fire department expenditures, injuries to civilians and firefighters, and net insurance costs. In 2011, the National Fire Protection Association (NFPA) estimated that the total cost of fires was $329 billion, which is significantly more than the entire 2011 budget for the National Aeronautics and Space Administration (NASA).[2] Looking specifically at industrial and manufacturing property fires, from 2006 to 2010 there were an estimated 42,800 fires, which caused approximately $951 million in property damage annually in the United States alone.[3]

Fires can be started by a variety of causes, which can be categorized into three major categories: intentional, unintentional/accidental, and natural. Infrastructure protection systems should be designed to deal with all three kinds. In 2013 intentional home structure fires represented an estimated 8 percent of the total, and from 2007 to 2011, intentional fires caused $1.3 billion in direct property damage annually.[4] Candles are an example of accidental fires. From 2007 to 2011, candles caused an average of 10,630 home fires and $418 million in direct property damage annually.[5] An example of a natural fire cause is lightning. Based on NFPA reports, from 2007 to 2011, an estimated 22,600 fires were caused by lightning each year.[6] These fires caused an estimated $451 million in direct property damage per year.

Within structure fires, an example of a compartment fire is a room in a residential structure. This type of compartment fire can grow very rapidly. *NFPA 1710 Standard for the Organization and Deployment of Fire Suppression Operations, Emergency Medical Operations, and Special Operations to the Public by Career Fire Departments* recommends that the initial arriving fire department company should be within four minutes of an alarm notification.[7] In four minutes time, many fires will have grown substantially, and this does not take into account the amount of time needed for an alarm to be sent to emergency services. A typical residential room with a compartment fire becomes unsustainable for civilians in about four minutes (the upper room layer rapidly exceeds 600°C) and can make firefighting activities difficult, which can lead to the onset of flashover. The impact of fires can be reduced by having an alarm that notifies emergency services and occupants faster, having passive systems to prevent fire spread, or having active systems that suppress the fire when the fire is detected.

Fire protection systems come in active forms, such as sprinkler systems, and passive forms, such as fire-rated walls and doors. Whether to use active systems, passive systems, and/or a combination of both will depend on the standards required in a given jurisdiction and the building designer.

Which codes and standards govern the requirements for fire protection systems vary by jurisdiction, but for the purposes of this text, the focus is on the NFPA standards. These standards can be found on the NFPA Web site.[8] As a place to start, *NFPA 1 Fire Code* provides minimum requirements for building construction, maintenance, fire department access, and others. This code has been adopted statewide in 19 states in the United States.[9] In a similar way, *NFPA 101 Life Safety Code* specifies minimum requirements for building design, construction, operation, and others to protect occupants from fire, smoke, and toxic fumes. This code has been adopted statewide in 43 states.[10]

Fire Protection Alarm Systems

Fire alarms and extinguishment systems can contribute greatly to both notification and protection of equipment and materials. *NFPA 72 National Fire Alarm and Signaling Code* provides minimum requirements for application, installation, location, performance, testing, maintenance of fire alarm systems, and so on. Fire alarms can be set up to notify not only the inhabitants of a structure but also outside agencies. Many fire alarms go directly into an area's 9-1-1 emergency system or other emergency communication systems but can be set up to notify private security firms as well. Commercial products are even being sold that listen for a residential fire alarm and notify homeowners on their smartphones if an alarm sounds in their home. Current systems can also be set up to detect many different kinds of threats. Smoke detectors are sometimes considered the most common type of detector, but there are also heat detectors, radiation detectors, ignitable gas detectors, water flow alarms, manual pull stations, and others. Fire alarm stations will typically have an auditory and visual component. Some modern building alarms will not only have a warning tone and flashing lights but will also provide people with information about the nature of the threat. The information is provided in an attempt to get occupants to react to the correct type of emergency and reduce the time required for people to begin to move after an alarm sounds.

External Agency Notifications

Fire alarm systems can be set up in a variety of ways. Systems can be set up to evacuate parts of buildings or the entire structure. Alarms can be set to notify only occupants of a building or notify external agencies as well. There are also multistage alarms; for instance, in labs that use ignitable gasses (such as propane), some flammable gas alarm systems will sound an audible alarm in the lab at a low percentage of the lower flammable limit (LFL) and a building evacuation alarm at a higher percentage of the LFL. The first alarm allows the laboratory technicians to find and fix small fuel leaks without having to evacuate the entire building.

Active Fire Protection Systems

There are many different types of commercial systems to protect structures from fire and even certain types of industrial explosions. This section provides a brief overview of many of the major kinds of fire and explosion protection systems. Due to the wide variety of available technology, not every type of system can be covered here.

Sprinkler Systems

Sprinkler systems can fall into a variety of categories. *NFPA 13 Standard for the Installation of Sprinkler Systems* describes requirements for design, installation, and testing of sprinkler systems in typical buildings. There are also *NFPA 13R Standard for the Installation of Sprinkler Systems in Low-Rise Residential Occupancies* and *NFPA 13D Standard for the Installation of Sprinkler Systems in One- and Two-Family Dwellings and Manufactured Homes*, which describe requirements for those specific occupancies. Many systems use a heat-activated sprinkler head, which will open one sprinkler as heat reaches it. This is done to release water specifically where the heat from a fire is, limit the amount of water used, and minimize water damage. An assortment of sprinkler heads are available for installation. Some use a glass bulb filled with a liquid that will expand and break the glass when heated, and others have fusible metal links, which will melt when heated to release the water. The amount of heat required to activate a sprinkler, and the amount of water the sprinkler puts out, depends on the design. Other sprinkler systems, known as deluge systems, will pump water out of every nozzle when an activation signal is sent. There are different kinds of water-based systems, including sprinkler, water mist, and deluge. Describing each of these is outside the scope of this chapter; for more information, see the references listed in Table 12.1 at the end of this chapter. These water-based systems work to extinguish a fire in the same way: The water cools the area by absorbing heat and displacing oxygen as the water turns to steam and expands approximately 1,700 times (the actual amount of expansion depends on the specific temperature change of the water).

In some situations, water alone is not a good method for putting out a fire. Examples of this are oil or metal fires. Adding water to these types of fires will make the situation worse rather than better. Many of these types of fires can be handled with water-foam mixtures or the application of dry powder chemical agents. There are multiple types of foam agents that are designed to work on different categories of fires. It is important that the fire emergency services in a given area have the appropriate foam to deal with the hazards in their jurisdiction. It is also important that users of foams are aware of any environmental hazards associated with the release of the agent into the environment. The toxicity of different foam extinguishing agents varies significantly.

Dry chemical powders can also be used on various kinds of fires. Many handheld fire extinguishers use a dry chemical extinguishing agent usable for class A (normal combustibles), B (ignitable liquids), and C (involving electrical equipment) fires. Other powders should be used for class D (metal) fires. This is important because putting water on a metal fire can result in a violent reaction.

In some situations, using water to put out a fire is either difficult due to a lack of access or the water would do significant damage to the equipment in the facility. In these cases, alternative extinguishing agents are used. Some of these alternative agents are described in the next section.

Water Foam Systems

Many fires will not extinguish easily with water alone. Applying water onto fires fueled by some materials, such as oil, will make the fire worse. In many of these cases, foam additives can be combined with water to effectively extinguish the fire. These foams will usually form a blanket over the surface of the fuel. This blanket of foam reduces the radiant feedback to the fuel and prevents oxygen from reaching the fuel surface. *NFPA 11 Standard for Low-, Medium-, and High-Expansion Foam* and *NFPA 16 Standard for the Instillation of Foam-Water Sprinkler and Foam-Water Spray Systems* specify requirements for a variety of expansion foam systems. There are many different types of firefighting foams, each with a corresponding use, cost, and impact to the environment. Describing the cost and use of all of the different types of foams is outside the scope of this chapter, but readers are referred to the *Fire Dynamics* textbook for more information.[11]

Handheld Extinguishers in Buildings

Several codes require the use of portable fire extinguishers depending on the structure type and occupancy classification. *NFPA 10 Standard for Portable Fire Extinguishers* specifies requirements for selection, installation, inspection, maintenance, and testing of portable extinguishing equipment. Common equipment examples include CO_2 and dry chemical (ABC) portable fire extinguishers. Aircraft have their own specific standard for portable fire extinguishers: *NFPA 408 Standard for Aircraft Hand Portable Fire Extinguishers.*

Alternative Extinguishing Agents

NFPA 2001 Standard on Clean Agent Fire Extinguishing Systems lists requirements for both total flooding and local application of clean agent fire extinguishing systems. This standard covers both halogenated agents, which disrupt the chemical reaction of a gas phase flame, and inerting agents, which reduce the oxygen level in an environment to a level low enough to prevent combustion from continuing. These types of systems are often used when water is in short supply, or if potential damage caused by using water would be significant, such as in a data storage facility.

Explosion Protection Systems

Industrial explosions are a major cause of property loss and damage around the world. Causes of recent industrial explosions include wood dust, iron dust, methane and coal dust, sugar dust, plastic dust, and many more.[12] *NFPA 68 Standard on Explosion Protection by Deflagration Venting* describes the requirements for allowing the overpressure created by an explosion to be vented adequately to prevent the structure from being damaged. These systems include such technologies as pressure releasing vents and blowout panels/walls. Preventing structural damage is important because the majority of injuries and fatalities are caused by flying/falling debris rather than the explosion itself. There are also systems specifically designed to prevent explosions from propagating. *NFPA 69 Standard on Explosion Prevention Systems* provides requirements for this technology, which is meant to control oxidant concentration, control combustible concentration, explosion suppression, deflagration pressure containment, and spark extinguishing systems. These systems are for dispersed fuel oxidizer mixtures rather than military grade explosives. For instance, some explosion suppression systems expel an extinguishing agent at high speed when activated by a detection system. This extinguishing agent quenches the flame front before significant overpressure can build up. Many people are not aware that organic dusts such as sawdust, woodmeal, or sugar can cause catastrophic industrial explosions.

Smoke Control Systems

Smoke control systems are used to remove smoke from a building or prevent smoke from entering / building up in part of a structure. Smoke control technologies are especially useful in the area of a building being used for evacuation but can also be important if sensitive equipment is located in specific portions of the building. The heating, venting, and air conditioning system in these areas can be designed to work in conjunction with a smoke control system so that combustion products will not contaminate delicate technology. For further information, *NFPA 92 Standard for Smoke Control Systems* specifies requirements for design, installation, and testing of smoke control systems.

Passive Fire Protection Systems

Passive fire systems typically include fire-rated walls, doors, door release mechanisms, wall pass through devices, sealants, and buoyancy controlled vents. *NFPA 80 Standard for Fire Doors and Other Opening Protectives* provides requirements for the installation and maintenance of assemblies and devices used to protect openings in walls, floors, and ceilings against the spread of fire and smoke. As an example of technology used to accomplish this, new constructed fire-rated doors use a magnetic coupling to close the door when a fire alarm is activated. The closed door is used to prevent smoke and combustion products from freely traveling throughout the building. Also of interest is the opening mechanism, which opens with a push in the direction the door swings. This prevents crowd crush from prohibiting the opening of the door in an emergency.

One interesting and often overlooked type of technology is how utilities pass through fire-rated walls without making a path for the fire to spread. Multiple kinds of hardware are commercially available along with fire-rated foam sealants. Many of these foam sealants are intumescent materials. Intumescent materials form an expanding char layer when exposed to the heat from a fire. This thickened char layer protects the underneath material from being exposed to the heat flux of the fire.

Design of Fire Protection Systems

Fire protection systems for typical structures are designed using a combination of NFPA codes and standards or a comparable set of standards by another agency. When a building does not conform to the design of a typical structure or an architect does not want to use designs required by typical safety standards, a performance-based design can be done to create a system that meets the safety requirements. This design is then approved by the authority having jurisdiction. The performance-based design is done in the planning stages of a potential building and can theoretically be built directly into an infrastructure protection plan. Computer modeling is often used for performance-based design. Some of these models are discussed below. Fire protection system design is important, especially to both provide safety and minimize the number of false alarms. In 2013 an estimated 2.3 million false alarm or false calls to fire departments were placed. These are often due to system malfunctions and unintentional system calls.[13]

Traditional elevators are not designed to be used by civilians in a structure fire, but there are built-in override capabilities for firefighters. Modern building designers are starting to use smoke control technologies to make elevators safe for civilians to use in a fire emergency. The use of an elevator during an evacuation is important in tall buildings because it is difficult for everyone to escape from the top of a skyscraper in a reasonable amount of time if people have to walk down stairs. The tallest building will soon reach over 1,000 meters in height. Tall buildings also present a challenge to transport water for fire suppression to the top floors. Pumps must sometimes be staggered along the height of the building to generate enough flow at upper floors. In some cases, water tanks are built on the roofs of tall buildings to provide firefighting water to overcome this challenge. *NFPA 72 National Fire Alarm and Signaling Code* describes requirements for firefighter use of elevators.

Computer Fire Modeling Technologies

There are multiple types of computer fire models, but the three most common types are spreadsheet models, zone models, and field models. Spreadsheet models can be considered the simplest type of computer model. An example of a set of spreadsheet models is the Fire Dynamic Tools created by the U.S. Nuclear Regulatory Commission.[14] These are Microsoft Excel files with built-in macro programming that provide such calculations as heat flux to an object from a fire, compartment upper layer temperature, burn duration of a confined liquid fire, and others depending on which file is used. A more complex method is zone modeling, such as Consolidated Model of Fire and Smoke Transport (CFAST) created by the National Institute of Standards and Technology (NIST).[15] This type of model divides a compartment into two layers—a hot zone and a cold zone—and solves conservation equations on each zone to determine the conditions in the room for a specified fire. The most complicated methods are field models such as Fire Dynamic Simulator (FDS) created by NIST.[16] This type of model breaks up the simulation environment into a multitude of cells and solves conservation equations on each cell to determine the conditions in the simulation environment. All of these different types of models can be used to predict the behavior of combustion products inside of a specific structure with a given design fire. One use of these models is to allow fire protection engineers to calculate the available safe egress time (ASET) versus the required safe egress time (RSET). The comparison of ASET versus RSET can be used to show that a system design will allow all of the occupants of a building to exit safely without being exposed to heat or combustion products.

Firefighter Personal Protective Equipment

Firefighters have a variety of personal protective equipment they use depending on the emergency being addressed. The type of gear can vary between structural/vehicle fires, surface water operations, wildland fire-fighting, hazardous material emergencies, and medical emergencies. People typically think of turnout gear as boots, pants, coat, hood, helmet, and gloves made to temporarily protect the wearer from the elevated temperatures inside of a structure fire. A self-contained breathing apparatus (SCBA) is worn to provide firefighters with air to breath when inside of a smoke-filled structure. The SCBA includes a mask that protects the firefighters face as well. There is a limit to the protection these garments can provide; firefighters cannot sustain existence inside a fully involved compartment fire. If the firefighters are exposed to elevated temperatures for too long, they will begin to experience hypothermia, which has significant negative consequences on the health and cognitive function of the firefighter.

There are multiple more specialized types of suits that can protect fire-fighters in various hostile environments. One of the most commonly seen is a suit with a shiny silver exterior. This type of suit is used to protect firefighters from higher-than-normal levels of radiative heat flux often found when close to large industrial fires. Other types of suits are used to protect against biological and radiological agents, among others. There are a variety of NFPA codes and standards that specify requirements for pro-tective clothing including:

- *NFPA 1952 Standard on Surface Water Operations Protective Clothing and Equipment*
- *NFPA 1971 Standard Protective Ensembles for Structural Fire Fighting and Proximity Fire Fighting*

- NFPA 1877 Standard on Protective Clothing and Equipment for Wildland Fire Fighting
- NFPA 1999 Standard on Protective Clothing and Ensembles for Emergency Medical Operations
- NFPA 1986 Standard on Respiratory Protection Equipment for Technical and Tactical Operations
- NFPA 1981 Standard on Open-Circuit Self-Contained Breathing Apparatus (SCBA) for Emergency Services

Hazardous Materials Technologies

Hazardous materials (HAZMAT) technologies come in a variety of forms. Some of these include suits, showers, tents, and storage facilities. HAZMAT suits allow specialized workers to operate in dangerous environments. Decontamination showers allow workers to clean the HAZMAT suits so that the workers are not exposed to the hazard that may have contaminated the suit during work. There are rigid and inflatable tents that can be used to separate workers from a hazardous area or contain infected individuals or materials. Specialized containers are also available to store hazardous materials, whether it be nuclear, chemical, or biological. There are numerous codes and standards that specify requirements for technology to be used in hazardous situations:

- NFPA 400 Hazardous Materials Code
- NFPA 471 Recommended Practice for Responding to Hazardous Materials Incidents
- NFPA 1953 Standard on Protective Ensembles for Contaminated Water Diving
- NFPA 1991 Standard on Vapor-Protective Ensembles for Hazardous Materials Emergencies
- NFPA 1992 Standard on Liquid Splash-Protective Ensembles and Clothing for Hazardous Material Emergencies
- NFPA 1994 Standard on Protective Ensembles for Fire Responders to CBRN Terrorism Incidents

Urban Search and Rescue Technologies

Urban search and rescue technologies have changed over the years, and standards have been created to provide guidance to emergency personnel and manufacturers. Firefighters are often called upon to rescue people out of trapped environments, such as a crumpled car after a crash, which can involve the use of specialized power tools. These power tools are governed by NFPA 1936 Standard on Powered Rescue Tools. Other incidents involve planes and other forms of transportation. There are a number of standards that cover search and rescue technologies relevant to urban environment, including:

- *NFPA 402 Guide for Aircraft Rescue and Fire-Fighting Operations*
- *NFPA 1670 Standard on Operations and Training for Technical Search and Rescue Incidents*
- *NFPA 1855 Standard Selection, Care, and Maintenance of Protective Ensembles for Technical Rescue Incidents*
- *NFPA 1951 Standard on Protective Ensembles for Technical Rescue Incidents*
- *NFPA 1670 Standard on Operations and Training for Technical Search and Rescue Incidents*

Special Topics

When operating in nonstandard atmospheric conditions such as in a submarine, aircraft, or spaceship, the behavior of combustion becomes different. Flammability limits change, burning rates differ, and smoke movement can change. When the pressure, temperature, or oxygen concentration varies, the way fire behaves can change. Describing the specifics of this behavior is outside of the scope of this text, but individuals should be aware of these variations. Microgravity combustion in spacecraft is an interesting topic. As humans spend more time in outer space, the problems of preventing fires becomes a major concern. This was especially true on early spacecraft that used pure oxygen atmospheres. Modern spacecraft typically use a normal earth atmosphere composition, but fires still need to be prevented or controlled quickly since the astronauts cannot simply leave the spacecraft to escape the fire. The placement of smoke detectors has to be chosen carefully since without gravity, smoke does not rise due to buoyancy. Often, smoke detectors are placed in ventilation intake ducts. Handheld water foam and CO_2 extinguishers are currently used on the International Space Station.[17] The materials taken to the space station are also limited to minimize the risk of an accidental fire. In 1997 the Russian space station MIR had a serious fire caused by an oxygen generation device that overheated. This fire is interesting because the source of the fire created its own oxygen to sustain the burning process. In this situation, both water and foam extinguishers were used in an attempt to put out the fire.[18] The smoke from this fire required the astronauts to wear personal breathing apparatus and put a strain on the station's atmospheric management system.

Conclusion

Fire protection technology has come a long way since its beginnings in the 20th century. This technology can be of significant benefit

Table 12.1 Resources for Fire Protection System Design

Book Title	Author
SFPE Handbook of Fire Protection Engineering	Philip J. Dinenno
Fire Protection Handbook	Arthur E. Cote
Industrial Fire Protection Engineering	Robert G. Zalosh
Fire Protection Engineering in Building Design (Plant Engineering)	Jane I. Lataille
Handbook of Fire and Explosion Protection Engineering Principles	Dennis P. Nolan
Fire Protection Systems	Maurice Jones Jr.
Industrial Fire Protection Handbook	Craig Schroll
Fire Protection: Systems and Response	Robert Burke
Fire Safety Engineering Design of Structures	John A. Purkiss
Structural Design for Fire Safety	Andrew H. Buchnan
Fire Detection and Suppression Systems	Ted Boothroyd
Fire Detection & Suppression Systems	IFSTA

to infrastructure protection when used appropriately. A wide variety of technology can be used to protect against fires and notify safety professionals if an emergency occurs. This chapter provided a brief overview of different technology and fire protection systems, and was meant as a general overview of the different fire protection technologies that can be used for infrastructure protection. For more in-depth information on these and other technologies, Table 12.1 lists a variety resources.

Discussion Questions

1. In six sentences, describe the differences between active and passive fire protection systems.
2. In six sentences, describe a fire or explosion that occurred near your hometown in the last five years.
3. What are three of the codes and/or standards that control what kinds of fire protection systems are required for a given structure?
4. Describe a situation in which a blowout panel would be used for explosion protection.
5. Describe a situation where a smoke control system would be used.

6. Describe the difference between the direct cost of a fire and the total cost of a fire.
7. What is the benefit of fire and explosion modeling software?
8. What is the purpose of a fire-rated door or wall?
9. What is the difference between natural, accidental, and intentional fires?

Notes

1. Haynes, *Fire Loss in the United States During 2014*.
2. Hall, *The Total Cost of Fire in the United States*; National Aeronautics and Space Administration, "Budget Information."
3. Evarts, *Fires in U.S. Industrial and Manufacturing Facilities*.
4. National Fire Protection Association, *NFPA's Latest Estimates of Intentional Home Structure Fires—2013*; Campbell, *Intentional Fires*.
5. National Fire Protection Association, *U.S. Home Candle Fires Fact Sheet*.
6. Ahrens, *Lightning Fires and Lightning Strikes*.
7. Flynn, *Fire Service Performance Measures*.
8. National Fire Protection Association, "Document Information Pages (List of NFPA Codes and Standards)."
9. National Fire Protection Association, *NFPA 1: Fire Code (Fact Sheet)*.
10. National Fire Protection Association, *NFPA 101: Life Safety Code (Fact Sheet)*.
11. Gorbett and Pharr, *Fire Dynamics*.
12. Rockwell and Rangwala, "Influence of Coal Dust on Premixed Turbulent Methane-Air Flames"; Rockwell and Rangwala, "Modeling of Dust Air Flames."
13. Karter, *Trends and Patterns of U.S. Fire Losses in 2013*.
14. U.S. Nuclear Regulatory Commission, *Fire Dynamic Tools*.
15. National Institute of Standards and Technology, "CFAST, Fire Growth and Smoke Transport Modeling."
16. National Institute of Standards and Technology, "FDS and Smokeview."
17. National Aeronautics and Space Administration, "Fire Prevention in Space."
18. National Aeronautics and Space Administration, "Fire and Controversy."

Bibliography

Ahrens, M. *Lightning Fires and Lightning Strikes*. Quincy, MA: National Fire Protection Association. 2013.

Campbell, R. *Intentional Fires*. Quincy, MA: National Fire Protection Association. 2014.

Evarts, B. *Fires in U.S. Industrial and Manufacturing Facilities*. Quincy, MA: National Fire Protection Association. 2012.

Flynn, J. *Fire Service Performance Measures.* Quincy, MA: National Fire Protection Association. 2009.

Gorbett, G., and J. Pharr. *Fire Dynamics.* Upper Saddle River, NJ: Prentice Hall. 2010.

Hall, J. *The Total Cost of Fire in the United States.* Quincy, MA: National Fire Protection Association. 2014.

Haynes, H. *Fire Loss in the United States During 2014.* Quincy, MA: National Fire Protection Association. 2015.

Karter, M. *Trends and Patterns of U.S. Fire Losses in 2013.* Quincy, MA: National Fire Protection Association. 2014.

National Aeronautics and Space Administration. "Budget Information." National Aeronautics and Space Administration. Last modified February 14, 2011. http://www.nasa.gov/news/budget/2011.html.

National Aeronautics and Space Administration. "Fire and Controversy." National Aeronautics and Space Administration. Accessed January 2016. http://history.nasa.gov/SP-4225/nasa4/nasa4.htm#fire.

National Aeronautics and Space Administration. "Fire Prevention in Space." National Aeronautics and Space Administration. Last modified November 22, 2007. http://www.nasa.gov/missions/shuttle/f_fireprevention.html.

National Fire Protection Association. "Document Information Pages (List of NFPA Codes and Standards)." National Fire Protection Association. Accessed January 2016. http://www.nfpa.org/codes-and-standards/document-information-pages.

National Fire Protection Association. *NFPA 1: Fire Code (Fact Sheet).* Quincy, MA: National Fire Protection Association. 2015.

National Fire Protection Association. *NFPA 101: Life Safety Code (Fact Sheet).* Quincy, MA: National Fire Protection Association. 2015.

National Fire Protection Association. *NFPA's Latest Estimates of Intentional Home Structure Fires—2013.* Quincy, MA: National Fire Protection Association. 2015.

National Fire Protection Association. *U.S. Home Candle Fires Fact Sheet.* Quincy, MA: National Fire Protection Association. 2015.

National Institute of Standards and Technology. "FDS and Smokeview." National Institute of Standards and Technology. Last modified November 9, 2015. http://www.nist.gov/el/fire_research/fds_smokeview.cfm.

National Institute of Standards and Technology. "CFAST, Fire Growth and Smoke Transport Modeling." National Institute of Standards and Technology. Last modified December 10, 2015. http://www.nist.gov/el/fire_research/cfast.cfm.

Rockwell, S., and A. Rangwala. "Influence of Coal Dust on Premixed Turbulent Methane-Air Flames." *Combustion and Flame* 160, no. 3 (2013): 635–640.

Rockwell, S., and A. Rangwala. "Modeling of Dust Air Flames." *Fire Safety Journal* 59 (2013): 22–29.

U.S. Nuclear Regulatory Commission. *Fire Dynamic Tools: Quantitative Fire Hazard Analysis Methods for the U.S. Nuclear Regulatory Commission Fire Protection Inspection Program.* Washington, DC: U.S. Nuclear Regulatory Commission. 2013.

CHAPTER THIRTEEN

Conclusion

The Future of Homeland Security Technology

Ryan K. Baggett and Chad S. Foster

Learning Objectives

After reading this chapter, readers should be able to:

- Identify and explain the Technology Life Cycle and Technology Readiness Levels and apply the phases to a specific technology.
- Distinguish between forecasted technological trends and recognize existing technologies exhibiting the trends.
- Evaluate technological trends and demonstrate how each of the trends may be used in homeland security technologies to carry out the identified mission.
- Identify the five U.S. Department of Homeland Security, Science and Technology Directorate visionary goals and analyze their importance to emergency responders throughout the United States.

Key Terms

Futurology/Future Studies
Research and Development
Technological Forecasting
Technology Life Cycle (TLC)
Technology Readiness Level (TRL)
Technology Trends

Introduction

FUTURE STUDIES OR FUTUROLOGY IS a growing field of study that examines the possible and preferable futures and the world views and myths that underlie them. Likely this field can be seen as part art and part science, but futurists seek to understand patterns of past and present and determine the likelihood of future events and trends.[1] Emerging technologies continue to be a common area of study for futurists due to the impact technology has on societal change. In 2015, Microsoft co-founder Bill Gates was asked his opinion of what the next 30 years holds in terms of technology. He stated:

> There will be more progress in the next 30 years than ever. Even in the next 10, problems like vision and speech understanding and translation will be very good. Mechanical robot tasks like picking fruit or moving a hospital patient will be solved. Once computers/robots get to a level of capability where seeing and moving is easy for them then they will be used very extensively.[2]

Technology Life Cycle

Technological forecasting is a subset of future studies that looks at technology deployment timelines and characteristics. Forecasters base predictions on the premise that the technology of the future depends on economic, ethical, social, and political considerations. An important concept used by technological forecasters is "stages of innovation."[3] Every technological advance passes through certain stages, with each stage representing a greater degree of practicality or use. While there are variations on the model, a popular framework is Technology Life Cycle (TLC) as identified in Figure 13.1.

As displayed in the TLC, the first phase of the cycle is research and development (R&D). Companies invest in the most promising technologies based on market research and other techniques. Based on this data, a calculated risk is taken where R&D is conducted to move a technology toward commercialization. Second, the Ascent Phase (A) follows R&D where a company recovers out-of-pocket costs and the technology begins to see rapid growth and distribution. The technology is the "latest and greatest" on the market at this point and companies can leverage the competitive advantage.[4] Next, technologies entering the Maturity Phase (M) have been on the market for an extended period and have seen other competitors enter and compete. The supply of the technology begins to surpass the demand, and financial returns begin to slow. This slowdown ultimately turns into the last phase of Decline or Decay (D). It's in this phase that sales

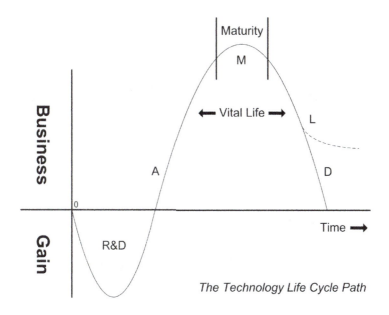

Figure 13.1 Technology Life Cycle (Source: Adapted from Jayalath, "Understanding S-Curve of Technology Innovation").

decline drastically until the technology fails to turn profit.[5] It should also be noted that it is during the decline phase that some companies may choose to License (L) out the technology so that it can still be attractive to firms in other markets.

Obviously the time period spent in each phase differs depending on the technology and the current financial market. Unfortunately, it should be noted that some technologies do not move past the R&D phase and some find their Decline or Decay phase much faster than others. In the end, this cycle allows futurists to better predict the adoption, acceptance, and eventual decline of new technological innovations.[6] As such, the final chapter of this textbook will examine future technology trends in both the private sector and the homeland security enterprise. The chapter is designed to encourage readers to think critically about the future development and consequences of emerging technologies.

Technology Readiness Level

Related to the TLC is the Technology Readiness Level (TRL), which allows for estimation of technology maturity based on critical technology elements. It can help management make informed decisions concerning R&D of technologies and allows for the consistent evaluation of technical maturity across different types of technology. As identified in Figure 13.2, there are nine technology readiness levels, with one being the lowest and nine being the highest.

TRL 1, the basic research phase, includes initial scientific research on the concept. Applied research begins at the TRL 2 level with the formulation of the technology concept and/or application to include the determination of what problems would be solved or what needs would be satisfied. At this level, practical applications are invented and basic principles are observed. The proof of concept or critical function level (TRL 3) then commences where active R&D occurs and analytical and laboratory studies are conducted. Next, TRL 4 is the lab testing/validation level in which technological components are integrated to form the system with subsequent system validation. The fifth TRL (TRL 5) evaluates the technology in a simulated operational environment to increase fidelity of the system. The beginning prototype phase takes place in TRL 6 with testing, which demonstrates a major step in a technology's demonstrated readiness. The last three TRLs place the technology in various operational environments.

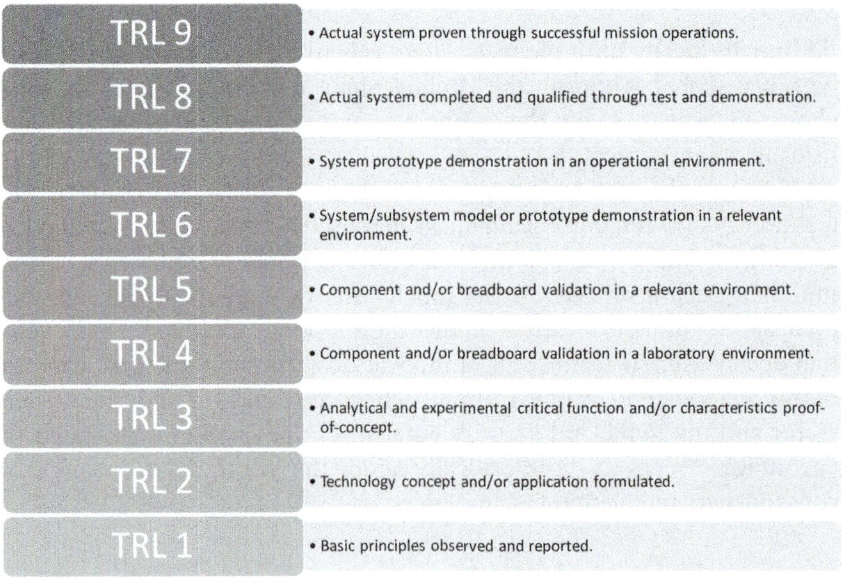

TRL 9	• Actual system proven through successful mission operations.
TRL 8	• Actual system completed and qualified through test and demonstration.
TRL 7	• System prototype demonstration in an operational environment.
TRL 6	• System/subsystem model or prototype demonstration in a relevant environment.
TRL 5	• Component and/or breadboard validation in a relevant environment.
TRL 4	• Component and/or breadboard validation in a laboratory environment.
TRL 3	• Analytical and experimental critical function and/or characteristics proof-of-concept.
TRL 2	• Technology concept and/or application formulated.
TRL 1	• Basic principles observed and reported.

Figure 13.2 Technology Readiness Levels (Source: Adapted from National Aeronautics and Space Administration, "Technology Readiness Level").

First, TRL 7 places the system prototype in its intended mission space. Next, TRL 8 incorporates the system into commercial design and qualifies it through testing and demonstration. Finally, TRL 9 is the level at which the system is proven and ready for full commercial deployment.[7]

Since the development of the TRL by the National Aeronautics and Space Administration (NASA) in the 1970s, it has been adopted and adapted by the U.S. Department of Defense, the oil and gas industry, the European Space Agency, and the European Commission. Although the foundation remains the same, these agencies have adapted the model to fit their particular mission space. Additionally, others have built interactive tools to assist with TRL determination, such as the Technology Readiness Level Calculator developed by the U.S. Air Force Research Laboratory.[8] In 2008, the Homeland Security Institute modified the existing U.S. Air Force calculator for use within the U.S. Department of Homeland Security (DHS) Science and Technology Directorate (S&T). The calculator allowed users to assess the readiness levels of technology as well as the RLs of manufacturing and programmatics independently of one another.[9]

Technology Trends

Earlier this year, David Cearley of Gartner, Inc. forecasted the top 10 technology trends.[10] Cearley's trends are neatly categorized into the three categories of the Digital Mesh, New Information Technology (IT) Reality, and Smart Machines. This section will highlight a few of those trends and provide highlights on which readers can future investigate.

- **The Device Mesh:** This term refers to endpoints people use to access applications and information or interact with people, social communities, governments, and businesses. This mesh includes all the Internet-connected devices a user possesses, which include mobile and home electronic devices. Gartner projects significant development in wearables and augmented reality, especially virtual reality.
- **Ambient User Experience:** Ambient means that information is always in the cognitive background and will always be available. Cearley notes that the "experience blends physical, virtual, and electronic environments, and uses real-time contextual information as the ambient environment changes or as the user moves from one place to another."
- **Three-Dimensional (3-D) Printing Materials:** Futurists anticipate that more materials will be utilized in 3-D printing to include nickel alloys, carbon fiber, glass, conductive ink, electronics, pharmaceuticals, and biological materials for practical applications expanding into aerospace, medical, automotive, energy, and the military. Additionally, it is anticipated that in the future these materials may be combined in a single build.

- **Advanced Machine Learning:** Machine learning has allowed smart machines the ability to learn and change their behavior. This advancement "is important because as models are exposed to new data, they are able to independently adapt. They learn from previous computations to produce reliable, repeatable decisions and results."[11]
- **Adaptive Security Architecture:** As the level of sophistication in technologies increases, coupled with increased reliance on technology by the public, developers work diligently to develop adaptive security architecture. Gartner notes that "comprehensive protection requires an adaptive protection process integrating predictive, preventive, detective, and response capabilities."[12]

A myriad of publications are available on the future of emerging technologies. Readers are encouraged to review related publications and determine the plausibility and consequence of the technology's implementation to current society. Many of the trends noted above can also be transferred to the homeland security enterprise in an effort to support the five mission areas[13] of:

- Preventing terrorism and enhancing security
- Securing and managing U.S. borders
- Enforcing and administering U.S. immigration laws
- Safeguarding and securing cyberspace
- Ensuring resilience to disasters

The remainder of this chapter will focus on several U.S. Department of Homeland Security, Science and Technology Directorate Apex programs that "look strategically at the nation's security and address future challenges while continuing to support today's operational needs."[14]

The Future of Homeland Security Technology

Entities across the world are applying science, technology, and creativity to develop technologies that will be used to thwart terrorism, to train emergency responders, to effectively respond to disease outbreaks, and in other homeland security-related activities.[15] In the United States, DHS is funding research and development to address these challenges. Specifically, DHS S&T has developed five visionary goals that will be accomplished partly through the implementation of technology.

Screening at Speed[16]

Ever since the 1988 bombing of Pan Am Flight 103 and the more recent 2009 "Underwear Bomber" who smuggled plastic explosives onboard

Northwest Airlines Flight 253, the ability to screen explosives in commercial aviation has been a significant challenge. In a 2016 House Committee Hearing, a DHS official noted the need to "implement unobtrusive screening of people, baggage, or cargo that will enable the seamless detection of threats while respecting privacy, with minimal impact to the pace of travel and speed of commerce."[17] One component of the advanced screening technology will be the development of the "Aviation Checkpoint of the Future."

The Aviation Checkpoint of the Future will more effectively and efficiently detect aviation threats with automated threat recognition/detection software implementation to lessen human error. The advanced software will better detect potentially harmful items in the midst of other items carried by passengers.[18] DHS hopes that the automated checkpoint features will lead to an expedited process for passengers and an overall safer travel experience.

Trusted Cyber Future

DHS predicts that "in a future of increasing cyber connections, the underlying digital infrastructure will be self-detecting, self-protecting, and self-healing. Users will trust that information is protected, illegal use is deterred, and privacy is not compromised with security operating seamlessly in the background."[19] The DHS Cyber Security Division identified three major challenges to protecting the nation's cyber infrastructure:

- Unknown system and network infiltration by adversaries
- Understanding of the cyber situation by owners/operators within the 16 critical infrastructure sectors is inaccurate, incomplete, or only achieved forensically and after the infiltration has occurred
- Network owners/operators lack strong ways to respond and mitigate the impact of adversarial infiltrations while still allowing for adequate operating capacity[20]

The primary technological and threat drivers within the cyber future include the continued growth of the Internet of Things (IoT), which will lead to a large magnitude of devices interacting with the Internet. The reliance on the Internet will increase based on daily activities, which will likely decrease the barriers for cyber criminals.[21]

Enable the Decision Maker

According to the DHS, "predictive analytics, risk analysis, and modeling and simulation systems will enable critical and proactive decisions to be made based on the most relevant information, transforming data into actionable information. Even in the face of uncertain environments involving chemical, biological, radiological, or nuclear (CBRNE) incidents, accurate, credible, and context-based information will empower the aware decision maker to take instant actions to improve critical outcomes."[22] One example of this capability is the DHS Apex Real-Time Biothreat Awareness program.[23]

The Real-Time Biothreat Awareness program is a bio-surveillance system that seeks to provide timely intelligence to multiple entities. This information will enable informed and confident decisions that will likely minimize the impact of a biological incident. Situational awareness is imperative for homeland security partners in their ability to identify, process, and comprehend the critical elements of information about what is happening at a scene.[24]

Responder of the Future (Protected, Connected, Fully Aware)

In order to carry out the mission, the future homeland security partner must have comprehensive physical protection, interoperable tools, and networked threat detection and mitigation capabilities. DHS's Next Generation First Responder (NGFR) program looks to enhance protective gear, hands-free communication devices, integrated trans-jurisdictional communications, and technology that provides enhanced situational awareness for decision support. The goal of the NGFR is to save lives and help homeland security partners do their jobs more safely and effectively.[25]

Resilient Communities

The current state of U.S. critical infrastructure is in decay and would likely not withstand various emerging threats. One objective is to design infrastructure that will be built and maintained to withstand naturally occurring and man-made disasters. Additionally, by using advanced analytics, authorities will anticipate the effects of disasters, and use various technologically advanced countermeasures to shield communities from negative consequences. By incorporating resilience (the ability to adapt in the face of adversity) into communities, society may be able to return to a state of normalcy (e.g., recover) faster and with less disruption than in the past.

An example of such a program is the DHS Flood Apex, which is designed to incorporate new technologies to reduce flood fatalities and property loss and enhance overall community resilience to flooding. A key premise of the program is to develop decision support tools to better enable communities to conduct pre- and post-event flood resiliency planning. The effort will include the identification and deployment of smart practices and collaboration with all levels of government to develop the National Flood Decision Support Toolbox.[26]

Dealing with Unknown Future

Despite the government's and futurists' best attempts at predicting the future of technologies, forecasts are largely based on conceptions of contemporary problems. Among other theories for homeland security, Chris Bellavita from the Naval Postgraduate School offered the issue-attention cycle[27] as one viable explanation for the homeland security enterprise.[28]

Essentially, the homeland security enterprise is ever-changing to meet the priorities and demands of the latest large-scale disaster. Each disaster results in a policy window that alters the trajectory of the nation, or even within different communities of practice. For example, solutions were sought to strengthen school safety and security following the 2012 shootings at Sandy Hook Elementary School in Connecticut. That same year, disaster resilience and infrastructure protection became a concern following Hurricane Sandy. According to the cycle, attention to problems eventually wanes as other events unfold such as wildfires, airplane accidents, and outbreaks of diseases such as Ebola. At least within the homeland security domain and given the difficulty conceiving future hazards and threats, a focus on technological solutions to current problems may be shortsighted.

Another challenge in predicting the future of technologies within the homeland security domain is the division of labor that exists among all enterprise partners. Homeland security is multidisciplinary, and homeland security problems may be unique based on one's perspective. The U.S. Border Patrol is certainly concerned with border security and related technologies, while a local hospital is focused on detecting infectious diseases and a state department of transportation is charged with inspecting the structural integrity of bridges. Especially for those who support an all-hazards view of homeland security, attempting to categorize homeland security technologies is problematic.

Many of the predictions noted in this chapter also reflect broad changes at the societal level. Roy Amara, past president of The Institute for the Future, is known for quoting the following axiom: "We tend to overestimate the effect of a technology in the short run and underestimate the effect in the long run."[29] In other words, it is extremely difficult to predict how changes will unfold 30, 20, or even 10 years into the future. Beginning in the early 1990s, research focused on the "digital divide" or those with and without access to the Internet. Attention quickly shifted in the first decade of the 21st century to the "broadband divide," or those with and without high-speed networks. Today, the rage is all about mobile broadband networks, streaming wireless video, connecting wireless devices and IoT, and so on. Certainly there were some who could foresee where we are today back in 1990; however, few would claim that it is an exact science.

Conclusion

Throughout this book, readers have been introduced to a plethora of homeland security technologies. It is noted that the array of homeland security technologies is as varied as the threats facing the United States. According to Kaplan, "during the post-9/11 security spending phase, small companies with a specialization in homeland security technologies enjoyed considerable gains. As the market for such technologies has grown, many large companies with a history of government contracting joined the field."[30] As the largest consumer of homeland security technologies, DHS plays a paramount role in defining the market. Obviously, DHS does not specify what products to buy but rather what functions products should perform. DHS has also worked diligently to encourage and adopt standards to ensure reliable, interoperable, and effective technologies and processes. In the end, the future of homeland security technology and the threats faced by the United States are unknown. However, the limitless possibilities that technology may bring to society are at the same time bewildering and exciting. As U.S. politician Christopher Bond noted:

> Advances in technology will continue to reach far into every sector of our economy. Future job and economic growth in industry, defense, transportation, agriculture, health care, and life sciences is directly related to scientific advancement.[31]

Discussion Questions

1. As a homeland security technologist, you are hired at a company that specializes in developing alert and warning technologies. The company currently produces several different technologies with varying degrees of success. How could you utilize the Technology Life Cycle to explain the stages of the company's products at an upcoming shareholder's meeting?
2. It's your first day on the job working as a staffer for a local congressman. He has asked you to identify technological trends so that he can evaluate

a technology project in his district for which he has a keen interest. He has asked you to put the trends in layman's terms and not include a bunch of "techno jargon." How would you explain the trends identified in this chapter to him (someone who is not tech-savvy)?

3. As a U.S. presidential hopeful, you are looking for a few talking points regarding technology projects to strengthen homeland security. Out of the five visionary goals and associated projects, which one would you talk about on the campaign trail? What would you say about it and why?

Notes

1. Princeton University, "Futurology."

2. Soper, "Bill Gates on the Future of Technology, His Biggest Regret and Microsoft's HoloLens."

3. Rutgers University, "Methods and Approaches of Future Studies."

4. Boundless, "The Technology Life Cycle."

5. Ibid.

6. Ibid.

7. U.S. Department of Defense, *Technology Readiness Assessment (TRA) Guidance*; Brookhaven National Laboratory, "Technology Readiness Levels Definitions and Descriptions."

8. Nolte, Kennedy, and Dziegiel, "Technology Readiness Calculator."

9. Homeland Security Studies and Analysis Institute, *Department of Homeland Security Science and Technology Readiness Level Calculator (ver. 1.1)*.

10. Cearley, "Top 10 Technology Trends for 2016."

11. SAS, "Machine Learning."

12. MacDonald and Firstbrook, "Designing an Adaptive Security Architecture for Protection from Advanced Attacks."

13. U.S. Department of Homeland Security, "Our Mission."

14. U.S. Department of Homeland Security, "Apex Programs."

15. Anser, "Science and Technology Roundup."

16. U.S. Department of Homeland Security, "Apex Screening at Speed."

17. U.S. Department of Homeland Security, "Written Testimony of S&T Homeland Security."

18. U.S. Department of Homeland Security, "Apex Screening at Speed Infographic."

19. U.S. Department of Homeland Security, "Visionary Goals."

20. U.S. Department of Homeland Security, "Protecting the Nation's Cyber Infrastructure."

21. U.S. Department of Homeland Security, *Science and Technology Strategic Plan 2015–2019*.

22. U.S. Department of Homeland Security, "Visionary Goals."
23. U.S. Department of Homeland Security, "Apex Programs—Realtime Bio-threat Awareness Infographic."
24. U.S. Coast Guard, "Team Coordination Training."
25. U.S. Department of Homeland Security, "Next Generation First Responder Apex Program."
26. U.S. Department of Homeland Security, "Flood Apex Program Infographic."
27. Bellavita applied the issue-attention cycle originally advanced by the economist and political scientist Anthony Downs to homeland security.
28. Bellavita, "Waiting for Homeland Security Theory."
29. Avery, "Remember Some Forecaster's Axioms."
30. Kaplan, "Homeland Security Technologies."
31. Bond, "Christopher Bond Quotes."

Bibliography

Anser. "Science and Technology Roundup." *Homeland Security Forum*. Accessed April 2016. http://www.anser.org/node/3353.
Avery, M. "Remember Some Forecaster's Axioms." Institute for the Future. Accessed April 2016. http://www.iftf.org/future-now/article-detail/remember-remember -some-forecasters-axioms/.
Bellavita, C. "Waiting for Homeland Security Theory." *Homeland Security Affairs* 8, article 15. 2012.
Bond, C. "Christopher Bond Quotes." *BrainyQuote*. Accessed April 2016. http:// www.brainyquote.com/quotes/quotes/c/christophe168795.htm.
Boundless. "The Technology Life Cycle." Boundless. Last modified April 13, 2016. https://www.boundless.com/management/textbooks/boundless-management -textbook/organizational-culture-and-innovation-4/technology-and-innovation -37/the-technology-life-cycle-202-3486/.
Brookhaven National Laboratory. "Technology Readiness Levels Definitions and Descriptions." Brookhaven National Laboratory. Accessed April 2016. https:// www.bnl.gov/techtransfer/docs/Technology-Readiness-Levels-Definitions-and -Descriptions.pdf.
Cearley, D. "Top 10 Technology Trends for 2016." *Forbes Magazine*. Last modified January 15, 2016. http://www.forbes.com/sites/gartnergroup/2016/01/15/top -10-technology-trends-for-2016/#708fe5515ae9.
Homeland Security Studies and Analysis Institute. *Department of Homeland Security Science and Technology Readiness Level Calculator (ver. 1.1)*. Arlington, VA: Homeland Security Institute.
Jayalath, C. "Understanding the S-Curve of Technology Innovation." ArticlesBase. Accessed April 2016. http://www.articlesbase.com/technology-articles/under standing-the-s-curve-of-technology-innovation-1229680.html.
Kaplan, E. "Homeland Security Technologies." *Council on Foreign Relations*. Last modified November 19, 2007. http://www.cfr.org/defense-technology /homeland-security-technologies/p14827.

MacDonald, N., and P. Firstbrook. "Designing an Adaptive Security Architecture for Protection from Advanced Attacks." Gartner. Last modified February 12, 2014. https://www.gartner.com/doc/2665515/designing-adaptive-security -architecture-protection.

National Aeronautics and Space Administration. "Technology Readiness Level." National Aeronautics and Space Administration. Last modified October 28, 2012. https://www.nasa.gov/directorates/heo/scan/engineering/technology/txt _accordion1.html.

Nolte, W., B. Kennedy, and R. Dziegiel. "Technology Readiness Calculator." Defense Technical Information Center. Last modified October 20, 2003. http:// www.dtic.mil/ndia/2003systems/nolte2.pdf.

Princeton University. "Futurology." WordNet. Accessed April 2016. http:// wordnetweb.princeton.edu/perl/webwn?s=futurology.

Rutgers University. "Methods and Approaches of Futures Studies." Rutgers University. Accessed April 2016. http://crab.rutgers.edu/~goertzel/futuristmethods .htm.

SAS. "Machine Learning: What It Is and Why It Matters." SAS. Accessed April 2016. http://www.sas.com/en_us/insights/analytics/machine-learning.html.

Soper, T. "Bill Gates on the Future of Technology, His Biggest Regret, and Microsoft's HoloLens." *GeekWire*. Last modified January 28, 2015. http://www .geekwire.com/2015/bill-gates-future-technology-biggest-regret-microsofts -hololens/.

U.S. Coast Guard. "Team Coordination Training." U.S. Coast Guard. Last modified January 12, 2016. https://www.uscg.mil/auxiliary/training/tct/.

U.S. Department of Defense. *Technology Readiness Assessment (TRA) Guidance.* Washington, DC: U.S. Department of Defense. 2011.

U.S. Department of Homeland Security. "Apex Programs." U.S. Department of Homeland Security. Last modified March 18, 2016. https://www.dhs.gov/science -and-technology/apex-programs.

U.S. Department of Homeland Security. "Apex Screening at Speed Infographic." U.S. Department of Homeland Security. Accessed April 2016. https://www .dhs.gov/science-and-technology/screening-speed-infographic.

U.S. Department of Homeland Security. "Flood Apex Program Infographic." U.S. Department of Homeland Security. Accessed April 2016. https://www.dhs.gov /science-and-technology/flood-apex.

U.S. Department of Homeland Security. "Next Generation First Responder Apex Program." U.S. Department of Homeland Security. Accessed April 2016. https:// www.dhs.gov/science-and-technology/ngfr.

U.S. Department of Homeland Security. "Our Mission." U.S. Department of Homeland Security. Last modified March 21, 2016. https://www.dhs.gov/our -mission.

U.S. Department of Homeland Security. "Protecting the Nation's Cyber Infrastructure." U.S. Department of Homeland Security. Accessed April 2016. https://www .dhs.gov/science-and-technology/apex-ngci.

U.S. Department of Homeland Security. "Real-Time BioThreat Awareness Apex Program Infographic." U.S. Department of Homeland Security. Accessed April 2016. https://www.dhs.gov/science-and-technology/apex-biothreat-awareness -infographic.

U.S. Department of Homeland Security. *Science and Technology Strategic Plan 2015–2019.* Washington, DC: U.S. Department of Homeland Security. 2015.

U.S. Department of Homeland Security. "Screening at Speed." U.S. Department of Homeland Security. Accessed April 2016. https://www.dhs.gov/science-and -technology/apex-screening-speed.

U.S. Department of Homeland Security. "Visionary Goals." U.S. Department of Homeland Security. Accessed April 2016. https://www.dhs.gov/science-and -technology/visionary-goals.

U.S. Department of Homeland Security. "Written Testimony of S&T Homeland Security Advance Research Projects Agency Explosives Division Director Steve Wallen for a House Committee on Homeland Security, Subcommittee on Transportation Security Hearing Titled, 'Transportation Security Acquisition Reform Act: Examining Remaining Challenges.'" January 7, 2016. https://www .dhs.gov/news/2016/01/07/written-testimony-st-house-homeland-security -subcommittee-transportation-security.

Bibliography

Abramovich, G. "15 Mind-Blowing Stats about the Internet of Things." *CMO by Adobe.* Last modified April 17, 2015. http://www.cmo.com/articles/2015/4/13 /mind-blowing-stats-internet-of-things-iot.html.

Adelman, T. "Under New Leadership, FAA's Unmanned Aircraft Systems Integration Office Meets Its Deadline." *UAS News.* Last modified May 14, 2012. https:// www.suasnews.com/.

Advanced Glass Technology. "Advanced Glass Technology: Advanced Glass Protection Systems." Advanced Glass Technology. Accessed January 2016. http:// www.agtwindowfilm.com/.

Advanced Perimeter Systems. "Security Systems and Detection Products." Advanced Perimeter Systems. Accessed January 2016. http://www.aps-perimeter -security.com/products/.

Ahrens, M. *Lightning Fires and Lightning Strikes.* Quincy, MA: National Fire Protection Association. 2013.

Allen, I., and J. Seaman. *Changing Course: Ten Years of Tracking Online Education in the United States.* Babson Park, MA: Babson Survey Research Group and Quahog Research Group, LLC. 2013.

American Civil Liberties Union. "Does the USA PATRIOT Act Diminish Civil Liberties?" American Civil Liberties Union. Last modified July 2008. http://aclu .pro con.org/view.answers.php?questionID=000716.

American Civil Liberties Union. "What's Wrong with Public Video Surveillance?" American Civil Liberties Union. Accessed March 2016. https://www.aclu.org /whats-wrong-public-video-surveillance.

American Society of Safety Engineers. "Industry Notes: Professional Development —USFA Announces New Online Training System." *Professional Safety* 52, no. 12 (2007): 20.

Ameristar Security Products. "High Security Perimeter Fences." Ameristar Security Products. Accessed January 2016. http://www.ameristarsecurity.com/perimeter -fence/.

Andison, M., S. Benge, N. Miller, L. Francis, and H. Cherry. "Transformation and Training for a Mobile Workforce: Sharing Lessons Learnt." *International Journal*

of Integrated Care 14, no. 8 (2014). Retrieved from http://www.ijic.org/index
.php/ijic/article/viewFile/1746/2573.

Andrew, T., and D. Petkov. "The Need for a Systems Thinking Approach to the
Planning of Rural Telecommunications Infrastructure." *Telecommunications
Policy* 25 (2003): 75–93.

Andronie, M. "Distance Learning Management Based on Information Technology."
Contemporary Readings in Law and Social Justice 6, no. 1 (2014): 350–361.

Anser. "Science and Technology Roundup." *Homeland Security Forum.* Accessed
April 2016. http://www.anser.org/node/3353.

Antal, J. "Augmented Reality for the Soldier." *Military Technology* 37, no. 7 (2013):
27–30.

Anthem, Inc. "How to Access and Sign Up for Identity Theft Repair and Credit
Monitoring Services." Anthem, Inc. Last modified August 25, 2015. https://
www.anthemfacts.com/.

Association of Public-Safety Communications Officials International. "APCO and
NENA Reach Consensus Plan with Major Wireless Carriers on Improvements to
Locating 9-1-1 Callers." *APCO International.* Last modified November 15, 2014.
http://psc.apcointl.org/2014/11/15/apco-and-nena-reach-consensus-plan-with
-major-wireless-carriers-on-improvements-to-locating-9-1-1-callers/.

Association of Public-Safety Communications Officials International. "Comm
Center and 9-1-1." *APCO International.* Accessed January 2016. https://www
.apcointl.org/resources/9-1-1.html.

Association of Public-Safety Communications Officials International. "Project 25."
Last modified 2016. https://www.apcointl.org/spectrum-management/resources
/interoperability/p25.html.

Atherton, E., and P. Sheldon. "Correctional Training and Technology: Keys to the
Future." *Corrections Today* 73, no. 6 (2012): 28–33.

Atkinson, S. *Psychology and the Hacker—Psychological Incident Handling.* Bethesda,
MD: SANS Institute. 2015.

Avery, M. "Remember Some Forecaster's Axioms." Institute for the Future. Accessed
April 2016. http://www.iftf.org/future-now/article-detail/remember-remember
-some-forecasters-axioms/.

Bacon, J. *The Art of Community: Building the New Age of Participation.* Boston, MA:
O'Reilly Media. 2009.

Baggett, R. "The Effectiveness of Homeland Security Training for Rural Communities: A Comparative Analysis of Web-Based and Instructor-Led Training Delivery." Dissertation, Eastern Kentucky University. 2012.

Bailey, R. "Technology and Ethics." Coursera. Accessed March 2016. http://www
.coursera.org/.

Balanced Scorecard Institute. "Strategic Planning Basics." Balanced Scorecard Institute. Accessed February 16, 2016. http://balancedscorecard.org/Resources
/Strategic-Planning-Basics.

Baldwin, T., and J. Ford. "Transfer of Training: A Review and Directions for Future
Research." *Personnel Psychology* 41, no. 1 (1988): 63–105.

Banerjee, B. "The Evolution of Video Analytics." *Security Technology Executive* 25, no. 4 (2015): 30–33.

Barnard, J. "High Tech Security Glass." *Popular Science*. Last modified March 23, 2009. http://www.popsci.com/scitech/article/2009-03/high-tech-security-glass.

Basse, S. *A Gift of Fire: Social, Legal, and Ethical Issues for Computing Technology* (4th ed.). Upper Saddle River, NJ: Pearson. 2012

Bauer, L., L. Cranor, M. Reiter, and K. Vaniea. *Lessons Learned from the Deployment of a Smartphone-Based Access-Control System*. Pittsburg, PA: Carnegie Mellon University, School of Computer Science, Institute for Software Research. 2007.

Beard, L., C. Harper, and G. Riley. "Online versus On-Campus Instruction: Student Attitudes and Perceptions." *TechTrends* 48, no. 6 (2004): 29–31.

Bell, D. "The Third Technological Revolution and Its Possible Socioeconomic Consequences." In *Industrialization: Critical Perspectives on the World Economy*, ed. P. O'Brien. New York, NY: Routledge. 1988.

Bellavita, C. "Waiting for Homeland Security Theory." *Homeland Security Affairs* 8, Article 15. 2012.

Bennett, B. *Understanding, Assessing, and Responding to Terrorism: Protecting Critical Infrastructure and Personnel*. Hoboken, NJ: John Wiley and Sons. 2007.

Bennett, W. *Issues in Governance Studies (Number 55)—Unmanned at Any Speed: Bringing Drones into Our National Airspace*. Washington, DC: The Brookings Institution. 2012.

Berlusconi, G. "Paul Ekblom: Crime Prevention, Security and Community Safety Using the 5Is Framework." *European Journal of Criminal Policy and Research* 17 (2011): 249–251.

Bernstein Global Wealth Management. *Black Book: The Art of Cyber War—Asymmetric Payoffs Lead to More Spending on Protection*. New York, NY: Bernstein Global Wealth Management. 2010.

Bertram, J., J. Moskaliuk, and U. Cress. "Virtual Training: Making Reality Work." *Computers in Human Behavior* 43 (2015): 284–292.

Blanchard, K. *e-Learning: An Effective, Engaging Solution for Boosting Training Participation and Completion*. Escondido, CA: The Ken Blanchard Companies. 2009.

Bodell, P. "Communications: Bluetooth vs. NFC." *Security Info Watch*. Last modified August 9, 2013. http://www.securityinfowatch.com/article/11034554 /smartphone-access-control.

Bond, C. "Christopher Bond Quotes." *BrainyQuote*. Accessed April 2016. http:// www.brainyquote.com/quotes/quotes/c/christophe168795.htm.

Boundless. "The Technology Life Cycle." Boundless. Last modified April 13, 2016. https://www.boundless.com/management/textbooks/boundless-management -textbook/organizational-culture-and-innovation-4/technology-and-innova tion-37/the-technology-life-cycle-202-3486/.

Boyette, C. "Robots, Drones, and Heart-Detectors: How Disaster Technology Is Saving Lives." *CNN*. Last modified October 5, 2015. http://www.cnn.com /2015/08/24/us/robot-disaster-technology/.

Broder, J. *Risk Analysis and the Security Survey* (3rd ed.). New York, NY: Butterworth-Heinemann. 2006.

Brookhaven National Laboratory. "Technology Readiness Levels Definitions and Descriptions." Brookhaven National Laboratory. Accessed April 2016. https://www.bnl.gov/techtransfer/docs/Technology-Readiness-Levels-Definitions-and-Descriptions.pdf.

Brown, T. "Police Radio History and Innovation: What Have We Learned?" *Journal of Law Enforcement* 3, no. 6 (2014).

Brown University. "A Framework for Making Ethical Decisions." Brown University. Last modified May 2013. https://www.brown.edu/academics/science-and-technology-studies/framework-making-ethical-decisions.

Burrus, D. "The Internet of Things Is Far Bigger Than Anyone Realizes." *Wired.* Last modified in November 2014. http://www.wired.com/insights/2014/11/the-internet-of-things-bigger/.

Business Dictionary. "Grant." Business Dictionary. Accessed September 5, 2015. www.businessdictionary.com.

Campbell, R. *Intentional Fires.* Quincy, MA: National Fire Protection Association. 2014.

Cardwell, D. "At Newark Airport, the Lights Are On, and They're Watching You." *The New York Times.* Last modified on February 17, 2014. http://www.nytimes.com/2014/02/18/business/at-newark-airport-the-lights-are-on-and-theyre-watching-you.html?_r=0.

Carter, D., and T. Martinelli. "Civil Rights and Law Enforcement Intelligence." *Police Chief Magazine* 74, no. 6 (2007).

CBS News. "These LED Smart Lights Are Tracking Your Moves." *CBS News.* Last modified June 30, 2014. http://www.cbsnews.com/news/technology-in-led-smart-lights-raises-privacy-concerns/.

Cearley, D. "Top 10 Technology Trends for 2016." *Forbes Magazine.* Last modified January 15, 2016. http://www.forbes.com/sites/gartnergroup/2016/01/15/top-10-technology-trends-for-2016/#708fe5515ae9.

Cha, M., S. Han, J. Lee, and B. Choi. "A Virtual Reality Based Fire Training Simulator Integrated with Fire Dynamics Data." *Fire Safety Journal* 50 (2012): 12–24.

Chapman, S. "How Digital Technology Is Revolutionising Disaster Response." *World Economic Forum.* Last Modified April 21, 2015. http://www.weforum.org/agenda/2015/04/how-digital-technology-is-revolutionising-disaster-response.

Cisco Systems, Inc. *Simplifying Physical Access Control with Cisco UPOE: Unleash the Power of Your Network.* San Jose, CA: Cisco Systems, Inc. 2011.

City of New York. "911 Performance Reporting." City of New York. Accessed January 2016. http://www.nyc.gov/html/911reporting/html/home/home.shtml.

Clubb, K., L. Kirch, and N. Patwa. "The Ethics, Privacy, and Legal Issues around the Internet of Things." University of California-Berkley. Last modified Spring 2015. http://www.ischool.berkeley.edu/files/projects/w231-internetofthingsfinalpaper.pdf.

Cohen, D., N. Sevdalis, D. Taylor, K. Kerr, M. Heys, K. Willett, A. Batrick, and A. Darzi. "Emergency Preparedness in the 21st Century: Training and Preparation Modules in Virtual Environments." *Resuscitation* 84, no. 1 (2013): 78–84.

Cohen, S., W. Eimicke, and T. Heikkila. *The Effective Public Manager: Achieving Success in Government Organizations* (5th ed.). San Francisco, CA: Jossey-Bass. 2013.

Colombo, A. "Checking Out the Latest Surveillance Technologies." *Campus Safety Magazine.* Last modified April 21, 2015. http://www.campussafetymagazine .com/article/checking_out_the_latest_surveillance_technologies.

Concannon, R. *COA How to Book.* Grand Forks, ND: Department of Aviation, University of North Dakota. 2008.

Cone, J. "Look before You Leap into Mobile Learning." *T+D* 67, no. 6 (2013): 40–45.

Congressional Research Service. *Intelligence, Surveillance, and Reconnaissance (ISR) Acquisition: Issues for Congress (CRS Report R41284).* Washington, DC: Congressional Research Service. 2011.

Congressional Research Service. *Unmanned Aerial Systems (CRS Report R42136).* Washington, DC: Congressional Research Service. 2012.

Cook, T. "A Message to Our Customers." Apple, Inc. Last modified February 16, 2016. http://www.apple.com/customer-letter/.

Coullahan, R., and R. Desourdis Jr. "Planning Considerations for Unmanned Aircraft Systems Deployment in the Public Safety Mission." *The CIP Report* 11, no. 7 (2013): 4–5, 14–16.

Coulombe, R. "New Technology Fashions: What's Hot on the Trade Show Floor." *Security Technology Executive* 25, no. 4 (2015): 10, 35.

Criminal Intelligence Systems Operating Policies. *Code of Federal Regulations,* Title 28, Chapter 1, Part 23.

Criminal Justice Information Systems. *Code of Federal Regulations,* Title 28, Chapter 1, Part 20.

Crowe, A. *Disasters 2.0: The Application of Social Media Systems for Modern Emergency Management.* Boca Raton, FL: CRC Press. 2012.

CS Staff. "What's Next for Physical Security Information Management Systems?" *Campus Safety Magazine.* Last modified January 11, 2016. http://www .campussafetymagazine.com/article/an_expert_gives_reflections_and _predictions_on_the_psim_world.

Cummins, K. "The Rise of Additive Manufacturing." *The Engineer.* Last modified May 24, 2010. http://www.theengineer.co.uk/the-rise-of-additive-manufacturing/.

Dabinett, G. "Reflections on Regional Development Policies in the Information Society." *Planning Theory and Practice* 3, no. 2 (2002): 232–237.

David Brower Center. "Welcome." David Brower Center. Accessed September 6, 2015. www.browercenter.org.

DeGarmo, M. *Issues Concerning Integration of Unmanned Aerial Vehicles in Civil Airspace.* McLean, VA: Center for Advanced Aviation System Development, MITRE Corporation. 2004.

Deltek, Inc. *Unmanned Aerial Systems Market Overview*. Reston, VA: Deltek, Inc. 2012.

Dempsey, J. *Introduction to Private Security* (2nd ed.). Belmont, CA: Wadsworth. 2010.

Dewey, C. "Almost as Many People Use Facebook as Live in the Entire Country of China." *The Washington Post*. Last modified October 29, 2014. https://www.washingtonpost.com/news/the-intersect/wp/2014/10/29/almost-as-many-people-use-facebook-as-live-in-the-entire-country-of-china/.

Diaz, O. "Augmented Reality: Merging the Real and Digital World." *Occupational Health & Safety*. 2014. http://ohsonline.com/Articles/2014/07/01/Rich-New-Training-Technologies-for-Professional-Development.aspx.

Dykman, C., and C. Davis. "Online Education Forum: Part Two—Teaching Online versus Teaching Conventionally." *Journal of Information Systems Education* 19, no. 2 (2008): 157–164.

Eastern Kentucky University Justice and Safety Center. *SAVER Program Report: Incident Decision Support Software Application Note (Cooperative Agreement #EMW-2005-CA-0378 awarded by DHS)*. Richmond, KY: Eastern Kentucky University. 2010.

Eastern Kentucky University Justice and Safety Center. *SAVER Program Report: Mobile Command Systems Application Note (Cooperative Agreement #EMW-2005-CA-0378 awarded by DHS)*. Richmond, KY: Eastern Kentucky University. 2010.

Eastern Kentucky University Justice and Safety Center. *SAVER Program Report: Mobile Computing through the Cloud (Cooperative Agreement #EMW-2005-CA-0378 awarded by DHS)*. Richmond, KY: Eastern Kentucky University. 2012.

Eastern Kentucky University Justice and Safety Center. *SAVER Program Report: Propagation Modeling Software Application Note (Cooperative Agreement #EMW-2005-CA-0378 awarded by DHS)*. Richmond, KY: Eastern Kentucky University. 2010.

Eastern Kentucky University Justice and Safety Center. *SAVER Program Report: Ruggedized Computers Selection and Procurement Guide (Cooperative Agreement #EMW-2005-CA-0378 awarded by DHS)*. Richmond, KY: Eastern Kentucky University. 2012.

Edgar, J., W. McInerney, E. Finneran, and J. Hunter. "Use of Locks in Physical Crime Prevention." In *Effective Physical Security* (4th ed.), ed. L. Fennelly, 117–168. New York, NY: Butterworth-Heinemann. 2013.

Eisenhower, D. "Annual Message to the Congress on the State of the Union (January 7, 1960)." The American Presidency Project. Accessed March 2016. http://www.presidency.ucsb.edu/ws/?pid=12061.

Ekblom, P. *The 5Is Framework: A Practical Tool for Transfer and Sharing of Crime Prevention and Community Safety Knowledge*. London, England: Design Against Crime Research Center, 2008.

Electronic Communications Privacy Act of 1986, Public Law 99-508 (1986): 2510–2522, 2701–2709.

Electronic Privacy Information Center. *Petition to the FAA: Drones and Privacy.* Washington, DC: Electronic Privacy Information Center. 2012.

Elias, B. *Pilotless Drones: Background and Considerations for Congress Regarding Unmanned Aircraft Operations in the National Airspace System (CRS Report 42718).* Washington, DC: Congressional Research Service. 2012.

Elky, S. *An Introduction to Information System Risk Management.* Bethesda, MD: SANS Institute. 2006.

Emerson, L., and B. MacKay. "A Comparison between Paper-Based and Online Learning in Higher Education." *British Journal of Educational Technology* 42, no. 5 (2011): 727–735.

Evarts, B. *Fires in U.S. Industrial and Manufacturing Facilities.* Quincy, MA: National Fire Protection Association. 2012.

Farra, S., E. Miller, N. Timm, and J. Schafer. "Improved Training for Disasters Using 3-D Virtual Reality Simulation." *Western Journal of Nursing Research* 35, no. 5 (2013): 655–671.

Federal Aviation Administration. AFS-407: *Evaluation of Candidate Functions for Traffic Alert and Collision Avoidance System II (TCAS II) on Unmanned Aircraft System (UAS).* Washington, DC: Federal Aviation Administration. 2011.

Federal Aviation Administration. *Fact Sheet—Unmanned Aircraft Systems (UAS).* Washington, DC: Federal Aviation Administration. 2011.

Federal Aviation Administration. *Law Enforcement Guidance for Suspected Unauthorized UAS Operations.* Washington, DC: Federal Aviation Administration. 2015.

Federal Aviation Administration. *NextGen Implementation Plan.* Washington, DC: Federal Aviation Administration. 2012.

Federal Aviation Administration. *Notice of Proposed Rulemaking Regulatory Evaluation, Small Unmanned Aircraft Systems, 14 CFR Part 107.* Washington, DC: Federal Aviation Administration. 2015.

Federal Aviation Administration. *Operation and Certification of Small Unmanned Aircraft Systems, Notice of Proposed Rulemaking, RIN 2120-AJ60, Docket No. FAA-2015-0150, Notice No. 15-01.* Washington, DC: Federal Aviation Administration. 2015.

Federal Aviation Administration. *Overview of Small UAS Notice of Proposed Rulemaking.* Washington, DC: Federal Aviation Administration. 2015.

Federal Communications Commission. *Wireless E911 Locations Accuracy Requirements (FCC 15-9; OS Docket No. 07-114).* Washington, DC: Federal Communications Commission. 2015.

Federal Emergency Management Agency. "FEMA Mobile Applications." *Federal Emergency Management Agency.* Last modified May 21, 2015. http://www.fema.gov/mobile-app.

Federal Emergency Management Agency. "IS-42: Social Media in Emergency Management." *Federal Emergency Management Agency, Emergency Management Institute.* Last modified October 31, 2013. http://www.training.fema.gov/is/courseoverview.aspx?code=IS-42.

Federal Emergency Management Agency. "Who Do We Serve?" Federal Emergency Management Agency. 2014. https://www.firstrespondertraining.gov/content .do?page=serve.

Federal Emergency Management Agency. *A Whole Community Approach to Emergency Management: Principles, Themes, and Pathways for Action (FDOC 104-008-1).* Washington, DC: Federal Emergency Management Agency. 2011.

Federal Emergency Management Agency. *Authorized Equipment List (CSV File).* Washington, DC: U.S. Department of Homeland Security. https://www.fema .gov/authorized-equipment-list.

Federal Emergency Management Agency. *National Training and Education System: Narrative Overview.* Washington, DC: Federal Emergency Management Agency, National Training and Education Division, 2014.

Federal Emergency Management Agency. *National Training and Education Division (NTED) Condensed Course Development Specifications Guide.* Washington, DC: Federal Emergency Management Agency, National Training and Education Division, 2014.

Federal Emergency Management Agency. *NIMS Standards Case Study: Los Angeles Regional Interoperability.* Washington, DC: Federal Emergency Management Agency. 2008. https://www.fema.gov/txt/emergency/nims/Los_Angeles_CAP %20EDXL.txt.

Federal Records Act, U.S. Code 44 (1976), Chapter 33, § 3301.

Felson, M. *Crime and Everyday Life: Insight and Implications for Society.* Thousand Oaks, CA: Pine Forge Press. 1994.

Fennelly, L. *Effective Physical Security* (4th ed.). New York, NY: Butterworth-Heinemann. 2013.

Fenrich, P. "Getting Practical with Learning Styles in Live and Computer-Based Training Settings." *Issues in Informing Science & Information Technology* 3 (2006): 233–242.

First Responder Network Authority. "About FirstNet." Reston, VA: First Responder Network Authority. http://www.firstnet.gov/about.

First Responder Network Authority. "Project Overview." FirstNet. Accessed January 2016. http://www.firstnet.gov/content/project-overview.

First Responder Network Authority. *How Will the FirstNet Network Work with Today's Land Mobile Radio Networks?* Reston, VA: First Responder Network Authority.

Fitchard, K. "One Day You Won't Need a Badge to Enter Your Building, Just a SIM Card." *Gigaom.* Last modified February 7, 2014. https://gigaom.com/2014 /02/07/one-day-you-wont-need-a-badge-to-enter-your-building-just-a-sim -card/.

FLIR Corporation: http://www.flir.com/US/.

Flynn, J. *Fire Service Performance Measures.* Quincy, MA: National Fire Protection Association. 2009.

Flynn, S., and S. Bates. *Connecting America: Building Resilience with Social Media.* Washington, DC: Center for National Policy. 2014.

Folk, C. "U.S. Cyber Command Moves Towards 'Lethal Cyber Weapons.'" *Syracuse University, Institute for National Security and Counterterrorism.* Last modified November 10, 2015. http://insct.syr.edu/us-cyber-command-moves-towards -lethal-cyber-weapons/.

Ford, J., M. Quinones, D. Sego, and J. Sorra. "Factors Affecting the Opportunity to Perform Trained Tasks on the Job." *Personnel Psychology* 45, no. 3 (1992): 511–527.

Foreman, K. "Getting the Word Out: Effectively Using Social Media in Kentucky Law Enforcement." *Kentucky Law Enforcement Magazine* 14, no. 4 (2014): 38–43.

Fox, L., and S. Rainie. *The Web at 25 in the U.S.* Washington, DC: Pew Research Center. 2014.

Franklin, B. *GoodReads.* Accessed September 6, 2015. www.goodreads.com.

Franklin, B. *Memoirs of the Life and Writings of Benjamin Franklin.* Philadelphia, PA: William Duane. 1818.

Friedl, K., and H. O'Neil. "Designing and Using Computer Simulations in Medical Education and Training: An Introduction." *Military Medicine* 178, no. 10S (2013): 1–6.

Frommer, D. "Here's How to Use Instagram." *Business Insider.* Last modified November 1, 2010. http://www.businessinsider.com/instagram-2010-11.

Galusha, J. "Barriers to Learning in Distance Education." 1998. http://eric .ed.gov/?id=ED416377.

Gigliotti, R., and R. Jason. "Approaches to Physical Security." In *Effective Physical Security* (4th ed.), ed. L. Fennelly, 77–92. New York, NY: Butterworth-Heinemann. 2013.

Gigliotti, R., R. Jason, and N. Cogan. "What Is Your Level of Physical Security?" *Security Management* (1980): 46–50.

Gilgoff, D., and J. Lee. "Social Media Shapes Boston Bombings Response." *National Geographic.* Last modified April 17, 2013. http://news.nationalgeographic .com/news/2013/13/130415-boston-marathon-bombings-terrorism-social -media-twitter-facebook/.

Goodier, R. "The Next Generation of Technology for Disaster Preparedness and Relief." *Engineering for Change.* Last modified October 10, 2014. http://www .engineeringforchange.org/the-next-generation-of-technology-for-disaster -preparedness-and-relief/.

Gorbett, G., and J. Pharr. *Fire Dynamics.* Upper Saddle River, NJ: Prentice Hall. 2010.

Goudlock, J. "First Line of Defense: New Technologies Help Meet the Demand to Ward Off Strangers." *Security Today.* Last modified April 1, 2013. https:// security-today.com/Articles/2013/04/01/First-Line-of-Defense.aspx.

Gouillart, F., and D. Billings. "Community-Powered Problem Solving." *Harvard Business Review.* Accessed February 2016. https://hbr.org/2013/04/community -powered-problem-solving.

Greisler, D., and R. Stupak (eds.). *Handbook of Technology Management in Public Administration.* Boca Rotan, FL: Taylor and Francis. 2007.

Gross, D. "Red Cross Text Donations Pass $21 Million." *CNN.* Last modified January 18, 2010. http://www.cnn.com/2010/TECH/01/18/redcross.texts/.

Guy, M. *Ethical Decision Making in Everyday Work Situations.* New York, NY: Wuorum Books. 1990.

Hall, J. *The Total Cost of Fire in the United States.* Quincy, MA: National Fire Protection Association. 2014.

Harris, K., and W. Romesburg. *Law Enforcement Tech Guide: How to Plan, Purchase and Manage Technology (Successfully).* Washington, DC: U.S. Department of Justice. 2002.

Harris, M., and S. Gibson. "Distance Education vs. Face-to-Face Classes: Individual Differences, Course Preferences, and Enrollment." *Psychological Reports* 98, no. 3 (2006): 756–764.

Harrison, V., and J. Pagliery. "Nearly 1 Million New Malware Threats Released Every Day." *CNN.* Last modified April 14, 2015. http://money.cnn.com /2015/04/14/technology/security/cyber-attack-hacks-security/.

Haynes, H. *Fire Loss in the United States During 2014.* Quincy, MA: National Fire Protection Association. 2015.

Heaton, B. "Making the Connection: The National Public Safety Broadband Network Moves Forward—But Hurdles Remain." *Government Technology* 26, no. 4 (2013): 18–22.

Heinrichs, W., P. Youngblood, P. Harter, and P. Dev. "Simulation for Team Training and Assessment: Case Studies of Online Training with Virtual Worlds." *World Journal of Surgery* 32, no. 2 (2008): 161–170.

Hickey, K. "Robots Guard Nuclear Test Site." *GCN.* Last modified October 14, 2010. https://gcn.com/Articles/2010/10/14/robots-guard-nuclear-test-site.aspx?Page=2.

HID Corporation. *Smart Cards for Access Control Advantages and Technology Choices.* Austin, TX: HID Corporation. 2005.

HID Global Innovation Team. "2016 Trends." *Security Today.* Last modified January 25, 2016. https://security-today.com/Articles/2016/01/25/2016-Trends .aspx?Page=1.

Hoang, R., M. Sgambati, T. Brown, D. Coming, and F. Harris. "VFire: Immersive Wildfire Simulation and Visualization." *Computers & Graphics* 34, no. 6 (2010): 655–664.

Hodgson, E., E. Bachmann, D. Vincent, M. Zmuda, D. Waller, and J. Calusdian. "WeaVR: A Self-Contained and Wearable Immersive Virtual Environment Simulation System." *Behavior Research Methods* 47, no. 1 (2015): 296–307.

Holderman, E. "Technology Plays an Increasing Role in Emergency Management." *Emergency Management.* Last modified June 26, 2014. http://www.emergency mgmt.com/training/Technology-Increasing-Role-Emergency-Management .html.

Holmes, R., and D. Wagner. *Flood of June 11, 2010, in the Upper Little Missouri River Watershed, Arkansas: Scientific Investigations Report 2011–5194.* Reston, VA: U.S. Department of the Interior, U.S. Geological Survey. 2011.

Homeland Security News Wire. "Barrier Systems, Robots Reduce Security Costs." *Homeland Security News Wire.* Last modified December 20, 2013. http://www

.homelandsecuritynewswire.com/barrier-systems-robots-reduce-security -costs.

Homeland Security News Wire. "Sensor Cable Monitors Fences—and Can Even Detect Low-Level Drones." *Homeland Security News Wire.* Last modified March 27, 2015. http://www.homelandsecuritynewswire.com/dr20150327-sensor-ca ble-monitors-fences-and-can-even-detect-lowlevel-drones.

Homeland Security Studies and Analysis Institute. *Department of Homeland Security Science and Technology Readiness Level Calculator (ver. 1.1).* Arlington, VA: Homeland Security Institute.

Honovich, J. "Is Public Video Surveillance Effective?" *Government Security News.* Last modified January 9, 2009. http://gsnmagazine.com/article/17888/public _video_surveillance_effective.

Hopkins, J. "Surprise! There's a Third YouTube Co-Founder." *USA Today.* Last modified October 11, 2006. http://usatoday30.usatoday.com/tech/news/2006 -10-11-youtube-karim_x.htm.

Howell, S., P. Williams, and N. Lindsay. "Thirty-Two Trends Affecting Distance Education: An Informed Foundation for Strategic Planning." *Online Journal of Distance Learning Administration* 6, no. 3 (2003).

Hoyt, B. "Predicting Training Transfer of New Computer Software Skills: A Research Study Comparing E-learning and In-Class Delivery." *Association for University Regional Campuses of Ohio (AURCO) Journal* 19 (2013): 83–111.

Hsieh, M., S. Chen, Y. Cai, Y. Chen, and J. Chiang. "Immersive Surveillance for Total Situational Awareness." In *2010 International Computer Symposium*: 300– 305. 2010. doi:10.1109/COMPSYM.2010.5685499.

Huesemann, M., and J. Huesemann (2011). *Technofix: Why Technology Won't Save Us or the Environment.* Gabriola Island, British Columbia: New Society Publishers. 2011.

Identity Theft Resource Center. "Identity Theft Resource Center Breach Report Hits Record High in 2014." Identity Theft Resource Center. Last modified January 12, 2015. http://www.idtheftcenter.org/ITRC-Surveys-Studies/2014 databreaches.html.

Instagram. "Instagram Press." Instagram. Accessed February 2016. https://www .instagram.com/press/.

Integration Innovation, Incorporated. *Technical Exchange Meetings with Mr. Jon Daniels.* Las Vegas, NV: Integration Innovation, Incorporated. 2012.

Interagency Board. "Standardized Equipment List." Interagency Board. Accessed September 7, 2015. https://iab.gov/SEL.aspx.

International Association of Chiefs of Police. *Recommended Guidelines for the Use of Unmanned Aircraft.* Washington, DC: International Association of Chiefs of Police. 2012.

International Telecommunication Union and the Organization for Economic Cooperation and Development. *M-Government: Mobile Technologies for Responsive Governments and Connected Societies.* Geneva, Switzerland: ITU. 2011.

Isaacson, W. *Einstein: His Life and Universe.* New York, NY: Simon and Schuster. 2007.

ITU. "Internet of Things Global Standards Initiative." ITU. Accessed March 2016. http://www.itu.int/en/ITU-T/gsi/iot/Pages/default.aspx.

Jackson, B. "Technology Strategies for Homeland Security: Adaptation and Coevolution of Office and Defense." *Homeland Security Affairs* 5, no. 1 (2009): 1–16.

Jarventaus, J. "Virtual Threat, Real Sweat." *T+D* 61, no. 5 (2007): 72–78.

Jass, B. "Take the Mobile Learning Plunge." *T+D* 67, no. 2 (2013): 29–31.

Jayalath, C. "Understanding the S-Curve of Technology Innovation." ArticlesBase. Accessed April 2016. http://www.articlesbase.com/technology-articles/under standing-the-s-curve-of-technology-innovation-1229680.html.

Jefferson, T., and P. Ford. *The Writings of Thomas Jefferson: 1788–1792*. New York, NY: G. P. Putnam's Sons. 1892.

John J. Reilly Center. "Emerging Ethical Dilemmas and Policy Issues in Science and Technology 2015." University of Notre Dame. Accessed March 2016. http://reilly.nd.edu/outreach/emerging-ethical-dilemmas-and-policy-issues-in-science -and-technology-2015/.

Johnson, E., E. Koski, W. Furman, M. Jorgenson, and J. Nieto. *Third-Generation and Wideband HF Radio Communications*. Norwood, MA: Artech House. 2012.

Jonas, H. *Towards a Philosophy of Technology*. Oxford: Blackwell Publishing. 2013.

Kangdon, L. "Augmented Reality in Education and Training." *TechTrends* 56, no. 2 (2012): 13–21.

Kaplan, A., and M. Haenlein. "Users of the World, Unite! The Challenges and Opportunities of Social Media." *Business Horizons* 53, no. 1 (2010): 61.

Kaplan, E. "Homeland Security Technologies." *Council on Foreign Relations*. Last modified November 19, 2007. http://www.cfr.org/defense-technology /homeland-security-technologies/p14827.

Karter, M. *Trends and Patterns of U.S. Fire Losses in 2013*. Quincy, MA: National Fire Protection Association. 2014.

Kaynar, B., and G. Sumerli. "A Meta-analysis of Comparison between Traditional and Web-Based Instruction." *Ekev Academic Review* 14, no. 43 (2010): 153–164.

Kelly, H. "After Boston: The Pros and Cons of Surveillance Cameras." *CNN*. Last modified April 26, 2013. http://www.cnn.com/2013/04/26/tech/innovation /security-cameras-boston-bombings/.

Knight, J., S. Carley, B. Tregunna, S. Jarvis, R. Smithies, S. Freitas, A. Dunwell, and K. Jones. "Serious Gaming Technology in Major Incident Triage Training: A Pragmatic Controlled Trial." *Resuscitation* 81, no. 9 (2010): 1175–1179.

Kovacich, G., and E. Halibozek. "Physical Security." In *Effective Physical Security* (4th ed.), ed. L. Fennelly, 339–354. New York, NY: Butterworth-Heinemann. 2013.

Kranz, G. "Learning Gets a Higher Degree of Attention at Workplaces." *Workforce* 93, no. 1 (2014): 44–47.

Krone, J. "Guest Column: 10 Reasons to Switch from Analog Cameras and DVRs to IP Cameras and NVRs." *Business Solutions*. Last modified August 15, 2013. http://www.bsminfo.com/doc/reasons-to-switch-from-analog-cameras-and -dvrs-to-ip-cameras-and-nvrs-0001.

Krum, D., E. Suma, and M. Bolas. "Augmented Reality Using Personal Projection and Retroreflection." *Personal and Ubiquitous Computing* 16, no. 1 (2012): 17–26.

Kumle-Hammes, M. "Transformational Leadership in the PSAP: The Importance of Being Change Ready," *Public Safety Communications* 81, no. 6 (June 2015): 18–21.

Luo, L., W. Cai, S. Zhou, M. Lees, and H. Yin. "A Review of Interactive Narrative Systems and Technologies: A Training Perspective." *Simulation* 91, no. 2 (2015): 126–147.

MacDonald, N., and P. Firstbrook. "Designing an Adaptive Security Architecture for Protection from Advanced Attacks." Gartner. Last modified February 12, 2014. https://www.gartner.com/doc/2665515/designing-adaptive-security-architecture -protection.

Malatesti, C. "Physical Security in the IT Space." *ISSA Journal* (July 2008): 32–35.

Martin, B. *Disaster Recovery Plan Strategies and Processes.* Bethesda, MD: SANS Institute. 2015.

Martin, S. "Final Comparison Study of Teaching Blended In-Class Courses vs. Teaching Distance Education Courses." *Journal of Systemics, Cybernetics & Informatics* 10, no. 6 (2012): 40–46.

Massachusetts Emergency Management Agency. *After Action Report for the Response to the 2013 Boston Marathon Bombings.* Boston, MA: Massachusetts Emergency Management Agency. 2014.

Matthews, B. "Physical Security: Controlled Access and Layered Defense." In *Information Management Security Handbook* (6th ed.), ed. H. Tipton and M. Krause, 1327–1338. Boca Raton, FL: Taylor and Francis. 2007.

Mayer-Schonberger, V., and K. Cukier. *Big Data: A Revolution That Will Transform How We Live, Work, and Think.* New York, NY: Houghton Mifflin Harcourt. 2013.

Mazmanian, A. "Twitter for Disaster Responders." *Federal Computer Weekly.* Last modified July 7, 2013. https://fcw.com/articles/2013/07/09/fema-social-media .aspx.

McCready, C. "Growing the Role of Analytics in Video Surveillance: Adding Value to Video Surveillance." *Security Today.* Last modified February 1, 2015. https:// security-today.com/Articles/2015/02/01/Growing-the-Role-of-Analytics-in -Video-Surveillance.aspx?Page=1.

McCrimmon, M. "The Ideal Leader." In *Cases in Leadership* (4th ed.), ed. W. Rowe and L. Guerrero, 115–119. Thousand Oaks, CA: Sage Publications. 2016.

McKay, J. "Welcome to the Future." *Emergency Management* 1, no. 11 (Winter 2016): 10.

McKinnon, S. "Alarms: Intrusion Detection Systems." In *Effective Physical Security* (4th ed.), ed. L. Fennelly, 191–212. New York, NY: Butterworth-Heinemann. 2013.

Mell, P., and T. Grance. *The NIST Definition of Cloud Computing (Special Publication 800-145).* Gaithersburg, MD: National Institute of Standards and Technology.

Mendonca, D., G. Beroggi, D. Gent, and W. Wallace. "Designing Gaming Simulations for the Assessment of Group Decision Support Systems in Emergency Response." *Safety Science* 44, no. 6 (2006): 523–535.

Merriam-Webster. "Technology." *Merriam-Webster.* Accessed February 2016. http://www.merriam-webster.com/dictionary/technology.

Miller, R. "Hurricane Katrina: Communications and Infrastructure Impacts." In *Threats at Our Homeland: Homeland Defense and Homeland Security in the New Century—A Compilation of the Proceedings of the First Annual Homeland Defense and Homeland Security Conference*, ed. B. Tussing, 191–204. Carlisle Barracks, PA: U.S. Army War College. 2006.

Montana Public Safety Communications Bureau. "Public Safety Communications [online slide show]." Helena, MT: Montana Public Safety Communications Bureau. http://www.broadband.mt.gov/js_objs/fg_slideshow/pub_safety/index.html.

Morozov, E. *To Save Everything, Click Here.* New York, NY: Public Affairs. 2013.

Moskaliuk, J., J. Bertram, and U. Cress. "Impact of Virtual Training Environments on the Acquisition and Transfer of Knowledge." *Cyberpsychology, Behavior, and Social Networking* 16, no. 3 (2013): 210–214.

Motorola Solutions, Inc. *White Paper: 5 Trends Transforming Public Safety Communications.* Schaumburg, IL: Motorola Solutions, Inc. 2015.

Motteram, G., and G. Forrester. "Becoming an Online Distance Learner: What Can Be Learned from Students' Experiences of Induction to Distance Programs?" *Distance Education* 26, no. 3 (2005): 281–298.

Moynihan, T. "The New Tech of Disaster Response, from Apps to Aqua-Drones. *Wired.* Last modified August 29, 2015. http://www.wired.com/2015/08/fema-disaster-tech/.

Mugford, R., S. Corey, and C. Bennell. "Improving Police Training from a Cognitive Load Perspective." *Policing: An International Journal of Police Strategies & Management* 36, no. 2 (2013): 312–337.

Nam, Y. "Designing Interactive Narratives for Mobile Augmented Reality." *Cluster Computing* 18, no. 1 (2015): 309–320.

National Aeronautics and Space Administration. "Technology Readiness Level." National Aeronautics and Space Administration. Last modified October 28, 2012. https://www.nasa.gov/directorates/heo/scan/engineering/technology/txt_accordion1.html.

National Aeronautics and Space Administration. *Topic 2: A2 Air Traffic Management Research and Development/A2.01 Unmanned Aircraft Systems Integration into the National Airspace System Research.* Washington, DC: National Aeronautics and Space Administration. 2012.

National Aeronautics and Space Administration. "Budget Information." National Aeronautics and Space Administration. Last modified February 14, 2011. http://www.nasa.gov/news/budget/2011.html.

National Aeronautics and Space Administration. "Fire and Controversy." National Aeronautics and Space Administration. Accessed January 2016. http://history.nasa.gov/SP-4225/nasa4/nasa4.htm#fire.

National Aeronautics and Space Administration. "Fire Prevention in Space." National Aeronautics and Space Administration. Last modified November 22, 2007. http://www.nasa.gov/missions/shuttle/f_fireprevention.html.

National Commission on Terrorist Attacks upon the United States. *The 9/11 Commission Report*. Washington, DC: National Commission on Terrorist Attacks upon the United States. 2004.

National Emergency Number Association. "9-1-1 Statistics." *National Emergency Number Association*. Last modified December 2015. https://www.nena.org/?page=911Statistics.

National Emergency Number Association. "Status of NG9-1-1 State Activity." *National Emergency Number Association*. Last modified May 18, 2015. http://www.nena.org/?NG911_StateActivity.

National Fire Protection Association. "Document Information Pages (List of NFPA Codes and Standards)." National Fire Protection Association. Accessed January 2016. http://www.nfpa.org/codes-and-standards/document-information-pages.

National Fire Protection Association. *NFPA 1: Fire Code (Fact Sheet)*. Quincy, MA: National Fire Protection Association. 2015.

National Fire Protection Association. *NFPA 101: Life Safety Code (Fact Sheet)*. Quincy, MA: National Fire Protection Association. 2015.

National Fire Protection Association. *NFPA's Latest Estimates of Intentional Home Structure Fires—2013*. Quincy, MA: National Fire Protection Association. 2015.

National Fire Protection Association. *U.S. Home Candle Fires Fact Sheet*. Quincy, MA: National Fire Protection Association. 2015.

National Institute of Standards and Technology. "Cybersecurity Framework." National Institute of Standards and Technology. Last modified February 9, 2016. http://www.nist.gov/cyberframework/.

National Institute of Standards and Technology. "FDS and Smokeview." National Institute of Standards and Technology. Last modified November 9, 2015. http://www.nist.gov/el/fire_research/fds_smokeview.cfm.

National Institute of Standards and Technology. "Fire Growth and Smoke Transport Modeling with CFAST." National Institute of Standards and Technology. Last modified December 10, 2015. http://www.nist.gov/el/fire_research/cfast.cfm.

National Institute of Standards and Technology. *Guide for Conducting Risk Assessments: NIST Special Publication 800-30, Revision 1*. Gaithersburg, MD: U.S. Department of Commerce, National Institute of Standards and Technology, Computer Security Division. 2012.

National Institutes of Health. *Principles of Community Engagement* (2nd ed.). Bethesda, MD: National Institutes of Health.

Nelson, J. "Access Control and Badges." In *Effective Physical Security* (4th ed.), ed. L. Fennelly, 257–268. New York, NY: Butterworth-Heinemann. 2013.

Newcombe, T. "Are Smart Street Lights the Future of Security Tech?" *Emergency Management*. Last modified February 27, 2014. http://www.emergencymgmt.com/safety/Smart-Street-Lights-Security-Tech.html.

Nolte, W., B. Kennedy, and R. Dziegiel. "Technology Readiness Calculator." Defense Technical Information Center. Last modified October 20, 2003. http://www.dtic.mil/ndia/2003systems/nolte2.pdf.

Nowarra, H. *German Guided Missiles.* Atglen, PA: Schiffer. 1993.

Olson, E. "Using Video Analytics with Pan-Tilt-Zoom Cameras." *Security Magazine.* Last modified February 1, 2015. http://www.securitymagazine.com/articles/86077-adding-thermal-cameras-for-better-intrusion-detection.

Orwell, G. *Nineteen Eighty-Four.* London, United Kingdom: Penguin Books. 2004.

Partnership for Public Warning. *The Emergency Alert System: An Assessment (PPW Report 400-1).* McLean, VA: Partnership for Public Warning. 2004.

Pearsall, B. "Predictive Policing: The Future of Law Enforcement?" *National Institute of Justice.* Last modified June 23, 2010. http://www.nij.gov/journals/266/Pages/predictive.aspx.

Pereira, O., and J. Rodrigues. "Survey and Analysis of Current Mobile Learning Applications and Technologies." *ACM Computing Surveys* 46, no. 2 (2013): 1–35.

Perrin, A. "Social Media Usage: 2005–2015." Pew Research Center. Last Modified October 8, 2015. http://www.pewinternet.org/2015/10/08/social-networking-usage-2005-2015/.

Peters, S., M. Barbier, D. Faulx, and I. Hansez. "Learning and Motivation to Transfer after an E-learning Program: Impact of Trainees' Motivation to Train, Personal Interaction, and Satisfaction." *Innovations in Education and Teaching International* 49, no. 4 (2012): 375–387.

Petty, G., D. Lim, and J. Zulauf. "Training Transfer between CD-ROM Based Instruction and Traditional Classroom Instruction." *Journal on Technology Studies* 33, no. 1 (2007): 48–56.

Piccoli, G., R. Ahmad, and B. Ives. "Web-Based Virtual Learning Environments: A Research Framework and a Preliminary Assessment of Effectiveness in Basic IT Skills Training." *MIS Quarterly* 25, no. 4 (2001): 401.

Pine, J. C. *Technology in Emergency Management.* Hoboken, NJ: John Wiley and Sons, Inc. 2007.

Pittman, E. "The Story Behind #530slide: Social Media During Emergency Response." *Emergency Management.* Last modified April 16, 2014. http://www.emergencymgmt.com/training/530slide-Social-Media-Emergency-Response.html.

Porter, E., J. Weisenford, and R. Smith. "A Journey through the Design of a Virtual Learning Environment." *Public Manager Summer* (2012): 64–68.

Prenzler, T. *Preventing Burglary in Commercial and Institutional Settings: A Place Management and Partnerships Approach.* Alexandria, VA: ASIS Foundation, Inc. 2009.

Princeton University. "Futurology." WordNet. Accessed April 2016. http://wordnetweb.princeton.edu/perl/webwn?s=futurology.

Privacy Act, U.S. Code 5 (1974), Part I, Chapter 5, Subchapter II, § 552a.

Quinn, R., D. Bright, S. Faerman, M. Thompson, and M. McGrath. *Becoming a Master Manager: A Competing Values Approach* (6th ed.). New York, NY: John Wiley & Sons. 2015.

Ramey, K. "What Is Technology—Meaning of Technology and Its Use." *Use of Technology.* Last modified December 12, 2013. http://www.useoftechnology .com/what-is-technology/.

Readiness Resource Group Incorporated. *Roadmap for a Public Safety Unmanned Aircraft Systems Technical Assistance Program.* Las Vegas, NV: Readiness Resource Group Incorporated. 2013.

Ritchey, D. "Using Smartphone-Based Access Control to Keep Students Happy." *Security Magazine.* Last modified December 1, 2014. http://www.securitymagazine .com/articles/85957-using-smartphone-based-access-control-to-keep-students -happy.

Roberts, D. *Law Enforcement Tech Guide for Creating Performance Measures That Work.* Washington, DC: U.S. Department of Justice. 2006.

Rockwell, S., and A. Rangwala. "Influence of Coal Dust on Premixed Turbulent Methane-Air Flames." *Combustion and Flame* 160, no. 3 (2013): 635–640.

Rockwell, S., and A. Rangwala. "Modeling of Dust Air Flames." *Fire Safety Journal* 59 (2013): 22–29.

Rosenwald, M. "Weapons Made with 3-D Printers Could Test Gun-Control Efforts." *The Washington Post.* Last modified February 18, 2013. https://www .washingtonpost.com/local/weapons-made-with-3-d-printers-could-test-gun -control-efforts/2013/02/18/9ad8b45e-779b-11e2-95e4-6148e45d7adb _story.html.

Rowe, W., and L. Guerrero. "Transformational Leadership." In *Cases in Leadership* (4th ed.), ed. W. Rowe and L. Guerrero. Thousand Oaks, CA: Sage Publications. 2016.

Rutgers University. "Methods and Approaches of Futures Studies." Rutgers University. Accessed April 2016. http://crab.rutgers.edu/~goertzel/futuristmethods .htm.

Saenez, A. "Robots Guarding U.S. Nuclear Stockpile." *Singularity HUB.* Last modified October 8, 2010. http://singularityhub.com/2010/10/08/robots -guarding-us-nuclear-stockpile-video/.

Sales, N. "The USA PATRIOT Act Is a Vital Weapon in Fighting Terrorism." *The New York Times.* Last modified May 23, 2014. http://www.nytimes.com/roomfordebate /2011/09/07/do-we-still-need-the-patriot-act/the-patriot-act-is-a-vital-weapon -in-fighting-terrorism.

Saptharishi, M. "The New Eyes of Surveillance: Artificial Intelligence and Humanizing Technology." *Wired.* Last modified August 2014. http://www.wired.com /insights/2014/08/the-new-eyes-of-surveillance-artificial-intelligence-and -humanizing-technology/.

SAS. "Machine Learning: What It Is and Why It Matters." *SAS.* Accessed April 2016. http://www.sas.com/en_us/insights/analytics/machine-learning.html.

Schaffer, G. (Panelist). "The National Broadband (Communications) Plan: Issues for Public Safety [National Institute of Justice conference transcript]." Washington, DC: National Institute of Justice. 2011. http://nij.ncjrs.gov/multimedia /audio-nijconf2011-national-broadband-plan.htm#tab2.

Schaffhauser, D. "Student-Invented Mobile App Could Replace Security Access Badges." *Campus Technology.* Last modified February 13, 2012. https://campustechnology.com/articles/2012/02/13/student-invented-mobile-app-could-replace-security-access-badges.aspx?=CTMOB.

Schmeeckle, J. "Online Training: An Evaluation of the Effectiveness and Efficiency of Training Law Enforcement Personnel over the Internet." *Journal of Science Education and Technology* 12, no. 3 (2003): 205–260.

Schwartz, M. "Lost Laptops Cost $1.8 Billion per Year." Information Week. Last modified April 21, 2011. http://www.informationweek.com/mobile/lost-laptops-cost-$18-billion-per-year/d/d-id/1097314.

Scientific American. "More about Balloons." *Scientific American* 4, no. 26 (March 17, 1849): 205.

Scott, A. "8 Ways the Internet of Things Will Change the Way We Live and Work." *The Globe and Mail: Report on Business Magazine.* Accessed March 2016. http://www.theglobeandmail.com/report-on-business/rob-magazine/the-future-is-smart/article24586994/.

Select Bipartisan Committee to Investigate the Preparation for and Response to Hurricane Katrina. *A Failure of Initiative, 109th Congress,* R. REP. NO. 109–377. 2006.

Serge, S., H. Priest, H. Durlach, and C. Johnson. "The Effects of Static and Adaptive Performance Feedback in Game-Based Training." *Computers in Human Behavior* 29 (2013): 1150–1158.

Shachar, M., and Y. Neumann. "Differences between Traditional and Distance Education Academic Performances: A Meta-analytic Approach." *The International Review of Research in Open and Distance Learning* 4, no. 2 (2003): 1–20.

Shachar, M., and Y. Neumann. "Twenty Years of Research on the Academic Performance Differences between Traditional and Distance Learning: Summative Meta-analysis and Trend Examination." *Journal of Online Learning and Teaching* 6, no. 2 (2010): 318–334.

Shallcross, J. "Your Hotel Key Is the Smartphone You Already Own." *Conde Nast Traveler.* Last modified September 9, 2015. http://www.cntraveler.com/stories/2015-09-09/your-hotel-key-is-the-smartphone-you-already-own.

Simic, G. "Constructive Simulation as a Collaborative Learning Tool in Education and Training of Crisis Staff." *Interdisciplinary Journal of Information, Knowledge, and Management* 7 (2012): 221–236.

Simpkins, B. *2014–2015 National Rural Training Needs Assessment—Volume II: Assessing Capability and Training Needs within Rural Communities.* Richmond, KY: Eastern Kentucky University. 2015.

Simpson, T. "Physical Safety Is Becoming Digital Security." *AVG.* Last modified September 2, 2015. http://now.avg.com/physical-safety-is-becoming-digital-security/.

Sitzmann, T., K. Kraiger, D. Stewart, and R. Wisher. "The Comparative Effectiveness of Web-Based and Classroom Instruction: A Meta-analysis." *Personnel Psychology* 59, no. 3 (2006): 623–664.

Sloan Security Group. "Specialized Solutions." Sloan Security Group. Accessed in January 2016. http://www.sloancompanies.com/sloan_security_group/solutions/.

Smith, A. "U.S. Smartphone Use in 2015." Pew Research Center. Last modified April 1, 2015. http://www.pewinternet.org/2015/04/01/us-smartphone-use-in -2015/.

Smith, S., and T. Carter. "A Sloan Security Group. Virtual Environment to Test Police and Public Awareness of Anti-social Behavior Indicators." *International Journal of Police Science & Management* 12, no. 4 (2010): 548–566.

Soper, T. "Bill Gates on the Future of Technology, His Biggest Regret, and Microsoft's HoloLens." *GeekWire.* Last modified January 28, 2015. http://www.geekwire .com/2015/bill-gates-future-technology-biggest-regret-microsofts-hololens/.

Southwest Microwave, Inc. "Buried Cable Detection Systems." *Southwest Microwave, Inc.* Accessed in January 2016. http://www.southwestmicrowave.com /products/buried-cable-detection-systems/.

Space and Naval Warfare Systems Center Atlantic. *SAVER Program Highlight: Video Analytics Systems.* Charleston, SC: Space and Naval Warfare Systems Center Atlantic. 2013.

Spain, R., H. Priest, and J. Murphy. "Current Trends in Adaptive Training with Military Applications: An Introduction." *Military Psychology* 24 (2012): 87–95.

Stanley, J., and B. Steinhardt. *Even Bigger, Even Weaker: The Emerging Surveillance Society.* New York, NY: American Civil Liberties Union. 2007.

Stober, D., and S. Putter. "Going Mobile and Micro." *Professional Safety* 58, no. 2 (2013): 41–43.

Stone, A. "A New World." *Emergency Management* 1, no. 11 (Winter 2016): 16–21.

Strohm, P. "Enterprise Level Systems Integration Delivers ROI." *Security Technology Executive* 25, no. 2 (2015): 16–19.

Swanson, M., P. Bowen, A. Phillips, D. Gallup, and D. Lynes. *Contingency Planning for Information Technology Systems: NIST Special Publication 800-34.* Gaithersburg, MD: U.S. Department of Commerce, National Institute of Standards and Technology, Computer Security Division. 2010.

Targamadze, A., and R. Petrauskiene. "The Use of Information Technology Tools to Reduce Barriers of Distance Learning." *Vocational Education: Research & Reality* 23 (2012): 64–75.

Taylor, G., and J. Barnett. "Evaluation of Wearable Simulation Interface for Military Training." *Human Factors* 55, no. 3 (2013): 672–690.

Teal Group Corporation. World Unmanned Aerial Vehicle Systems. Fairfax, VA: Teal Group Corporation. 2012.

"Technologies to Watch." *Tech & Learning* 31, no. 1 (2010): 14.

Terdiman, D. "Why Fear of 3D-Printed Guns Is Overblown." *C/NET.* Last modified May 9, 2013. http://www.cnet.com/news/why-fear-of-3d-printed-guns-is -overblown/.

Thirunarayanan, M., and A. Perez-Prado. "Comparing Web-based and Classroom-based Learning: A Quantitative Study." *Journal of Research on Technology in Education* 34, no. 2 (2001): 131–137.

Thomas, S. "Social Media Changing the Way FEMA Responds to Disasters." *National Defense Magazine.* Last modified September 2013. http://www .nationaldefensemagazine.org/archive/2013/September/Pages/Social MediaChangingtheWayFEMARespondstoDisasters.aspx.

Tsai, M., P. Liu, and N. Yau. "Using Electronic Maps and Augmented Reality-based Training Materials as Escape Guidelines for Nuclear Accidents: An Explorative Case Study in Taiwan." *British Journal of Educational Technology* 44, no. 1 (2013): 18–21.

Tucker, S. "Distance Education: Better, Worse, or as Good as Traditional Education?" *Online Journal of Distance Learning Administration* 4, no. 4 (2001).

Twitter. "Twitter Company Facts." *Twitter.* Last modified December 31, 2015. https://about.twitter.com/company.

Tyco. "IP: Taking Video Surveillance to a New Level." *Tyco.* Last modified 2016. http://www.tyco.com/resource-library/articles/ip-taking-video-surveillance -to-a-new-level.

Tyco. "The New Age of Video Surveillance: Not Just Security Anymore." *Tyco.* Last modified 2016. http://www.tyco.com/resource-library/articles/the-new-age-of -video-surveillance-not-just-security-anymore.

Understanding the Power of Social Media as a Communication Tool in the Aftermath of Disasters: Hearing before the Ad Hoc Subcommittee on Disaster Recovery and Inter- governmental Affairs of the Committee on Homeland Security and Governmental Affairs, U.S. Senate. 112th Cong. 2011. https://www.gpo.gov/fdsys/pkg/CHRG -112shrg67635/pdf/CHRG-112shrg67635.pdf.

United States Code, Title 42, Chapter 140, Subchapter II, § 14611.

U.S. Coast Guard. "Team Coordination Training." *U.S. Coast Guard.* Last modified January 12, 2016. https://www.uscg.mil/auxiliary/training/tct/.

U.S. Computer Emergency Readiness Team. "Home Page." *U.S. Computer Emer- gency Readiness Team.* Accessed January 2016. https://www.us-cert.gov/.

U.S. Department of Defense. *Military Standard 810G (MIL-STD-810G): Environ- mental Engineering Considerations and Laboratory Tests.* Washington, DC: U.S. Department of Defense. 2008.

U.S. Department of Defense. *Technology Readiness Assessment (TRA) Guidance.* Washington, DC: U.S. Department of Defense. 2011.

U.S. Department of Defense. *Unmanned Systems Integrated Roadmap: FY2011–2036 (Reference Number: 11-S-3613).* Washington, DC: U.S. Department of Defense. 2011.

U.S. Department of Homeland Security, Office of Inspector General. *DHS Uses Social Media to Enhance Information Sharing and Mission Operations, but Additional Oversight and Guidance Are Needed (OIG-13-115).* Washington, DC: U.S. Department of Homeland Security, Office of Inspector General. 2013.

U.S. Department of Homeland Security. "Apex Programs." U.S. Department of Homeland Security. Last modified March 18, 2016. https://www.dhs.gov /science-and-technology/apex-programs.

U.S. Department of Homeland Security. "Apex Screening at Speed Infographic." U.S. Department of Homeland Security. Accessed April 2016. https://www.dhs .gov/science-and-technology/screening-speed-infographic.

U.S. Department of Homeland Security. "Civil Rights and Civil Liberties." U.S. Department of Homeland Security. Last modified October 5, 2015. https:// www.dhs.gov/topic/civil-rights-and-civil-liberties.

U.S. Department of Homeland Security. "DHS Authorized Equipment List." U.S. Department of Homeland Security. Accessed September 7, 2015. https://www .fema.gov/media-library/assets/documents/101566.

U.S. Department of Homeland Security. "DHS Launches YouTube Channel and Redesigns DHS.gov." U.S. Department of Homeland Security. Last modified July 22, 2009. http://www.dhs.gov/news/2009/07/22/dhs-launches-youtube -channel-and-redesigns-dhsgov.

U.S. Department of Homeland Security. "Flood Apex Program Infographic." U.S. Department of Homeland Security. Accessed April 2016. https://www.dhs.gov /science-and-technology/flood-apex.

U.S. Department of Homeland Security. "Fusion Center Locations and Contact Information." U.S. Department of Homeland Security. Accessed March 2016. http://www.dhs.gov/fusion-center-locations-and-contact-information.

U.S. Department of Homeland Security. "Imaging System for Immersive Surveil-lance: New Video Camera Sees It All." U.S. Department of Homeland Security. Last modified August 24, 2015. http://www.dhs.gov/imaging-system-immersive -surveillance-new-video-camera-sees-it-all.

U.S. Department of Homeland Security. "National Network of Fusion Centers Fact Sheet." U.S. Department of Homeland Security. Last modified August 21, 2015. https://www.dhs.gov/national-network-fusion-centers-fact-sheet.

U.S. Department of Homeland Security. "Next Generation First Responder Apex Program." U.S. Department of Homeland Security. Accessed April 2016. https://www.dhs.gov/science-and-technology/ngfr.

U.S. Department of Homeland Security. "Our Mission." U.S. Department of Homeland Security. Last modified March 21, 2016. https://www.dhs.gov/our -mission.

U.S. Department of Homeland Security. "Protecting the Nation's Cyber Infrastruc-ture." U.S. Department of Homeland Security. Accessed April 2016. https:// www.dhs.gov/science-and-technology/apex-ngci.

U.S. Department of Homeland Security. "Real-Time BioThreat Awareness Apex Program Infographic." U.S. Department of Homeland Security. Accessed April 2016. https://www.dhs.gov/science-and-technology/apex-biothreat-awareness -infographic.

U.S. Department of Homeland Security. "Screening at Speed." U.S. Department of Homeland Security. Accessed April 2016. https://www.dhs.gov/science-and -technology/apex-screening-speed.

U.S. Department of Homeland Security. "Terrorist Hazards." *Ready.gov.* Accessed February 2016. http://www.ready.gov/terrorist-hazards.

U.S. Department of Homeland Security. "Visionary Goals." U.S. Department of Homeland Security. Accessed April 2016. https://www.dhs.gov/science-and-technology/visionary-goals.

U.S. Department of Homeland Security. *Baseline Capabilities for State and Major Urban Area Fusion Centers: A Supplement to the Fusion Center Guidelines.* Washington, DC: U.S. Department of Homeland Security. 2008.

U.S. Department of Homeland Security. *Civil Rights/Civil Liberties Impact Assessment: DHS Support to the National Network of Fusion Centers.* Washington, DC: U.S. Department of Homeland Security. 2013.

U.S. Department of Homeland Security. *Comprehensive Preparedness Guide (CPG) 201: Threat and Hazard Identification and Risk Assessment Guide.* Washington, DC: U.S. Department of Homeland Security. 2013.

U.S. Department of Homeland Security. *Imaging System for Immersive Surveillance.* Washington, DC: U.S. Department of Homeland Security, Science and Technology Directorate. 2014.

U.S. Department of Homeland Security. *Innovative Uses of Social Media in Emergency Management.* Washington, DC: U.S. Department of Homeland Security, System Assessment and Validation for Emergency Responders (SAVER). 2013.

U.S. Department of Homeland Security. *National Emergency Communications Plan.* Washington, DC: U.S. Department of Homeland Security. 2014.

U.S. Department of Homeland Security. *National Incident Management System.* Washington, DC: U.S. Department of Homeland Security. 2008.

U.S. Department of Homeland Security. *National Infrastructure Protection Plan: Partnering for Critical Infrastructure Security and Resilience.* Washington, DC: U.S. Department of Homeland Security. 2013.

U.S. Department of Homeland Security. *National Preparedness Goal* (2nd ed.). Washington, DC: U.S. Department of Homeland Security. 2015.

U.S. Department of Homeland Security. *Next Steps: Social Media for Emergency Response.* Washington, DC: U.S. Department of Homeland Security. 2012.

U.S. Department of Homeland Security. *Recommended Protective Measures and Response Procedures for Remote Controlled Model Aircraft / Unmanned Aircraft System at Stadiums and Mass Gatherings.* Washington, DC: U.S. Department of Homeland Security. 2014.

U.S. Department of Homeland Security. *Request for Information (RFI) Number DHS 13-01: Robotic Aircraft for Public Safety (RAPS).* Washington, DC: U.S. Department of Homeland Security. 2012.

U.S. Department of Homeland Security. *SAVER Program Assessment Process.* Washington, DC: U.S. Department of Homeland Security. 2009.

U.S. Department of Homeland Security. *Science and Technology Strategic Plan 2015–2019.* Washington, DC: U.S. Department of Homeland Security. 2015.

U.S. Department of Homeland Security. *Science and Technology: A Foundation for Homeland Security.* Washington, DC: U.S. Department of Homeland Security, Office of Science and Technology Policy. 2005.

U.S. Department of Homeland Security. *Social Media Strategy.* Washington, DC: U.S. Department of Homeland Security. 2012.

U.S. Department of Homeland Security. *The 2014 Quadrennial Homeland Security Review.* Washington, DC: U.S. Department of Homeland Security. 2014.

U.S. Department of Homeland Security. *Using Social Media for Enhanced Situational Awareness and Decision Support.* Washington, DC: U.S. Department of Homeland Security. 2014.

U.S. Department of Transportation, National Highway Traffic Safety Administration. *Emergency Medical Dispatch: EMD Program Implementation and Administration—Manager's Guide.* Washington, DC.: U.S. United States Government Printing Office. 1995.

U.S. Federal Aviation Administration: http://www.faa.gov/.

U.S. Fire Administration. *Funding Alternatives for Emergency Medical and Fire Services.* Washington, DC: Federal Emergency Management Administration. 2012.

U.S. Forest Service. *Recreation Visitor Safety Report: October 18, 2010.* Washington, DC: U.S. Forest Service. 2010.

U.S. Government Accountability Office. *Unmanned Aircraft Systems: Measuring Progress and Addressing Potential Privacy Concerns Would Facilitate Integration into the National Airspace System (GAO-12-981).* Washington, DC: 2012.

U.S. Nuclear Regulatory Commission. *Fire Dynamic Tools: Quantitative Fire Hazard Analysis Methods for the U.S. Nuclear Regulatory Commission Fire Protection Inspection Program.* Washington, DC: U.S. Nuclear Regulatory Commission. 2013.

USA PATRIOT Act, Public Law 107-56 (2001).

Wadhwa, V. "Laws and Ethics Can't Keep Pace with Technology." *MIT Technology Review.* Last modified April 15, 2014. https://www.technologyreview.com /s/526401/laws-and-ethics-cant-keep-pace-with-technology/.

Walsh, M. "Using a Simulated Learning Environment." *Emergency Nurse* 18, no. 2 (2010): 12–16.

Waugh, D. "Why Law Enforcement Should Be Using Instagram." *International Association of Chiefs of Police Center for Social Media.* Last modified September 10, 2014. http://blog.iacpsocialmedia.org/Home/tabid/142/entryid/395/Default.aspx.

Webel, S., U. Bockholt, T. Engelke, N. Gavish, M. Olbrich, and C. Preusche. "An Augmented Reality Training Platform for Assembly and Maintenance Skills." *Robotics and Autonomous Systems* 61 (2013): 398–403.

Wehr, J. "Instructor-Led or Computer-based: Which Will Work Best for You?" *Training and Development Journal* 42, no. 6 (1988): 18–21.

West, D. *A Vision for Homeland Security in the Year 2025.* Washington, DC: The Brookings Institute. 2012.

The White House. *Presidential Policy Directive 21: Critical Infrastructure Security and Resilience.* Washington, DC: The White House. 2013.

The White House. *The National Strategy for the Physical Protection of Critical Infrastructures and Key Assets.* Washington, DC: The White House. 2003.

Wilson, R., S. Smith, J. Markovic, and J. LeBeau. *Geospatial Technology Working Group Meeting Report on Predictive Policing (NCJ 237409)*. Washington, DC: U.S. Department of Justice, National Institute of Justice. 2009.

Wilt, G. "Argus Oversees and Protects All." *Science and Technology Review* (April 1998): 13–15.

Winter, J. "Homeland Security Bulletin Warns 3D-Printed Guns May Be Impossible to Stop." *Fox News*. Last modified May 23, 2015. http://www.foxnews.com /us/2013/05/23/govt-memo-warns-3d-printed-guns-may-be-impossible-to -stop.html.

Wire and Electronic Communications Interception and Interception of Oral Communications, U.S. Code 18 (1994), Part 1, Chapter 119, §§ 2510–2522, 2701–2709, and 3121–3125.

Woodyard, D., H. Young, M. Amos, and J. Bandy. *Review Team Report: Inquiry Regarding June 11, 2010 Flash Flood Incident Albert Pike Recreation Area Ouachita National Forest*. Washington, DC: U.S. Department of Agriculture. 2010.

Zengerle, P., and M. Cassella. "Millions More Americans Hit by Government Personnel Data Hack." *Reuters*. Last modified July 9, 2015. http://www.reuters .com/article/us-cybersecurity-usa-idUSKCN0PJ2M420150709.

About the Editors and Contributors

Editors

Ryan K. Baggett, EdD, is an associate professor of homeland security at Eastern Kentucky University (EKU) in Richmond, Kentucky. In this capacity, his instruction focuses on critical infrastructure protection, risk analysis, and technology applications. He formerly served as a contractor to the U.S. Department of Homeland Security for six years. His published works include Praeger's *Homeland Security and Critical Infrastructure Protection* as well as several book chapters and journal articles. Dr. Baggett is a 2013 EKU Critical Thinking Teacher of the Year award recipient, a 2014 EKU Award of Teaching Excellence recipient, and the 2015 EKU eCampus Faculty Advocate for Student Success award recipient. Dr. Baggett holds a doctorate in leadership and policy studies as well as graduate and undergraduate degrees in criminal justice.

Chad S. Foster, PhD, is an assistant professor of homeland security at Eastern Kentucky University (EKU) in Richmond, Kentucky, where he supports student learning in the homeland security and emergency management fields of study. Previously, Dr. Foster managed U.S. Department of Homeland Security projects at EKU, including software development and testing and responder-driven assessments of systems. Dr. Foster has managed the development and implementation of two national conformity assessment programs for promoting data interoperability. His background is in the military, emergency management, and public policy fields of study. Dr. Foster holds a BS degree from the United States Military Academy and graduate-level degrees in public administration and urban and public affairs from the University of Louisville.

Brian K. Simpkins, EdD, is the associate director of research and evaluation of the Eastern Kentucky University (EKU) Justice and Safety Center where he provides daily oversight of the Center's research support to federal grant programs. He also serves as the associate director of the Bluegrass State Intelligence Community Center of Academic Excellence, which is funded through the Office of the Director of National Intelligence. Dr. Simpkins is also an adjunct faculty member with the EKU Homeland Security Degree Program and provides consulting services to the American Public University System, School of Security and Global Studies related to faculty and student research engagement. Prior to EKU, Dr. Simpkins worked on federal critical infrastructure protection programs as a contractor to DHS in the Washington, DC area. He obtained a doctorate of education and an MS degree in criminal justice from EKU and a BA in criminal justice from Marshall University.

Contributors

S. Kristopher Bowerman, MS, serves as a network analyst for the Kentucky Department of Criminal Justice Training in which he provides support to the Information Systems Branch in the area of information systems and physical security. Mr. Bowerman is also an adjunct faculty member with Midway College and Eastern Kentucky University (EKU). Mr. Bowerman is also a network administrator/information systems consultant for several firms in the medical and financial industries. In this capacity, he is responsible for maintaining and updating the networking infrastructure, overseeing data and cybersecurity, and meeting the information systems security compliance requirements with regard to HIPPA and the Securities and Exchange Commission. He holds an MS degree in Loss Prevention and Safety and a BS degree in Police Administration from EKU.

Robert Coullahan, MA, MS, president of Readiness Resource Group Incorporated, is a senior executive with more than 38 years of experience in national preparedness, environmental security, infrastructure protection, and special technologies integration. Mr. Coullahan served 20 years with Science Applications International Corporation where he was senior vice president, leading complex programs in C4ISR, crisis management, and homeland security. Mr. Coullahan also served five years as vice president for the Consortium for International Earth Science Information Network, a NASA-sponsored research organization focused on environmental security and disaster assistance. Mr. Coullahan obtained a BA degree from the University of California and graduate-level degrees in telecommunications and security management from the George Washington University. Mr.

Coullahan is board-certified in emergency management and security management and served nine years with the U.S. Army.

Jay English has more than 30 years of public safety, communications, and technology experience, including command of three emergency communications centers and several law enforcement divisions as a sworn officer. He currently serves as the director of Communications Center and 9-1-1 Services for the Association of Public-Safety Communications Officials (APCO) International. Mr. English served on active duty with the U.S. Air Force in airborne electronic warfare and intelligence billets and with the U.S. Marine Corps Reserve while attending college. He is a Lt. Colonel with the U.S. Air Force Auxiliary. His assignments have included Wing Inspector General and Deputy Chief of Staff.

David Lamensdorf is the chief executive officer, president, and founder of Safe Environment Engineering (http://www.safeenv.com/) in Valencia, California, which offers network-based telemetric safety and environmental solutions. Previously, Lamensdorf served as vice president and director of engineering for Confined Space Safety Products and as an electrical engineer and project manager for the Bently Engineering Company. He earned his degree in electrical engineering from California Polytechnic University. Lamensdorf served as chairman of the Emergency Interoperability Consortium, focused on development of open data interoperability standards. He also served as co-chairman of the Organization for the Advancement of Structured Information Standards Emergency Interoperability Steering Committee.

Scott Rockwell, PhD, is an assistant professor at Eastern Kentucky University (EKU), where he teaches classes on fire behavior, combustion, hydraulics, and fire dynamics along with conducting research and supervising graduate student thesis projects. Dr. Rockwell has earned a BS degree in aerospace engineering along with graduate-level degrees in fire protection engineering. His current research includes active learning teaching techniques that minimize the students' cognitive load, use of digital media in fire science education, alternative flame extinguishing techniques, radiation from dust flash fires, and investigations into the mathematical scaling of fire whirls. Among others, he serves on the Society of Fire Protection Engineers Subcommittee for Higher Education and the Association for Fire Safety Science Education Subcommittee. He also created the Fire Science Tools, which is a Web site that provides freely available fire science educational material (http://www.firesciencetools.com/).

Index

Made in the USA
Monee, IL
15 January 2023

25362129R00177